Audacious Women

Dear Mother

I haven't read any of these stories, but I know of a British woman in our lineage who could probably tell one just as interesting

Hope you enjoy these.

Love, Cheryl

(mother's Day 1998)

Audacious Women
Early British Mormon Immigrants

Rebecca Bartholomew

Signature Books ❖ Salt Lake City ❖ 1995

To John

Cover design: Rebecca Jacoby

Cover photo: John and Sophia Thomas Phillips, parents
of Elizabeth Phillips Thomas and third great
grandparents of the author.

∞ *Audacious Women* was printed on acid-free paper
and was composed, printed, and bound in the United States.

95   96   97   98   99   6   5   4   3   2   1

Library of Congress Cataloging-in-Publication Data
Audacious women : early British Mormon immigrants /
Rebecca Cornwall Bartholomew.
p.   cm.
Includes index.   ISBN 1-56085-066-3
1. Mormon women—Great Britain—History—19th century.
2. Mormon women—Utah—History—19th century. 3. Utah—
Emigration and immigration. 4. Great Britain—Emigration and
immigration. 5. Immigrants—Utah—History—19th century.
6. British—Utah—History—19th century. 7. Utah—
Church history—19th century. I. Title.
BX8641.B294 1995
289.3'41'082—dc20   94-23624
CIP

Contents

Introduction   vii

A Note on Sources   xv

Chapter 1. The Stereotypes   1

Chapter 2. Who Were They? 25

Chapter 3. The Conversion Experience . . . 57

Chapter 4. The Branches 81

Chapter 5. Women Organize 103

Chapter 6. Plural Marriage 119

Chapter 7. Emigration 133

Chapter 8. America and the Great Plains 161

Chapter 9. Monogamous Lives in Zion . . 187

Chapter 10. The Polygamous Minority . . . 215

Conclusion 249

Bibliography 259

Index 275

Introduction

In 1975, while employed as a research historian for the Mormon Trust Foundation in Salt Lake City, I was assigned to search out contacts between Brigham Young and the British/American literati of his day. While noting what William Hepworth Dixon, Samuel Bowles, Mark Twain, Sir Charles Wentworth Dilke, Solomon Carvalho, Richard Burton, General Philip DeTrobriand, and others had to say about the great colonizer, I encountered an obscure novel entitled *John Brent*. Its author, Theodore Winthrop, a Yale graduate, won recognition for his fiction and travel accounts about the time he won immortality as the first Northern officer to be killed in the Civil War.

John Brent is the story of a puritanic minister's son who finds himself while crossing the Great Plains. He also finds his true love. She happens to be a Mormon lass until rescued from this disgrace by the hero, who knows sham religion when he sees it.[1]

Winthrop's opinion of Mormonism did not surprise me—most of his generation considered Mormonism synonymous with polygamy, as heinous a crime against the Victorian (hence God's) mind as slavery. What did surprise me was the novel's priggishness. After all, here was an antebellum author sophisticated enough to take a stab at realism and even local color—yet by and large *John Brent* is drivel.[2]

Perhaps I took overweening offense because the poor immi-

1. Eugene T. Woolf, *Theodore Winthrop: Portrait of an American Author* (Washington, D.C.: University Press of America, 1981), gives the most thorough and appreciative assessment of Winthrop as both a writer and a character.
2. Most readers of Winthrop's day did not consider him drivel. Woolf discusses the Philip Sydneyian "cult of the gentleman" to which Winthrop subscribed. Poesy, action, Christian conduct, and chivalry were its codes, and with such an outlook Mormon polygamy must have been as remote to Winthrop's understanding as Martian law.

grants who people Winthrop's story and act as foil to his delicate-skinned heroine happen to be my ancestors—refugees from the coal mines and factories of Wales and England. And he described them in phrases not likely to set a descendant burbling and cooing: "a withered set of beings," "hardly men if man means strength," "hardly women if woman means beauty." Their leaders are greasy, self-serving, even murderous. In the company of women whose sensitivities aspire to those of oxen, his heroine is lonely, and it is only through high chivalry that the hero is able to forbear the other creatures long enough to rescue her.

Blaaggh, I thought. If Winthrop's superciliousness toward the (albeit Mormon) tired and poor was representative, no wonder God spoke so scathingly of the Victorians in his revelations to Joseph Smith. To these rebukes he might have added a little literary criticism. It didn't placate me to realize that, as the genre went, Winthrop's anti-Mormonism was bland, or to later learn that Winthrop's literary knife had scored targets besides Mormons.

Then in 1985 another research assignment sent me to Latter-day Saint church archives looking for histories of British Mormon women. Other than a few notable sources, and the valuable if sometimes vague writings of the Daughters of the Utah Pioneers, I found that the collection of women's biographies, diaries, letters, and autobiographies was extremely limited compared to men's, even though women have always comprised more than 50 percent of Mormon church membership and in spite of recent efforts in gathering and writing Mormon women's history.

Nineteenth-century Mormon church records in Britain were kept by men, which may explain why they dealt 96 percent with men. Only one women's Relief Society minute book survived to reach church archives, and Welsh women did not keep diaries at all, not even in Cymric. I have since been told that they could read the Bible but could not write. Whether it is strictly true that they *could* not write, most *did* not. Their husbands meanwhile authored voluminous personal notes, autobiographies, poetry, astrological studies, patriotic hymns, treatises on mathematics, and letters to editors.[3]

The less I found, the hungrier I became. Were these women the fishwives portrayed by Winthrop? Were they, as depicted in other works, even worse: dupes, low-lifes? A few stories handed down by my grandmother and great-aunt, both members of the Salt Lake Cambrian Society, left more questions than answers, and both women by then had passed away so that I could not ply them for details.

Once in a search mode, however, I found that new sources presented themselves. A whole body of private histories exists, written by family genealogists (many of them women), with as many life stories of matriarchs as of patriarchs. Most of these are thoroughly researched, some are documented, and copies of many have been donated to the Family History Library of the LDS church in Salt Lake City. Yet many of these exhibit the same tendency as more professional histories to brush over a woman's early life in Britain. So the problem remained of a still hazy picture of pre-immigration Latter-day Saint women.

Hence this study. It is a search for my mothers. If at times I despair of portraying anything real about them beyond their births, marriages, and deaths, perhaps it is because even today, with the modern reality before us, my generation can't agree on

3. Ronald D. Dennis, in his study of the Mormon Welsh emigration, states: "Most of the Welsh, including women, were literate, thanks to the "circulating schools" from the previous century. These schools consisted of brief training in reading skills from various nonconformist ministers who traveled the countryside out of an intense desire to get people to read the Bible . . . Little attention was given to writing . . . Consequently, many of the Welsh could read or quote the scriptures, while at the same time being totally incapable of writing their names" (*The Call to Zion: The Story of the First Welsh Emigration* [Provo, UT: Religious Studies Center, Brigham Young University, 1987], 19).

My ancestress, Elizabeth Phillips, signed an X on her marriage certificate. But exceptions include Mrs. Elizabeth Lewis, whose very literate letters were published in the Welsh Mormon newspaper and are reprinted by Dennis, and Priscilla Merriman Evans, whose prolific diary has been widely cited by Mormon historians.

the identity of women. As in the 1800s, twentieth-century literature has favored extremes: either we Mormon women are repressed, depressed, and demeaned—brainwashed sacrifices to an
outmoded patriarchal system—or we must be the last of the
fortunates, protected, honored, and fulfilled by men raised to more
virtuous manhood through the doctrines of the priesthood.

Both extremes rankle. Yet the simplism must be acknowledged
and dealt with, for in a hundred years this polarism in Mormon-
watching has not changed much. Samuel Bowles, Horace Greeley,
Maria Ward, Kate Field, and others who visited Zion—either to
study the "Mormon Question" or as an important stop on a
Western tour—encountered here, and then exhibited in their
works, the same duality of voice and attitude. Some visitors more
adeptly grappled with the conflict than others who, perhaps unable to reconcile contradictory, emotionally pungent impressions,
went home to fabricate an entirely new, personal reality which
presumably made sense to themselves. They then published their
reality as *Mormonism Unveiled* or *The Truth About the Mormons* or
another such ambitious title.[4]

All this is pertinent to a study of British Mormon women
because, by and large, what happened in Utah happened to participants and observers throughout the missions. Utah was popu-
lated by immigrants, and more importantly, British Mormons
were closely attuned to church headquarters. It might accurately
be stated that as Utah went, so went the British Mission. Church
policy was centrist, with mission leaders fully in accord with the
prophet. Since church doctrine stressed The Gathering, most converts probably began planning emigration before they were baptized. Also, the strain of dwelling in an unsympathetic society
made Utah seem even more attractive. That British Mormons

4. The title "Mormonism Unveiled" was used by several writers over
the decades, including Eber D. Howe for his original, virulent history of
the fledgling sect (*Mormonism Unvailed* [sic] [Painesville, Ohio: by the
author, 1834]); John D. Lee's confessions as purportedly told to his
journalist/lawyer (*Mormonism Unveiled* [St. Louis: Byran, Brand, & Co.,
1877]; and Orvilla S. Belisle's romance (*Mormonism Unveiled* [London:
Charles Clark, 1855].

looked to Utah in most matters was one fact wholly grasped by outsiders.

And there are further reasons why it is difficult to find and study the British church as a separate unit. As Mormonism was an American church, and after 1847 even more isolated than in Ohio and Illinois, British observers often obtained their information about it from the American press. Thus a London editor who wished to visit the Whitechapel branch would have already read the body of American-originated literature and formed a number of impressions. Perhaps there were times (such as the public acknowledgement in Salt Lake City of polygamy) when some British Saints wished they were less closely linked in the public mind to Utah—but logic, loyalty, and faith bound them as relentlessly as did public opinion.

There were distinct differences between the Utah and British churches, however. One was that no such faction as the Godbeites developed in the English church, although a number of the dissenters, including William Godbe himself, were of British origin.[5] I will propose in a later chapter that this was not due to the embattled situation of Mormons in the mission field, but rather to the simple fact that devoted converts—among whom schisms rise—emigrated.

Another difference was the absence of female self-observation and support groups in the British church. In the mainstream of Utah culture there arose the new Relief Society, later the *Women's Exponent* magazine, and a whole network of suffragists, feminists, and commentators. In Britain the *Millennial Star* was written, edited, and published by male missionaries. Only rarely did a woman venture comment via editorial letter, and then very self-consciously. Not a single Relief Society germinated until 1869, and even then the societies were sporadically conceived and short-lived. As a result, relatively few women's records, minutes, founders' portraits, and diaries were produced, although many were

5. For information on the Godbeites, see Ronald W. Walker, "The Godbeite Protest in the Making of Modern Utah," Ph.D. diss., University of Utah, 1977.

written retrospectively in Utah. Thus a century later the mass of contemporary wordage favors the anti-Mormon press as one's chief source of printed information about British Mormon women.

So this book begins with impressions not by the women themselves or by mission writers, but by non-Mormons, mostly hostile writers. One of my conclusions is that the private lives of these women did not fit one pattern but revealed nearly as many styles of education, family roles, and interests as there were personalities. Unfortunately, images of these women created by nineteenth-century writers were far more limited in range and color.

Scope of the Study

The original concept of this study was to find one hundred quality records of women who were involved with Mormonism in the first fifty years of the British Mission, 1838-88. By quality I wanted "Type A" records: contemporary documents created by a directly-involved party. It could be a diary, letter, birth or marriage certificate, newspaper report, etc., so long as it was immediate to the events described. Such records would contain fewer of the mental editings caused by time and distance. When I could not see an original source itself, I used a published article based upon the source. But I have tried not to repeat work already well covered by other writers, which is why stories about some prominent early Mormon women such as Ruth May Fox and Martha Hughes Cannon are not recounted here.

Type B sources are further removed from the actual events but still close to the women's lives, including autobiographies written by the women or their husbands or biographies by a spouse or another contemporary after the fact—often years after and usually late in life. Some of these are more reliable than others, as when the writer referred to an earlier diary or letters.

A third class of sources, Type C, is far more numerous and includes biographies written by children or descendants even further removed. These are mainly found in encyclopedias compiled by the Daughters of the Utah Pioneers (DUP), early LDS biographical collections, and family histories. While DUP publications have been a splendid help, most are undocumented. I have tried to use these only when I could verify the information through a second source.

While I had hoped to find one hundred Type A records, this proved too formidable. Eventually I had to settle for thirty-four. Type B sources proved even scarcer: sixteen. The remaining fifty are Type C. Some day, given greater resources, I propose to contact descendants of each of the fifty women in an effort to uncover further information, perhaps copies of diaries, letters, and other vital records which may still be held by the families.

Most of the primary source records are in the women's collection of the Utah State Historical Society in Salt Lake City. These were inventoried and registered in 1985 by Linda Thatcher. Many would never have come to exist but for the efforts of Works Progress Administration writers hired for make-work projects by the federal government during the Great Depression. These writers interviewed female pioneers still living throughout the state and made carbon typescripts of their interviews.

A second major repository is the library of the LDS church historical department. During Church Historian Leonard Arrington's tenure, a massive effort was made to itemize and register all documents held in archives, in the process of which a women's register was created. I believe Maureen Ursenbach Beecher was a leader in this effort. I encountered some of these sources during my eight years with the Mormon Trust Foundation.

A few sources are held by Brigham Young University's Harold B. Lee Library (Provo, Utah), the University of Utah's Marriott Library Special Collections (Salt Lake City), and Utah State University's library (Logan).

While I felt underprivileged by not being able to work in Great Britain, probably the best place anyway for my project was the LDS genealogical library (since renamed the Family History Library), which contains a world-class collection of genealogical reference works, background texts on British history, family histories, and, best of all, what were once called "family group sheets." Before computerization, these genealogical charts were submitted by family researchers as hard copies and compiled in notebooks. They are now on microfilm and microfiche. These records are now being entered on computer as the library's Ancestral File. I was able to find family group records giving documented vital statistics on thirty-one of my women, not as many as I'd hoped but a helpful number especially since these sheets name sources. However, I discovered that records in the computerized Ancestral File are not as reliable as information on those earlier, hand-written family group sheets.

Although its limitations are mine alone, I am grateful to those who have assisted this study. Leonard J. Arrington and the Mormon Trust Foundation supported several chapters through a grant. Linda Thatcher of the Utah State Historical Society went beyond her duties in helping me root out sources on Victorian women and women's studies. Rodello Hunter provided continual encouragement and an interested ear through rough drafts. Carol Kowallis Onyon donated hours of research along with an astute sensitivity to telling detail. Ron Dennis of Brigham Young University shared his considerable insights into Welsh history and culture. My husband helped with research besides fixing dinner, washing dishes, and spending hundreds of evenings entertaining himself while I persisted at the computer. I am grateful to these people, and if ever I am able I will repay them in some way.

I am painfully aware of the limitations of this work, which I will not enumerate, as the reader will discover them soon enough. They are due partly to my limited gifts and partly to not enough time and money. Because of them, at times I despaired of the project but finally decided to wrap it up and submit it before I grow old.

A Note on Sources

For most of the one hundred women surveyed for this study I was able to locate only two sources each, usually a brief biography or autobiography and a genealogical record. Because of this, it seemed to me that repeating full bibliographical citations in the footnotes on the women as they appear from chapter to chapter was unnecessarily cumbersome.

Instead I decided to list the sources on each woman in an alphabetically-organized bibliography at the end of the book. I use parentheses in the text to reference this bibliography. If the woman is not named in the text, her name follows in parentheses in lieu of a footnote. However, when a woman is named in connection with a piece of information or quotation, I use neither footnote nor parenthetical reference because the source is self-evident.

When citing all other sources, I use standard footnotes.

Chapter 1.

The Stereotypes

Stereotypes of Mormons do not at first seem to be limited. At least fifty novels, five histories, scores of short stories, hundreds of newspaper articles, and several per-year essays in each major American and European magazine kept Mormonism in the public mind between 1834 and 1900. True, the articles were contradictory in tone and conclusions, but two things help to simplify analysis of this literature: first, its content and quantity ebbed and flowed in discernible cycles; second, the massive wordage boiled down to a few themes.

Cycles of anti-Mormon publicity have been recognized by various historians. Sandra Myres, comparing anti-Mormon writing of the 1830s and 1840s to that of later decades, perceived it as "increasingly virulent," especially during the 1850s when a wave of travel accounts and popular novels took up the Mormon theme.[1] Gail Casterline noted that the literature of the 1870s brought a shift in approach from scorn to pity for polygamous wives.[2]

1. Sandra L. Myres, *Westering Women and the Frontier Experience, 1800-1915* (Albuquerque: University of New Mexico, 1982), 87.
2. Gail Farr Casterline, "'In the Toils' or 'Onward for Zion': Images of the Mormon Woman, 1852-1890," M.A. thesis, Utah State University, 1974, 20.

Both observations could be further refined into four cycles described by Dennis Lythgoe. (1) The earliest and most sustained cycle, characterized with few major exceptions by invective, was set in the 1840s following the Mormon wars in Missouri and Illinois and continued through the 1860s. Perhaps its bitterness was due to regional American roots. The proponents were often amateur authors of midwest sectarian attitude, hot with the reformist fire which characterized American letters before the Civil War.[3]

(2) By the 1870s cooler emotions prevailed in works of broader interest by writers less concerned with sectarian religion than with social reform. This change in the tenor of attitude may have been influenced by Mormon apostate writers Fanny Stenhouse and Ann Eliza Young whose autobiographies appeared in 1870 and 1872 and who personally did not fit the sensationalist mold of the depraved, mindless Mormon wife.

(3) The "humanitarianism" fermented into new militancy and brought in the 1880s passage of the Edmunds-Tucker anti-polygamy act, as well as serious consideration of a Constitutional amendment against bigamy and polygamy.

(4) By 1890, the reform nearly accomplished, considerable sentiment against Mormonism and Utah persisted so that two Mormon electees had to fight in the federal courts (one unsuccessfully) for seats they had already won in their districts.[4]

But a number of maverick pieces, and many cases of borrowing, clipping and enlarging over seventy-five years of anti-Mormon writing, blur the lines between cycles. For this reason we should consider the mass of Mormon-related literature as one body and analyze it primarily according to stereotypes: themes or ideas which repeated themselves in work after work between 1838 and 1888.

One feels sheepish attempting to catalog and analyze ideas

3. Dennis L. Lythgoe, "The Changing Image of Mormonism in Periodical Literature," Ph.D. diss., University of Utah, 1969. I have added my own interpretations of the four phases.

4. See Davis Bitton, "The B. H. Roberts Case of 1898-1900," *Utah Historical Quarterly* 25 (1957): 27-46.

which were not logical. But since so much of the fanciful in such literature came to be accepted as fact, the content ought to be approached methodically. The method chosen here is mostly chronological: what did Victorians say about the origins of Mormon converts (geographic, socio-economic, family and marital, educational and cultural, religious and moral)? What did they imagine to be the circumstances and motives for peoples' attachment to Mormonism, the rights and treatment of women within the Mormon branches, the Mormon emigration experience, and proselytes' ultimate situation in Zion? This organization provides the structure for the remainder of this study.

Geographic Origins: Rude Foreigners

We find in the literature three theories as to where and from what classes Mormonism obtained its followers. The dominant theory was that Mormon converts came primarily from the industrial cities of Europe. One writer characterized Mormons as "Europeans of low class who greatly improved their lot in life by coming to Utah."[5] This assumption was an almost universal one among nineteenth-century reporters and indeed is accepted (possibly prematurely) as fact by many twentieth-century historians.

American John Beadle, author of those famous dime novels which were the equivalent of our century's television sitcoms, had already written several Mormon romances when he abandoned fiction momentarily to produce *Life in Utah: Mysteries and Crimes of Mormonism* (Cincinnati, 1870). Here he created an indelible image of Mormons as socially inferior. Mormon men, he said, were "rude, discourteous and boorish" but very nearly justified in their boorishness by "the [Mormon] women themselves": "Nearly all of them are of foreign birth, English, Welsh and Scandinavian, and of that class, too, among which men have never been accustomed to respect women very highly." He continued, "Polygamy could never have been established in a purely American community," implying that monogamy was the property of the United States

---

5. *Nation*, 13 Dec. 1883, cited by Lythgoe, 38.

and that only un-American immigrants could produce such an aberration.

Other writers couched their cynicism in anti-immigrant, anti-masses, or anti-papist sentiment. Theodore Winthrop took a swipe at all three in *John Brent*. When his hero and narrator happens upon a caravan of Mormon immigrants, the sidekick notices that all the emigrants speak in the Lancashire dialect and represent the "poorest class of townspeople from the manufacturing towns." "The Pope and Brigham Young are the rival bidders for such weaklings in the nineteenth century," he concludes.

Some of this grew out of the American fashion of disparaging the Old World and could not have set very well with a second set of theorists, British writers and those with British sympathies. Yet the trend was so prevalent that an independent-minded observer like Ellen Browning Scripps, founder of Scripps College but first a Californian who wrote travel letters from Europe in 1881-83, had to defend her praise of European social customs.[6] Maria Ward (pseudonym for Cornelia Woodcock Ferris) was another Old World-apologist, although her intent was not objectivity but a need for literary contrast as a polemic device. Ward established the motif of an idealized British homeland, a woman discontented with the idyllic beauty of her surroundings, and Mormon opportunists who found her a sitting duck.[7]

6. Ellen Clark Revelle, ed., *A Sampling of Travel Letters, 1881-1883, by Ellen Browning Scripps* (Claremont, CA: Scripps College, 1973), 42.

7. Maria Ward's book, *Female Life Among the Mormons* (New York: J.C. Derby, and London: C. H. Clarke, 1855), was the most-read of all Mormon commentaries. It went through several English editions between 1855 and 1880 and was reprinted in five languages. Maria's real name was Cornelia Woodcock Ferris or Mrs. Benjamin G. Ferris.

Within a year or two after the appearance of *Female Life*, a companion volume by Maria and Austin Ward—supposedly her nephew but probably her husband—depicted *The Husband in Utah; or, Sights and Scenes Among the Mormons* (New York: Derby and Jackson, London: James Blackwood, 1857). Another 1857 volume entitled *Male Life Among the Mormons, or The Husband in Utah* lists Artemus Ward as author, and one of humorist Charles Farrar Browne's popular lecture sketches was, "Among the Mormons." *Male Life* appeared during Browne's early career, while he was still writing for the *Cleveland Plain Dealer*. Ward and Browne were the same person.

A third theory, a variation of the first, had Winthrop, Beadle, and Austin Ward (pseudonym for Benjamin G. Ferris) as proponents. It portrayed Mormons as an entirely separate stock: "a low-browed, stiff-haired, ignorant, and stolid race," in Beadle's words. Ward noted that all classes of English society were represented in Mormondom, even some "intelligent, refined" beings, but his most memorable observation was that the majority of Mormon women were of "uncouth shape and feature . . . more decidedly ugly than women of any age or country."

This is the school to which Winthrop's picaresque report on a Mormon emigrant caravan belongs: "A puny, withered set of beings," he described them. Even their children were aged and wrinkled. Unlike Beadle and Ward, however, he was kind enough to attribute this to the harshness of conditions in England: the drudgery of shop (factory) life, of a day-to-day existence of all work and no play.

A report in *DeBow's Review*, purported to be a direct observation by a member of the New Orleans Academy of Science, provides the most graphic expression of this theory. Although the report should have been authentic, New Orleans being a major way station second only to Liverpool along the Mormon immigration route, the treatise was of dubious validity. It assumed that all Mormons were either polygamist or polygamist offspring and constituted "a new race" distinguished by "yellow, sunken, cadaverous visage; greenish-colored eye; the thick protuberant lips, the low forehead; the light-yellowish hair, and the lank, jangular person."[8]

One longs to know the seeds of such a report. Perhaps the three- to nine-week voyage actually left land-lubbing passengers green-faced. Or the correspondent may have encountered Mormons not as they disembarked but later, camping along the Mississippi River after the ravages of cholera had set in. Or perhaps there was no experiential basis, only the incipient yellow press. Whatever the inspiration, this and other highly-specific, seemingly-authentic word pictures helped create an unflattering image

8. Cited by Lythgoe, 29.

which some readers accepted as reality. As late as the 1960s, Utahns of my acquaintance were still meeting people in the American Midwest who serio-comically quizzed them about Mormon physiological abnormalities.

Socio-Economic Origins: Women and Men of Small Property

Stereotypes about economic conditions contradict the new race theories. "Documentarist" Maria Ward personalized the idea that Mormons came from the British middle class with her storyline of the proselyte who abandons her "idolizing" and property-owning husband and "almost [breaks] the hearts" of her children to marry a Mormon. Austin's counterpart to the foolish British wife was a male convert who becomes bishop of "Bricktown," Utah. He is said to have been "a man of small property" in England until a Mormon tempter came into his Eden and teased him with glowing accounts of the New World and he became dissatisfied with the simple pleasures of home and emigrated. On the way, like the poor, foolish women of Mormondom, the man falls into want, discomfort, and disorganization.[9]

Other theorists were more or less realistic than the Wards. Robert Richards (pseudonym) claimed to have converted to Mormonism himself, and characterized most Mormon converts as "honest dupes like myself . . . day-labourers, weavers, carpenters, shoemakers, masons, shipwrights, sawyers, gun-makers, basket-makers." They went to Utah expecting to find a spiritual and economic Zion and commonly returned home with shattered expectations.[10]

In novelist Mayne Reid's *The White Huntress*, one of his romance novels in which the hero must choose between an earthy, dark-haired love and a more delicate, light-haired girl of his own ethnic background, the damsel is in distress because of the profligacy of her father. Made desperate by debt, he betrays her to the

9. Ward, 120.

10. Robert Richards (pseud.), *The Californian Crusoe, or The Lost Treasure Found* (London: J. H. Parker, and New York: Stanford and Swords, 1854).

{6}

horrible Stebbins, Mormon-Danite-polygamist, in whose hands she helplessly faces a fate worse than death.[11]

Joaquin Miller toyed with the same type in his novel, *The Danites in the Sierras*, which was made into a hit Broadway play and later, almost unrecognizably, into the movie "Paint Your Wagon." Miller was a Californian with direct knowledge not only of the Mormon movement but of Pikers, or '49-ers, some of whom had helped expel Mormons from Missouri and Illinois in 1846. Furthermore, Miller was a free-love advocate without the usual indignation toward polygamy. Thus the stereotype took on some new twists: his damsel and her brothers are educated, soon-to-be affluent, several cuts above Pikers in culture and intelligence. Miller deserves credit for verisimilitude rare in anti-Mormon literature and for characterization of a Mormon woman that very nearly pokes its shoulders above the mire of stereotype.[12]

Family Characteristics: Disagreeable Countenances

Most nineteenth-century writers equated Mormonism with polygamy. Clichés about polygamy ranged from the genuinely documentarist approach of Jules Remy and Richard Burton to dramatic (for the sake of circulation) reports sobered by reserved disapproval from Horace Greeley and William Hepworth Dixon, to the ludicrous accounts of the Wards. Among the less sensational was an account in *Nation* magazine which said, "Polygamy can only work when women are under delusion or constraint," inferring that given a real choice Mormon women would slough off their shackles like new patriots. For fiction writer Robert Richards, who was relatively fair in portraying Mormon laborers as artisans

11. Captain Mayne Reid, *The Wild Huntress* (New York: R. M. DeWitt, 1861).

12. Joaquin Miller (pseud. for Cincinnatus H. Miller), *First Families in the Sierras* (London: G. Routledge and Sons, 1875), revised as *The Danites in the Sierras* (N.p.: Jansen, McClurg & Co., 1881). For analysis of the "Mormon" writings of Marryat, Reid, Winthrop, Miller, and A. Conan Doyle, see Rebecca F. Cornwall and Leonard J. Arrington, "Perpetuation of a Myth: Mormon Danites in Five Western Novels, 1840-90," *Brigham Young University Studies* 23 (Spring 1983). "Piker" referred to Pike County, Missouri, residents who joined the Gold Rush of 1848 and later.

with hopes and skills but no place in the socially- and economi-cally-petrified Old World,[13] polygamy was "the chief lure" for sensual but not lustful lower-class immigrants "honored" by the prospect of an earthly kingdom with several wives and many children.

In the realm of the absurd, there are Austin Ward's Bricktown caricatures of older wives with "disagreeable countenances" and "coarse and disgusting" laughter. Younger wives had bruised faces, and not from *husbandly* abuse. The real-life Maria Ward (writing as Mrs. B. G. Ferris) portrayed the typical Mormon woman as "a coarse, blowzy, greasy specimen of womanhood who delighted in bullying other wives."

Somewhere between the dignified and ludicrous fell the com-ment received by Zina Huntington Young, a wife of Brigham Young, at a women's suffrage meeting in the East. According to Susa Young Gates, daughter of another of Brigham's wives, the easterner looked at Zina, resplendent in a sealskin cape, and concluded, "You don't *look* depraved."[14]

Literarily in a class by itself is Mark Twain's satirical look at Mormon family life in his 1872 volume, *Roughing It*.[15] Actually,

13. Richards, 14.

14. From Susa Young Gates Collection, Utah State Historical Society, Salt Lake City.

15. Mark Twain (pseud. for Samuel Langhorne Clemens), *Roughing It* (Hartford, CT: American Publishing Co., 1872). I will consider Twain in depth not only because of his enormous influence in Britain but because his treatment of Mormons put the lie to the more blatant untruths circulating in his time. One way to discover just what the stereotypes were is to study Twain's satire of them.

Roughing It recalls a tour which young Twain made in 1860 with his brother, a federal appointee to Nevada. In America the book sold 40,000 copies its first month in publication (many by prior subscription) and went on to sell another 60,000 over the next nine years. It sold well in England as well, where Twain anticipated Joaquin Miller as a popular lecturer and darling of literary circles.

Here at last was a subtlety equal to the perplexing realities of Mormonism. While having his fun (particularly with Mormon women), Twain ridiculed the national obsession and distorted notions. As points of takeoff, he used several of the stereotypes, giving them new names and

Twain was temperate in his ridicule of Mormon men. His Destroy-ing Angel (Danite) is "murderous enough" but mostly just "de-void of dignity" in an unclean shirt, horse-laugh and swagger. Brigham Young is a benevolent monarch who coerces lesser Mor-mons into honoring business contracts with gentiles.[16]

Unfortunately, and as usual, Mormon women get the blunt end of Twain's pen. His narration begins with mild, self-bemused curiosity:

> We walked about the streets some . . . This was fairy land to us . . . land of enchantment, and goblins, and awful mystery. We felt a curiosity to ask every child how many mothers it had, and if it could tell them apart; and we experienced a thrill every time a dwelling-house door opened and shut as we passed, disclosing a glimpse of human heads and backs and shoulders—for we so longed to have a good satisfying look at a Mormon family in all its comprehensive ampleness . . .

The passage ends with the typical image of the uncouth, homely Mormon wife. Invited to an apostle's home, Twain saw:

> A lot of slatternly women [who] flitted hither and thither in a hurry, with coffeepots, plates of bread, and other appurtenances to supper, and these were said to be the wives of the Angel—or some of them, at least. And of course they were; for if they had been hired "help" they would not have let an angel . . . storm and swear at them as he did . . .

Finally, his oft-quoted conclusion:

twists with Twain's blessings: the Destroying Angel (previously referred to by many writers as the Ruthless Danite), the fatherly Brigham Young (nationally known as the tyrannical Brigham Young), the Marrying Elder (for the Seducing Elder), and the polygamous fishwife (for the Naive Shopgirl). To these he added a new type, the Tale-Telling Gentile. See James D. Hart, *The Popular Book: A History of America's Literary Taste* (New York: Oxford University Press, 1950), 140.

16. Young does not come off so well in a version of the Mountain Meadows massacre by Catherine Van Valkenburg Waite. See Mrs. C. V. Waite, *Adventures in the Far West* (Chicago: by the author, 1882). Possibly anticipating criticism for appearing too soft on the Mormons, Twain appended Waite's piece to at least one edition of *Roughing It*.

Our stay in Salt Lake City amounted to only two days, and therefore we had no time to make the customary inquisition into the workings of polygamy and get up the usual statistics and deductions preparatory to calling the attention of the nation at large once more to the matter. I had the will to do it. With the gushing self-sufficiency of youth I was feverish to plunge in headlong and achieve a great reform here—until I saw the Mormon women. Then I was touched. My heart was wiser than my head. It warmed toward these poor, ungainly and pathetically "homely" creatures, and as I turned to hide the generous moisture in my eyes, I said, "No—the man that marries one of them has done an act of Christian charity which entitles him to the kindly applause of mankind, not their harsh censure—and the man that marries sixty of them has done a deed of open-handed generosity so sublime that the nations should stand uncovered in his presence and worship in silence.

Religious Origins: Murderers and Thieves

One finds very little in the anti-Mormon literature about religious origins of Mormon converts. Fanny Stenhouse wrote about her personal religious experiences before and after conversion and speculated on factors which predisposed others toward Mormonism, but I have chosen to include Fanny among Mormon rather than anti-Mormon voices.

On the other hand, a good deal was written and implied about the moral propensities of Mormon converts. So much was said on this subject, most of it derogatory, that John Greenleaf Whittier personally studied Mormons in Illinois to discover how much was true. He concluded that "the Mormons were not at all as their Missouri detractors pictured them," but that the writers "were calling Mormons murderers and thieves so as to justify murdering and stealing from them."[17]

Much of the wordage on the moral theme was obviously imaginative, along the line of John Beadle's tale of the young Scot who supposedly came to Brigham Young asking the prophet to

17. Cited by Leonard J. Arrington and Jon Haupt in "The Missouri and Illinois Mormons in Ante-Bellum Fiction," *Dialogue: A Journal of Mormon Thought* (Spring 1970): 37-50.

marry him to his half-sister. Young solved the dilemma by marrying the girl to himself, only to discover that she was already "in a delicate condition." Divorce and consent for the original union allowed the couple to raise three children together. But in the end the girl "saw the degradation of her position and left for the States."[18] This was the vein from which A. Conan Doyle drew in his first Sherlock Holmes novel, *A Study in Scarlet* (London, 1887), in which the Mormon men, when they wanted wives, snatched them from non-Mormon caravans bound for Oregon and California.

Much of the later moralizing was just name-calling. In 1895, five years after the church's Manifesto which ostensibly stopped plural marriages among the vast majority of Mormons, *The Congregationalist* was still referring to "the Mormon ulcer." And in 1900 *Outlook's* correspondent, after a cursory look at the state, wrote: "Sexual morality in Utah was much lower than in any other American communities I had visited, but a little higher than in Continental Europe."[19]

Cultural Roots: Gullible Fishwives

Theodore Winthrop took apparent delight in portraying Mormon women as fishwives. While his masculine mail contractor is an honest, likable fellow in spite of his "lands and beeves and wives without number," the principal wife is represented as a "dowdy" woman who speaks "in tones that she must have learned from a rattlesnake." It is among such women that the hero meets the "high-bred" Ellen, and his first reaction is, "What a woman to meet in a Mormon caravan!" Ellen and her father, that rare miner with the soul of a gentleman, are "desolate souls in this forlorn environment." Ellen especially is "worn and sad" not from frontier drudgery but from the quality of companionship.

Lower-class, low-class Mormon women were said by other writers to be usually gullible. John Beadle wrote, "Brigham Young tells the women . . . 'If you see a dog run by the door with your

18. Beadle, 262.
19. *Century*, Jan. 1882, and *Outlook*, 3 Feb. 1900, cited by Lythgoe, 44, 49.

husband's head in its mouth, say nothing until you have consulted with the bishop.'" Maria Ward, too, portrayed the women as less ugly than stupid. In her view Mormon preachers had difficult-to-resist charisma: "Beware of their arts. Enter not into the circle of their fascinations; their charms are like those of the serpent, and lead to the death of all that is holy and beautiful in this life . . . " An intelligent woman would see through such charms. "One scarcely knows whether to be amazed most at the profane profligacy of the leaders, or the superstitious credulity of their dupes."[20]

The Ferris (a.k.a. Ward) family apparently found Mormon-bashing a lucrative field, publishing books under five different names. Benjamin Ferris, for a short time Utah territorial secretary and for a longer time husband of Cornelia, called Mormon wives "weak-minded." Cornelia, in a work published under her real name, Mrs. Ferris, wrote snidely that Mormon women would "gulp down the most preposterous proposition, merely saying, perhaps, 'Du tell'."[21]

Robert Richards took a similar jab at his supposedly deceased wife whose powers of reasoning told her that a Mormon preacher "could not speak so very positively unless he knew he spoke the truth." She is represented as having recanted her belief on her Nauvoo deathbed.

Such a body of supposed factual literature was a ready vein for the harem writers who used stereotypes as backdrop to imagined heroes and heroines. One of the first of the romancers was Orvilla Belisle, author of *The Prophets, or Mormonism Unveiled* (Philadelphia, 1855).[22] Although her title suggested a factual treatment, neither the setting, characterization, nor plot is remotely accurate. The setting is Wales, the main character a Welsh chieftain, and the villain a Lady MacBethian chieftainess who drives the village to a Mormon doom. Some of Belisle's images are especially memorable, particularly her bewildered bird of a hero-

20. This time Maria was writing in *Putnam's Monthly*, an 1855 issue cited by Lythgoe, 26.
21. As cited in Casterline, 12.
22. This was also published as *Mormonism Unveiled; or a History of Mormonism from Its Rise to the Present Time* (London: Charles Clarke, 1855).

ine who falls for a dashing but false young Mormon elder who uses religion to beguile this Welsh girl. Mouthing scriptures, he is soon winding his fingers "among those wondrous curls . . . dropping them one by one off her wax-like shoulders." With burning lips, he kisses her forehead, promising peace and a cherished position in his Mormon kingdom. Finally the bird, "bewildered, fascinated, but powerless," sinks into the open arms of the fowler.

Women's Status: Degradation

Some anti-Mormon works were no doubt inspired by a concern for woman's rights and station. Yet, Jane Austen-like, they did not question Christian society and its treatment of women but saw mistreatment only as the inevitable consequence of deviation from Christian standards. The wife who left her happy hearth and idolizing husband of course ended up "on the dump heap . . . abused shamefully" when the polygamous husband tired of her.[23] The foreign-born women of Zion were of a class which tended towards ungodliness and invited neither respect nor honor.

There were more careful writers who still helped to feed the misconceptions. Horace Greeley commented that he never saw any evidence in Great Salt Lake City that a woman had an opinion or was listened to if she did. William Hepworth Dixon helped introduce the association of Mormonism with the oriental harem, an analogy widely made afterwards in cartoons and editorials: "[Mormon wives] are brought into the public room as children are with us; they come in for a moment, curtsey and shake hands; then drop out again, as though they felt themselves in company rather out of place. I have never seen this sort of shyness among grown women, except in a Syrian tent."[24] Although Greeley's and Dixon's comments were made in the spirit of honest inquiry, they were influenced by preconception and cursory examination which reinforced the image of the doltish Mormon wife.

One doubts that literate people swallowed whole the sensationalist pulp. But, as I have pointed out, some more literate treatments distorted the truth just as severely if in a more pal-

23. Maria Ward, 61.
24. *New America*, 2 vols. (London, 1867); cited by Casterline, 14.

atable way. Reporters assigned to cover the trek of Johnston's army to Utah sometimes sent back copy more wishful than accurate. For instance, *Littell's Living Age* printed with sublime presumption, "Had Johnston's Army come in [that first winter], Brigham Young would have lost half his wives within a month."[25] Other correspondents thought they perceived an unheard-of yet timid trend among Utah women toward "inquiring and thinking for themselves," or that younger Mormon women felt a new-found shame "because of their degraded status in the eyes of the world."[26]

If a new wave of free-thinking, anti-polygamist women emerged in Utah in 1858, it had submerged by the 1880s when federal laws put high pressure on polygamist families and brought about an end to the practice of plural marriage. At three different times—1869, 1878, 1886—ladies rallied throughout Utah territory to let the world know that they were loyal to their husbands and faith. Some signed petitions, others sang hymns and attended caucuses, a few wrote letters to officials. Perhaps a silent majority stayed home, but (as the rare observer recognized) clearly few were clamoring to be free.[27]

25. From an 1858 issue, cited by Lythgoe, 27. In 1857 U.S. president James Buchanan, responding to complaints that Mormons were in a state of civil rebellion, sent a large force to invade the territory. This campaign was known as the Utah Expedition and more popularly as the "Utah War." A brief but helpful explanation of the Utah Expedition is found in Leonard J. Arrington and Davis Bitton, *The Mormon Experience: A History of the Latter-day Saints* (New York: Alfred A. Knopf, 1979), 164-69.

26. Annie Morris in *Lippincott's Magazine* 3 (July 1870): 49, and *Century*, Jan. 1882, cited by Lythgoe, 32, 38.

27. For a touching defense of plural marriage, see Artemesia Snow's speech cited by Leonard J. Arrington and Davis Bitton in *The Mormon Experience* (New York: Alfred A. Knopf, 1979), 201.

Casterline includes John Gunnison, Jules Remy, Sarah Wood Kane, Richard Burton, Phil Robinson, Solomon Carvalho, and a few others as writers whose observations were not marred by preconception and bias. If polygamy was "regrettable, perhaps even appalling," Mormon women were not miserably abused under the system but were clean, nice-looking and generally accepting if not elated about the doctrine practiced by 10-20 percent of Mormon families of that day.

It is difficult to talk about characteristics of Mormon women without including their men. By some writers men were portrayed as drunken, abusive husbands, by others as kidnappers and white-slave-procurers. A few found them lecherous, bearded old patriarchs "who continued marrying young girls as long as they were able to hobble about."[28]

Novelist Mayne Reid's men were "Yankee foxes . . . vulgar, brutal and cunning." California poet Joaquin Miller's Danites were hawk-nosed, with a bookishness terrifying to the rough, uneducated Pikers. Late in the century Fanny and Robert L. Stevenson spoofed all the above by redesigning the Mormon terrorist as a lovelorn oaf and the damsel a liberated woman capable of defending herself against almost anyone.[29]

It is significant that men were allowed comprehensible if not admirable motives. Female converts were almost never credited with intelligence or a will to think. With almost universal sexism, both male and female writers of the day characterized Mormon women as ignorant and naive. Sometimes the women were seen as victims, more often as fools, rarely as ambitious spiritualists, never as adults capable of knowledgeably choosing a life course. Sexism must paradoxically be admitted as one of the prominent forces in the creation of nineteenth-century anti-polygamist literature, and among the most guilty were female journalists writing in defense of womanhood.

The Conversion Experience: Seduction

By now the variations on the stereotypes are pretty warmed-over. Robert Richards, in *The California Crusoe*, gave a little more detail than usual to the "modest property owner" by having the man, prior to hearing of Mormonism, fall to schisms in the Church of England. In this way Richards came closer to the truth about some proselytes' backgrounds than most. He also has an entire congregation convert in a few preaching services in one locality, another resemblance to actual events in the very early history of the British mission.

28. Myres, 87.
29. *The Dynamiter* (New York: H. Holt and Co., 1885).

{ 15 }

According to Richards, Mormon proselyting appealed to its listeners' idealism. One elder promised his audience a holy city in Nauvoo, picturing America's rivers as "groaning with the weight of emigrants borne on the face of the water to the beautiful city of rest." Richards recreated the alleged actual sermon by an Elder Smart: "Cast off your traditions and your superstitions. By the hundreds and by the thousands in the Old World and the New, mankind are hearing and obeying the glad tidings of salvation." This does not sound too far-fetched, although a real Mormon elder would not have tended to use society or the opinions of men as his authorities. The type of listener attracted to Mormonism was more susceptible to scriptural allusions than to social enthusiasm.

Other conversion images are on the order of Belisle's seduction scene, flavored not by sermons pretended or real (these would have been boring) but by drama: villains and heroines.

The Mormon Emigration: Abduction

Theodore Winthrop provided the most vivid if fanciful image of a Mormon emigrant caravan. Unlike most Mormon novels, the leader of Winthrop's emigrants does not hold his caravaners in subjection through brutality. They are there because "what has England done for them?" Indeed, the emigrant leader is not even the villain. Instead it is the lecherous old Sizzum, a sort of renegade elder with Danite tendencies who rides into the caravan and kidnaps the aquiline Ellen. Yet Sizzum became the stereotype of the Mormon emigration leader.

It is a Sizzum-like Mormon who kidnaps the southern damsel in Mayne Reid's novel, skirting her across the plains with the hero in pursuit. This was how fiction said Mormonism obtained its female followers. If a Mormon woman wasn't a dolt, she was a hostage.

One is hard put to find a realistic or even semi-realistic treatment of the Mormon emigration. One of the few came from Charles Dickens, who was at the Liverpool docks as a company of Mormons (mostly Welsh, mostly women) departed for New Orleans. Dickens wrote, "Had I not known that the passengers were

Mormons, I might have called them, in their degree the pick and flower of England."[30]

The Mormon Holy Land: No Virgins in Zion

If a Mormon woman were fortunate (or unfortunate) enough to reach Zion, her old terror of abductors and deceivers was replaced by a new one. Ward called Nauvoo, Illinois, an early Mormon gathering site, "a Victorian nightmare of broken families and broken hearts."[31] Mayne Reid was writing during the Nauvoo period when he penned, "There are no virgins in Zion, only wedlock loveless and unholy."[32]

Promised a holy city, Robert Richards's Californian Crusoe finds Illinois reality disillusioning. His wife's last words to her husband are "that horrible, horrible prophet." Crusoe pens a fictional interview with the second mate on a ship back to Liverpool. The mate reportedly says: "they have taken lots of LDS people from Liverpool to America, happy and full of confidence, but on the homeward trip to Liverpool were scores of LDS people having tried being LDS and now hate the very name." The Californian Crusoe, Beadle's Scotswoman, Reid's and Winthrop's and the Stevensons' damsels together created the view of Zion as a prison of unhappy souls and the trail east as crowded with Mormons clamoring to get back to the homeland.

It was from these romances and the press that Arthur Conan Doyle, with no direct knowledge of Mormons, hit upon the unfortunate British damsel and the Danite as characters for *A Study in Scarlet*, the first Sherlock Holmes mystery. He imagined a Utah located in an alkaline basin where no birds chirp but coyotes skulk and buzzards flap dully.

His Mormon caravan is driven by grave, hard-lipped men;

---

30. From *The Uncommercial Traveller* (London: Chapman and Hall, 1865), as cited by Richard L. Jensen, "The British Gathering to Zion," in V. Ben Bloxham et al., eds., *Truth Will Prevail: The Rise of the Church of Jesus Christ of Latter-day Saints in the British Isles, 1837-1987* (Cambridge: University Press, 1987) 186; and Richard L. Evans, *A Century of Mormonism in Great Britain* (Salt Lake City: Deseret Book Co., 1936).
31. Cited in Arrington and Haupt.
32. Reid, 228.

meek, pale-faced women; ragged, dusty children—in contrast to a British child discovered on a hillside who, though abandoned and starving, is plump, snowy-toothed, and white-stockinged. Among such people it is "a dangerous matter to express an unorthodox opinion."[33]

Austin Ward reinforced the ugly image of Utah and the idea that women were kept there in degradation and bondage through his depiction of a fictional Mormon community. Ward's Bricktown wives are of several types: the shopgirl now ensconced in a Mormon harem and rapidly becoming disillusioned; the middle wife whose mind is becoming an irredeemable vacuum; and the elder wife/myrmidon, as ambitious as Belisle's chieftainess, harnessing her husband's younger concubines for the sake of glory in some eventual heavenly realm. All Bricktown citizens live in filth and squalor, eat off wooden boxes, go without food two out of every three days, and do not bother to edit windows or doors into their hovels.

Even Fanny Stenhouse, who had been a missionary's wife in an unsympathetic land, in the end turned her hand against her former colleagues with exaggerations such as: "One thing I am certain of; if . . . horrible deeds were ever perpetrated within those walls, there remains no *living* witness to testify of them."[34]

Fanny refers to rites performed in the Endowment House—a large log structure used until the Salt Lake temple was completed for sacred ordinances including marriages, baptisms for deceased ancestors, and "endowments" for the living. While an entire genre of folklore has arisen around Mormon temple rites, there is no

33. Arthur Conan Doyle, *A Study in Scarlet* (London: Ward, Lock & Co., 1858). Charles Higham believes he has found the immediate inspiration for *Scarlet*: a news report in the *London Times* published 20 March 1879, just before Doyle began his novel, titled, "The Last Struggle of the Mormons." See Higham, *Adventures of Conan Doyle* (New York: Norton, 1976), 71-72.

34. I use both an early edition and the 1971 facsimile edition: Mrs. T. B. H. (Fanny) Stenhouse, *Tell It All: The Story of a Life's Experience* (Cincinnati: Queen City Publishing Co., 1874); and T. B. H. Stenhouse, *Tell It All: The Tyranny of Mormonism, Or An Englishwoman in Utah* (New York: Travellers Classic [Praeger Publishers], 1971).

evidence that disemboweling, murders, human sacrifices, or erotic ceremonies took place in the Endowment House, as Fanny insinuates here.

Mark Twain's humorous comments on Salt Lake City contradicted those of Austin Ward and others in most respects. His Mormon capital has broad, level streets; pure streams; "no visible drunkards or noisy people"; block after block of neat homes with plush orchards and gardens; and "a general air of neatness, repair, thrift and comfort."

Even in jest he comes close to the truth when he hit upon the source of at least some sensationalist reports about closed Mormon society: those pleasant, cigar-filled talks in the back rooms of gentile homes and offices where are told "thrilling evening stories about assassinations of intractable Gentiles . . . how heedless people often come to Utah and make remarks about Brigham, or polygamy, or some other sacred matter, and the very next morning at daylight such parties are sure to be found lying up some back alley, contentedly waiting for the hearse."[35]

Modern Vermin

We also have Metta Victoria Victor who under the subtitle *A Narrative of Facts Stranger than Fiction* outdid even Maria and Austin Ward. Mormon women, she said, were "modern vermin perpetuating their kind in the disgusting ratio of other loathsome creatures."[36]

Her judgment represented extreme anti-Mormonism, more intense than most of the invective of the 1840s and 1850s. The 1870s and 1880s brought a different, more reasonable kind of myth-making. Yet Victor reminds us that, as reluctant as the modern student may be to take seriously Mormon or anti-Mormon literature of a century ago, much of it was in earnest, and deadly enough that it helped inspire the dispatch of between one-third and one-half of the American army sent to Utah to oversee a population thought

---

35. *Roughing It.*
36. Metta Victoria (Fuller) Victor, *Lives of Female Mormons; A Narrative of Facts Stranger than Fiction* (Philadelphia: G. G. Evans, 1859), cited by Casterline, 11.

to be in utter rebellion against the United States. A decade after Johnston's army marched on Utah, popular lecturer Kate Field claimed she knew personally of a Utah woman who was disemboweled—with her young sons looking on—for speaking about the temple rites![37]

A Puzzling Voice

Among Victorians who more or less declined to stereotype the Mormons, Fanny Stenhouse's voice is unique. Her autobiography, published in the United States in 1870 with a preface by Harriet Beecher Stowe, reads mostly as an open, pained introspection into her twenty years as a Mormon wife.[38] When she speaks with personal knowledge about her conversion, her romance with the intellectual young Elder Stenhouse, her experiences in the St. Helier's Branch where "things were had in common," her saucy insider tales of life in Salt Lake City are funny, intelligent, occasionally poignant.

Indeed, to a modern reader her long personal struggle to reconcile "womanly feelings" with desire toward husband and church are more damning of polygamy and patriarchal authority than any diatribe. After ten years in Utah her husband, by then an influential newspaper editor, succumbed to pressure to take an extra wife, and Fanny tried to accept the inevitable. By her account, many times she knelt by her bed as her husband slept, praying to the Lord to "subdue my rebellious heart."

But this personal account is mixed with malinformed narratives of political events of which she could only have been a third-hand witness at best. It was the old ambivalence. The majority of Mormon women were not, as Stenhouse chose to believe, in company with her in a slow-born distaste for the Mormon faith. Yet she undeniably shared some of their feelings and experiences.

37. Leonard J. Arrington, *Kate Field and J. H. Beadle: Manipulation of the Mormon Past* (Salt Lake City: University of Utah, Center for Studies of the American West, 1971).

38. I am citing *Tell It All*, one of two books she wrote about Mormonism. She also lectured and published newspaper and magazine articles about her polygamous experiences.

Should her autobiography be included among the one hundred life histories or placed with the anti-Mormon tale-tellers of this chapter? Because she was so long associated with Mormonism, and because her report was, overall, at least a cut above other self-acclaimed authentic studies, I include her with the voices of Mormon women—though she may well turn over in her grave at my decision.

Fiction Becomes Fact

In some of the works mentioned Mormon themes were used humorously, with sophistication, while in many others they were used soberly, even stupidly. Several forces were operating. Documentarists were religious and secular journalists who, with varying scruples, aimed for at least a facsimile of realism in their studies. William Mulder has noted that Mormonism was once a national pastime, the sect a subject of routine commentary in the dailies, weeklies, and monthlies of the last century. It was these recurring reports that provided the grains of truth around which the romancers wove their stories and through which public curiosity was kept alive. Some of the documentarists were reformers and politicos who encouraged or catered to mass preference for exaggeration and hysteria, addressing "the Mormon question" for its marketability.

Then there were the harem writers—romance novelists who borrowed rumors from hearsay, the daily press, and superficial observation which they turned into literary archetype. Most of these were hack writers using such titles as *Saved From the Mormons*, *Apples of Sodom*, and *The Little Gentile: A Desert Romance of Captive and Exile*, but some were of more formidable reputation, including Francis Marryat, Mayne Reid, Joaquin Miller, and A. Conan Doyle.[39]

Finally there were the literati who laughed at but nevertheless courted the public preference for entertainment, if in a saner and more circumspect manner. There were few sympathetic treat-

---

39. Anonymous, *Saved from the Mormons* (New York: n.p., 1872); and Rosetta Luce Gilchrist, *Apples of Sodom: A Story of Mormon Life* (Cleveland: W. W. Williams, 1883).

ments of Mormonism, none reaching the broad audiences of the virulent works, so that almost nothing was published to counteract the sensationalism.

Critical attitudes varied. Writers such as Jules Remy, Sarah Wood Kane, Phil Robinson, and others realized that Mormon women were not generally abused nor were they clamoring to be free. But according to Gail Casterline, "the depravity view dominated." If not weary and repressed, Mormon women were mentally deficient and lacked the higher instincts. The domestic novel popularized the plot of the genteel girl (or man) from an eastern or European city who was somehow lured out West to face ultimate disillusionment and escape to freedom or . . . death.[40] The fact is that most real-life converts to Mormonism were working-class women—shopgirls, factory workers, home pieceworkers.

Somehow the fiction of Mormon elders luring young women to their harems braided with real Mormon demographics until in the 1880s there were serious press reports of Mormon missionaries abducting young women off the streets of Liverpool, London, and Paris! Exactly how this transmutation of reality took place is not the subject of this book, only that it did occur. The novels, romances, short stories, plays, and poems accumulated into the force of fact in the public mind so that as people watched or heard of the one-half percent of their countryfolk converting to Mormonism they interpreted this reality through the eye of romance-inspired fiction.[41]

The stereotyping process was not simple, for the romancers and journalists were aided by the clergy, embittered spouses,

40. Casterline, 10-11.

41. One-half percent may be fanciful thinking myself. But another researcher, in stating that Great Britain humiliatingly lost the equivalent of its entire population in the migrations between the Napoleonic and first world wars, lists the 1821 British population as 21 million (Wilbur S. Shepperson, "The Place of the Mormons in the Religious Emigration of Great Britain, 1840-60," *Utah Historical Quarterly* 20 [1952]: 207-18). Several encyclopedias give the 1851 population of Great Britain as about the same, 21 million. Assuming Mormon baptisms totalled 125,000 (as discussed in the next chapter), .006 percent of Britons became Mormons while about half that many emigrated.

disillusioned converts, and the undeniable fact of spiritual wifery and accompanying abuse and neglect. How did the Mormon myth affect Victorian life, culture, and politics? At the very least, writes Casterline, it "drew attention to the reality of polygamy, which by implication was a direct threat to all women of America."[42] Maria Ward's exposé, with its thirty-four-plus supposedly factual instances of sadism in polygamist families, "familiarized an image of suffering Mormon womanhood." The romancers further embellished this image, creating "a true sense of fear" in their readers. Emotionalism dominated public thinking, public rhetoric, and public decision-making of the day. It was not analogous to a modern public enjoying a horror novel; it was a case of mass libel and quiet but prolonged mass hysteria.

British Mormon women endured along with their American sisters the bad press which plagued them during the first century. One result is that, while we know who Utah women were because they spoke for themselves, we still do not know much about British Mormon women. Were they seduced by handsome, ardent, hypocritical Mormon elders; girls with weak minds who, once on the lawless frontier, sank into primitivism? Were they naive married ladies, easily duped into slavery to one or another two-faced Danite? Did they represent the rude life of London and Manchester, seeking their level in a decadent, unsavory subculture? How many of them actually became plural wives, and did they turn into Lady MacBeths, domineering and brainwashing sister-wives?

If they weren't the above, who were they, the roughly 60,000 British women who gave up reputation for a disreputable religion? What classes did they represent, and what had been their childhood experiences and upbringings? Why and how did they attach themselves to Mormonism? What took place in the little British Mormon branches? What was the relationship of convert to elder, female to male, member to priesthood leader? How much input, if any, did women have in the way the British church operated? What were the characters of the missionaries who converted and led them to America?

42. Casterline, 20.

Why did British Mormon women emigrate in such numbers—at least 25,000 of them? In what numbers did they become disenchanted with the faith and at what stage of their pilgrimage? Were they happy or unhappy or—what?—ten, twenty years after arriving in Zion?

Could they read? Did they know what was being written about them? Did they never speak for themselves? Wasn't there a British Patty Sessions (a New England convert whose lifelong diaries have been widely read and cited by Mormon historians)? What did they think of themselves, of British society, of priesthood doctrine and custom?

Twentieth-century American folk singer Burl Ives sings a folksong with these lyrics: "That's about the size . . ./ where you put your eyes . . ./ that's about the size of it . . ." We know what their detractors chose to see. Where did the women themselves put their eyes?

Chapter 2.

Who Were They?

Just before World War II Kate B. Carter, president of the Daughters of Utah Pioneers and compiler of three encyclopedias of Utah history, tried to repair the image of the British Mormon. Her statistics, she claimed, proved that Mormon elders got no response in "the slums of the larger cities" but instead drew from "the great middle-classes, farmers and skilled tradesmen." She went on: "Even though many [converts] did not have enough money to carry them across the ocean, they were far from poverty. They had good positions, happy homes, and were in love with their country and their queen."[1]

I hope to prove Carter substantially right, but her claim first poses several problems. One, she did not elaborate statistics to support her. Second, her frame of reference was probably not that of pioneer mothers. She wrote in a more tactful age, when the Latter-day Saint church was conciliatory toward secular society and when society for its part had come a long way toward cleaning up its massive underside. Earlier Mormons than Carter were unashamed of poverty and unhesitant to blame it on godless and

1. Kate B. Carter, *Heart Throbs of the West* (Salt Lake City: Daughters of Utah Pioneers, 1947), 3:106.

{ 25 }

inhumane government—the society of David Copperfield and Oliver Twist.

In the mid-1990s we are still not sure how many Britons converted to Mormonism. One researcher cited by Carter claimed that the number exceeded 126,000 of whom 52,000 emigrated to America.[2] But Richard O. Cowan, writing in 1987, would consider such figures over-generous. He could find only 110,301 total baptisms for the entire century, with 46,054 emigrations.[3]

We have less idea how many of these convert emigrants were women. Records show that males and females almost equally manned the emigrant companies. If this held true for the British branches (congregations) as well, then between 55,000 and 63,000 British women were baptized. But this balance may well not have held in the branches. There is some indication that women joined the church more readily than men.[4]

Thus Carter's middle-class theory will be hard to prove with numbers. That may be just as well, since numbers and facts often do not tell the story. Yet since they pose the easier task in my detective work, I will begin with facts.

Geographic Origins: Industrial Cities

The easiest question to answer is where in Great Britain Mor-

2. Ibid., 74. She cited her source only as Evans, probably Richard L. Evans, author of *A Century of Mormonism in Great Britain* (Salt Lake City: Deseret Book Co., 1937). Compare Frederick S. Buchanan, "Scots Among the Mormons," *Utah Historical Quarterly* 36 (1968): 328-49; Philip A. M. Taylor, "Why Did British Mormons Emigrate?" *Utah Historical Quarterly* 22 (1954): 249-60. All three used charter ships records in computing their totals and about a 50-percent emigration rate.

3. Richard O. Cowan, "Church Growth in England, 1841-1914," in V. Ben Bloxham et al., eds., *Truth Will Prevail: The Rise of the Church of Jesus Christ of Latter-day Saints in the British Isles 1837-1987* (Cambridge: University Press, 1987), 199-217.

4. Kate Carter said that in the European emigration women predominated by a slim margin. Of 12,477 emigrants from Europe during the second half of the century, 5,796 were men, 6,681 women, a difference of 885 or 7 percent. But of the general British emigration between 1840 and 1855, 57.73 percent were male, 42.27 female. Kate B. Carter, ed., *Our Pioneer Heritage* (Salt Lake City: Daughters of Utah Pioneers, 1965), 13:109-61.

mons had their greatest success. To summarize, most converts were picked from England, the next largest groups came from Wales and Scotland, while Ireland contributed a small minority. British converts throughout the nineteenth century outnumbered Scandinavian converts several times over, and southern European baptisms were as scarce as Irish.

Actually, the small Irish numbers are misleading. Ten-20 percent of converts from Glasgow, Liverpool, Merthyr Tydfill, and probably even London itself were Irish refugees. Americans are aware of their 1 million ancestors who emigrated to the eastern seaboard during the potato famine but not so aware that three times that many simply migrated to other parts of Britain. One Mormon elder working in Glasgow in the 1850s claimed to have more Irish than Scotch converts.[5]

It was as if the sheep had been pre-gathered. My one hundred women's histories bear out P. A. M. Taylor's 1954 finding that the majority of baptisms were made in cities and counties which form a corridor about the shape of a woman's skirt down the western and lower parts of Britain.[6] Specifically, six areas contributed heavily: London to South Wales (at the slightly-flared hemline), the West Midlands and new West Riding of Yorkshire (at the thighs), Lancashire (at the hips), and far up to Glasgow and central Scotland (at the slim waist).

To be more precise, a sample of over 5,000 emigrants claimed these cities of origin:

London	1301	24 percent
Merthyr Tydfill	844	16
Birmingham	741	14
Liverpool	702	13
Glasgow	530	10
Manchester	485	9
Sheffield	385	7
Bristol	332	6

The numbers for Liverpool and Bristol may be inflated, for

5. Brent A. Barlow, "The Irish Experience," in Bloxham, 305.
6. See n2.

these were the embarkation ports for 95 percent of Mormon emigrant companies. Members commonly moved to these cities weeks or even months before emigrating, then reported their *in transit* addresses rather than places of origin.[7]

If converts came predominantly from this western corridor of mining and manufacturing counties rather than from England's rural east, north, and south, one would expect Mormon branches of the last century to have been predominantly urban—as indeed they were. Three out of four emigrants hailed from a city or large town, only one from the country or a village of under 10,000 people.[8]

Admittedly, few Britons were far removed from the village, for the northwest industrial cities had tripled in population only since 1800, and the typical city dweller was a transplant from a neighboring town, availing herself of metropolitan job opportunities.[9] Yet it is surprising that in a land still half-rural, Mormonism was three-quarters urban. Why should city more than rural Victorians be attracted to the new American religion?

Taylor poses this urban phenomenon as evidence that urban poverty was a motive for conversion and emigration. But urbanization could just as well have been a result rather than a cause. Mormon elders tended to work the towns and cities, finding it easier to obtain meeting halls and draw crowds.

Another reason for greater success in the cities was Britain's religious climate. City life loosened the bonds of extended family and parish church. Although well indoctrinated in the Bible, urbanites were somewhat less likely to be churched, were exposed to a greater variety of sectarian influences, and were freer to make personal choices about religious activity without affecting job,

7. Taylor, 260. See also P. A. M. Taylor, *Expectations Westward: The Mormons and the Emigration of their British Converts in the Nineteenth Century* (Edinburgh and London, 1965).

8. Taylor, "Why Did British Mormons Emigrate?" 260.

9. Malcolm R. Thorp, "The Setting for the Restoration in Britain: Political, Social and Economic Conditions," in Bloxham, 58. Also, R. F. Foster, ed., *The Oxford Illustrated History of Ireland* (New York: Oxford University Press, 1991).

housing, and social status. The opposite applied for villagers whose actions had more sure consequences in a more restrictive social atmosphere.

Among those heavily-urban counties which contributed converts, Lancashire was the first center of the British mission. The shipping and industrial city of Liverpool and the factory city of Birmingham were in Lancashire until it was restructured in 1974. But Brigham Young, Heber C. Kimball, later Joseph Fielding and Willard Richards, established their headquarters in Preston, in the northwest corner near the Irish Sea.

Preston was a textile town of 45,000 residents in 1837, the year missionaries arrived. It was growing by nearly 2,000 residents per year, much as modern Evanston, Wyoming, grew during the oil boom of the 1970s, with similar results: shortage of housing, inundated churches and schools, few social agencies, and public utility construction far behind needs. To the above add conditions peculiar to pre-modern towns: unpaved streets, backyard privies, and drainage facilities that during storms overflowed and carried odor and disease.[10]

Another Mormon stronghold was the mining country of central England. The Staffordshire Potteries yielded converts in the 1840s, but its branches declined by the 1850s through emigration, the vagaries of mining economics, and lack of attention to the waxing and waning branches.[11]

In Scotland the urban pattern held. With 3,291 members in 1851, Scotland had seventy branches, almost half of these in four counties: Lanark (Glasgow being its mining center, a city which throughout the century provided as many converts as all other Scottish counties combined), Fife (a coal-mining and agricultural area), Clackmannan (an industrial and agricultural hub), and Edinburgh (heavily industrial but a cultural center as well).

It was not that missionaries did not scour the Scottish countryside for proselytes. William Mackay volunteered in 1846 to preach

10. Thorp, 48.
11. Sherry Dew, "Mormonism in the Staffordshire Potteries," photocopy in archives, Historical Department, Church of Jesus Christ of Latter-day Saints, Salt Lake City, Utah (hereafter LDS archives).

in the Highlands where Gaelic was a barrier to English-speaking elders. He was unsuccessful. Later Peter McIntyre tracted through Argyllshire and some of the Western Isles where he too found few listeners willing to be baptized. Mormonism just did not do as well "in the heather hills as in the smoke stacks, mine shafts, and factories of central Scotland."[12]

Wales furnished most of its converts from its industrialized southern counties where three-quarters of its population still live. Cardiff, in the mid-1800s the world's most important coal shipper, had been a small town until 1794 when the Glamorganshire Canal connected it to coal deposits. While North Wales remained mostly agricultural (sheep and cattle), South Wales became mostly urban.

Yet it was in Herefordshire, a rural county on the border of Wales, that Wilford Woodruff found a congregation of 600 United Brethren and baptized all but one in 1837-38. Many of these men and women had Welsh surnames. Missionaries in 1840 established two branches in northeast Wales, but the elders were stoned and the branches quickly depopulated by emigration.

In 1845 Dan Jones, a Mississippi River steamboat captain born in northern Wales, began his mission in his home area. At the end of a year he had won only three baptisms.[13] Transferred to the south, he established a Cambrian newspaper and was directly or indirectly responsible for over 1,000 baptisms by 1848. Baptisms in Wales varied from 150 a month in the late 1840s to 90 per month in the early 1850s before they waned.[14] The emigrant group Jones led to Utah in 1849 was said by a non-Mormon editor to include "substantial farmers." What the editor did not mention is that most of the company were colliers, urbanites like their Scotch and English brothers.[15]

Ireland was different. While many Irish were converted in

12. Buchanan, 329-20, 273.
13. Ronald D. Dennis, *The Call to Zion: The History of the First Welsh Mormon Emigration* (Provo, UT: BYU Religious Studies Center, 1987), 236.
14. Ibid., 255-62.
15. Wilbur S. Shepperson, "Place of the Mormons in the Religious Emigration of Great Britain, 1840-60," *Utah Historical Quarterly* 20 (1952): 216.

England, Ireland itself never contained more than a couple of hundred members at a time, less than 3 percent of church membership in Britain.[16] In Dublin missionaries met with greater resistance and intolerance than almost anywhere in Britain. Their meetings were crashed by heckling crowds, tracting was disrupted by bands of "camp followers" who grabbed tracts out of would-be readers' hands and tore them up, and anyone who showed interest or pity for the elders was ("in thousands of instances," said George Q. Cannon) turned out of house and job. Members could not keep leases on their homes, the missionaries complained. Magistrates would not intervene. Most opposition came from non-conformist Protestant groups rather than from Roman Catholics. The hecklers effectively stifled proselyting in Ireland decade after decade, which is probably why a diary or history written by an Irish Mormon is exceptionally rare today.[17]

Socio-economic Origins: Mixed Circumstances

One might expect to see in the increasingly industrialized society of early Victorian Britain a developing middle class such as that described by Carter. If it existed, the early elders did not take notice. Barely middle-class themselves in America, they were shocked by living standards in England. Wilford Woodruff wrote of the Preston poor going to and from the factories, their wooden clogs making "a great rattling on the pavement." Heber C. Kimball was struck by the class discrepancy he saw in Liverpool, where one met "the rich attired in the most costly dresses, and the next minute was saluted with the cries of the poor with scarce covering sufficient to screen them from the weather."[18]

It should be remembered that in 1837 England was entering its severest depression of the nineteenth century. In good times,

16. Barlow, 310.
17. Ibid., 299-326.
18. Manuscript History of the British Mission, 14 Jan. 1840 and 20 July 1837, LDS archives. Such histories, hereinafter referred to as Mission History, were compiled by the LDS Church Historian's Office early in the twentieth century from mission minutes, missionary journals, and the *Millennial Star* (the mission magazine). Manuscript histories were also compiled for many of the conferences and branches.

writes Malcolm Thorp, factory workers earned wages adequate for a living, but in bad times wages fell. He estimates that one-half of the working force of Preston did not have enough to eat during such times as 1837-42.[19] To help families survive, women and children entered the work force, some children working thirteen-hour days without warm clothing or shoes, women leaving small children in the care of a shoemaker or blacksmith husband who had to spend the day in the shop.

Our women's histories reflect these conditions, not only in the 1840s, 1850s, and 1860s, but as late as 1900. Throughout the century over 90 percent of Britons were landless and in economic bondage to some degree. The Reform Act of 1832 lowered voting require-ments to include those not of the aristocratic class who owned land or rented property worth ten pounds or more. This meant that now 7 percent of the population could vote. The masses were locked into a system in which land was controlled in the country by local squires, in the cities by factory magnates, and in the mining villages by the mine proprietor. Not until the Reform Act of 1850 was franchise based on occupation rather than ownership of prop-erty.

Thus the elders obtained their converts primarily from among the unfranchised working classes and the poor. Many Mormon families resembled the Ewers—Hannah Taylor Ewer and John—who with their eleven children "struggled constantly for a meager living." They lived in rented quarters in Banbury, Oxfordshire, a beef processing and metal manufacturing town. They themselves were hand-loom weavers at a time when cottage industry was succumbing to competition from the factories. Ewer, his wife, and the older children all did piece work on two looms at home. That this provided a marginal living is revealed by their daughter's recollection of being pressed into winding bobbins when only six years old. When her fingers bled, torn by the warp, her mother wrapped them in linen so that Mary Jane could continue (Mary Jane Ewer Palmer).

Although from our biographies it appears that many families

19. Thorp, 50.

prospered a little better, the Ewers' situation was common. Taylor's study included 10 percent variously-skilled textile workers like the Ewers, 22 percent in perhaps a worse situation as "general laborers," 16 percent miners, and 4 percent farm or village workers such as wool combers. This gives a sub-total of 52 percent under-privileged.

That leaves 48 percent unlike the Ewers. According to Taylor, only a few of these came from the bourgeoisie of professionals and shopkeepers—those who fit today's conception of the middle class, who often lived above their own shop or office and some-times became monied. The majority of them was what we would now call "blue-collar workers"—artisans and skilled tradesmen considerably better off than their semi-skilled peers. They were carpenters, blacksmiths, shoemakers, tailors, stone masons, and iron workers. They comprised Carter's "great middle class," some of whom were far from poverty, had good positions and happy homes, and were in love with their queen.

Just how prominently they figured in the total Mormon popu-lation is debatable. Taylor's sample seems to represent emigrants of the 1840s and 1850s—those with resources to help themselves to Zion soonest. Malcolm Thorp compared a Mormon group to a Primitive Methodist group and found that 50 percent of Methodist emigrants were skilled artisans compared to 32 percent of Mor-mons. "These skilled workers, often the most prosperous group among the common people, were also the most numerous mem-bers of the evangelical sects" generally, but he concluded that the Mormons attracted converts from a lower socio-economic status than did the other proselyting churches. "Here were the meek and lowly being gathered."[20]

Yet the evidence is not all in. Among our narrower sample of one hundred, this second class of slightly more prosperous, skilled workers is more noticeable than in either Taylor's or Thorp's study. This may be because our sample was self-selected: that is, those who left records were more literate, higher-status converts. But if so, then why would one of the most articulate, vividly-de-

20. Thorp, 57.

tailed records be that of Mary Jane Ewer Palmer—who was all but illiterate and left her story only through dictation to her daughter? Literacy was not an exclusive factor in leaving histories.

Another statistic strengthens this argument. Whereas 22 percent of Taylor's Mormons were listed by emigration clerks as "general" (rather than "skilled") laborers, among British emigrants as a whole the percentage was 65. This would bear out Dickens's observation that the Mormon company included "the pick and flower of England," and it partially vindicates Carter.

Whatever the economic status of these women, their own records do not usually dwell on poverty in their pre-lives in Britain. Margaret McNeil Ballard, who emigrated with her family when she was ten, remembered in later years not hunger or drudgery but "the beautiful scenes of grasses and waters" of the coal mining village of Tranent, Heddingtonshire, Scotland. Other histories tell matter-of-factly of economic conditions which today might seem rather bleak but which then were unexceptional (Margaret McNeil Ballard).

Elizabeth Horrocks Jackson Kingsford wrote, "I was the eldest of a family of eleven children; when I was about eleven years of age I was placed to work in a silk factory and was thus enabled to earn a little to assist my parents in the support of the family." She seemed to view her job as an opportunity, while others saw it simply as a fact of life much as attending school for children today. My own ancestors, two Thomas families of Carmarthenshire, Wales, each had listed on the 1851 census a fourteen-year-old son at work, one as a coal miner, the other as a tailor's apprentice. A Welsh boy who could work beside his collier father in the mine increased his father's production and the daily family income.[21]

Even Mary Jane Ewer's reminiscences are not embittered, though there is a hint of resentment. It seems that after five or more years of working in a dress goods factory, all that time paying a strict tithe and sending a few cents each day through her father to the church emigration clerk, Mary Jane contracted smallpox. Two

---

21. LeNora Thomas Foster, "Notes on 1851 Census—Wales," Thomas family papers in my possession.

others in the family, her younger siblings, died, whereupon her father begged her for her savings to bury them. Mary Jane deliberated a full day before deciding not to postpone emigrating any longer. Her father obtained burial money from a town officer, and Mary Jane set out for Utah alone.

So much is unsaid in this story. In conflict were her duty to family and her impassioned desire to get to Utah. There is just the suggestion that she felt used by her family, that they expected her to sacrifice whatever present and future she might hope for. She must have given the bulk of her five-year earnings to her parents or it would not have taken so long to save emigration expenses. But her resentment is milder than Charles Dickens's, put to work at age twelve in a blacking warehouse while his father sat in debtor's prison. One has to wonder if in later years Ewer might not have rethought her decision, for her life in Utah as an oft-abandoned plural wife in an isolated desert outpost seems as bleak as her youth in Banbury.

Some women state conditions of hardship bluntly. Sarah Lewis Davies's husband, a stone cutter, died of what the children believed resulted from "lifting too hard" and "inhaling dust." This is an indictment of the labor system of the day, and it was meant to be (Mariah Davies Davies).

A few of our women describe people who were "making it" financially. Jane Graham Laidlaw, later portrayed by a Utah neighbor as "above average in intelligence and culture," remembered comfortable growing-up years in Annan, Dumfriesshire, Scotland, with an aunt and uncle. Jean Rio Baker Pearce, a widow with seven children, had either been left cash and property by her husband or earned sufficient as a dressmaker to buy a house ("only four rooms, but it will do for the winter") with twenty acres in Utah. Margaret Mitchell Blythe's father was a mine inspector entrusted by the Sydney Mining Company to open its new holding in Nova Scotia where the family lived in middle-class respectability.

Henrietta Bullock's husband was a law clerk, then tax exciseman whose work took him from port to port and provided a steady and satisfactory if modest income. Hannah Tapfield King lived the depressive but materially comfortable life of "an upper middle class lady" before becoming a Mormon. Among our sample, seven out of twenty-one who directly reported on socio-economic conditions appear to have been middle class or better.

Thus neither the stereotype of the poor, working girl nor Carter's picture of the happy, middle-class family is entirely satisfactory—yet both apply. Those attracted to Mormonism ranged the spectrum of class origin. Converts with some investiture in the British establishment seem to have been almost as numerous as those who might well have grasped an alternative to twelve-hour days, seventy-two-hour weeks, and no hope of ever owning land or rising above their stations.

Family Characteristics: Young and Married

Another of Taylor's conclusions is that the emigration was overwhelmingly young and whole-family. For every 100 emigrants, thirty-three were infants and children, sixteen were middle-aged or elderly, while fifty-one were between the ages of sixteen and forty. Whether youth was also a characteristic of those who converted is less certain but probable.

Again out of each 100, seventy-five belonged to some kind of family. Of these, twenty-five were attached to a large family of six or more members—often an extended family of a grandparent or two, an aunt and uncle, or cousins. Thus the idea that the gospel would call one of a household and two of a city applied to only 25 percent of Saints, and these did not remain isolated for long.[22]

The biographies bear out the fact that people joined the Mormon church as families. If a wife were baptized, chances were very good that within the year her husband would follow. If their family was young, all of the children would be baptized as a matter of course. If some children were grown, several if not all of these would also join with their spouses.

Alicia Allsley Grist provides an example of the core, two-parent family.[23] She was born in Birmingham in 1827, obtained at least a basic education as evidenced by her articulate letters to the *Latter-day Saints' Millennial Star* and *Woman's Exponent*, and mar-

22. Taylor, 259.
23. Some sources spell her given name as Elicia.

ried John K. Grist when she was about twenty-three. Five years later they were both baptized. After several months he was made an elder, and subsequently the family followed him to Dublin, perhaps on a mission for the church. By 1861 (six years later) they were in Liverpool Center Ward preparing to emigrate. It was another year and a half before the family, including at least four daughters, sailed for America with no mention of any extended family accompanying them. Other biographies encapsulate this family experience in the phrase, "the whole family was converted," meaning parents and children (Emily Ann Parsons Barker, Margaret McNeil Ballard, Alice Maw Poulter, and Mary Foster).

Another pattern was extended families who converted and helped one another emigrate. Henrietta Rushton married Thomas Bullock, whom she had known for years, when both were about twenty-two. Two years later her family "heard and believed" the gospel, and the following year she and Thomas converted. All of them emigrated together, sharing berth and wagon.

A third family pattern was that of the widow, widower, or divorced man or woman with children. Out of the twenty-seven biographies with enough detail to reveal family status at the time of conversion or emigration, seven subjects were single heads of families, including four widows, one divorcee, and two widowers. There were others who traveled singly but were technically still married. Most remarried either during emigration or within a year after arriving in Utah.

Remarriage as a product of church affiliation was so common it should be considered as a motive for both conversion and emigration. Reconstituted families were more numerous than those with single heads. Adults left alone by death prior to joining the church often remarried before emigrating. Reconstituted families comprise one-third to one-half of our 100 families. The experience of losing a spouse to death or divorce was at least as common during this period as in our day.

Single people, or those emigrating singly, formed the least typical pattern. Taylor's study shows them comprising only one-

My Grandmothers Ambrosine

fourth of emigration companies. In the histories I encountered they are less than one-tenth. Most singles were young and would marry soon after reaching Zion, if not on the way. Others became single through death of a spouse at sea or on the plains. And among the histories in this study are three or four stories of men and women who joined the LDS church, met with resistance from a spouse, and went to Zion alone—some divorcing first, most not. These incidents inspired tremendous hostility from outsiders and helped reinforce the image of home-breakers.

One suspects that for every person who abandoned a spouse for religion's sake there was one who did not but remained in Great Britain in varying degrees of involvement with the church. Stories about these women are hard to find, but they occasionally surface in subsequent chapters.

Large, Landless Families Acquainted with Grief

What were other characteristics of these Mormon families? First, if they were not large families at the time of emigration, they would become so in Zion. Couples with only three or four children were either young, fatherless, or had lost infants through death. Most would soon have six or more children, the average being eight.[24]

With so many children, there was little spacing between pregnancies and a woman's childbearing years were prolonged. When birth dates of the children are available, one typically sees the birth of the first child seven to twelve months after marriage, three or four subsequent children born in close succession (sixteen to twenty-four months apart), then later children born at 2.5 to four-year intervals. Women married between ages sixteen and twenty-three and, if not widowed, bore children for the next sixteen to twenty-eight years.

The case of Elizabeth Phillips Thomas's in-laws, while probably not typical, is instructive. Her mother-in-law was at marriage twenty-three, vocation not known, from Merthyr Tydfill. Her father-in-law was twenty-five, a weaver, of Pontgwynfe, Llan-

---

24. This is based on information from genealogical charts on thirty of the 100 women—the total found in LDS genealogical archives.

deusant Parish, Carmarthenshire, Wales. They were married "by banns" in 1831, according to the parish records, and were probably Church of England (unlike 80 percent of their countrymen) because they had each of their children christened. Legitimacy in marriage was necessary, but few Methodists cared to anglicize their children as well.[25]

By the time of the 1851 census the mother was thirty-three and had seven living children ranging from one to sixteen years. Thomas, the eighth child listed in the family record (and later the husband of Elizabeth Phillips), told his children that his parents had twenty-one children. Because the family record stops in 1841, and we have only the 1851 census, many of the mother's childbearing years are unaccounted for. With continued, nearly uninterrupted pregnancies, she may well have had twenty-one births.

It is tempting to believe that this was an extremely prolific family even for the nineteenth century—but was it? The first baby was born and died on Christmas Day. The second died sometime in infancy. We have no marriage or death dates for the fifth, sixth, and seventh children as well, suggesting that they may have died in infancy or early childhood. Since Thomas would not likely have fabricated a family tradition of twenty-one children, there must have been others, perhaps some stillbirths, that went unrecorded. Had the family record listed only those siblings who lived beyond infancy, the list might have been closer to the average of eight. Perhaps other subjects who reported only ten or twelve children did not include stillbirths. In other words, sixteen, eighteen, or twenty-one births might not have been remarkable.

Death was a common experience in these families. Most lost infants or older children to illness and accident in addition to the loss of a parent or step-parent. Clara Alice Robinson Allred's father

---

25. Marriages could be officially performed only by the established church—in England, the Church of England; in Wales, the Church of Wales; etc. Thus, if a Methodist couple wished to be married in the eyes of the law, they had no choice but an Anglican ceremony. Christenings and blessings, on the other hand, did not need a government stamp, so members of dissident sects were free to have such rites performed by their own ministers.

lost one wife at thirty-five, remarried but lost her too, then married a milliner who outlived him by seven years. "Wee Granny" Murdoch lost her husband when he went to rescue a young miner caught in a shallow shaft near their home. Perhaps out of consideration for his heroism, the company loaned her land on which her sons built her a stone cottage where she lived out her life (Mary Murray Murdoch).

Examining the childbearing history of eight women chosen at random from 100 histories shows that of sixty-four children born, thirteen died before the age of five, two died in their late teens, and one died unmarried at age thirty-one. An unusual case is the family of Elizabeth Phillips Thomas herself, whose own parents had eleven children between 1835 and 1852. Two died in infancy, one was stillborn, another died at age seven, and four others died by the age of twenty (one at sea, another killed by a team of horses). Out of eleven children, only Elizabeth lived to marry and raise a family, and she emigrated to Utah, leaving her parents childless.[26]

Another characteristic of these families is that they were landless. The Thomas family lived in the "Furnace Cottages," row houses leased out by a Carmarthen refinery. Even if the opportunity to buy land had arisen, many would have passed because they moved from mine to mine as one pit retired and another opened. Country residents were no more likely to own other than small parcels, sharecropping or hiring out to larger landowners.

It was in the larger towns and cities that shopkeepers and others of the middle class had a better chance of owning property. In our sample, several families owned shops with living quarters above, including London dressmaker Jean Rio Baker Pearce and Priscilla Merriman Evans's fancy milliner-sister who a gypsy had predicted would wear silk and satin and live in a big house in the city. Jane Benbow, whose husband was a yeoman farmer with a

26. From Thomas family papers, specifically my grandmother's research notes taken from "Births & Baptisms of Llannelly Branch Record of Members" and "Carmarthen Parish Records and Bishops Transcripts, 1686-1889," records found in LDS archives.

gracious house and property in Castle Frome, Herefordshire, was an exception.

Family Relations: The Histories Are All but Mute

What of the emotional fabric of these families? In the histories not much is overtly said about relationships, either between father and mother or parent and children. Hannah King, the upper-class lady, almost alone wrote in detail about her inner world. There was her idolized father, a kindly, expressive land steward to the Earl of Gogmagog near Cambridge. Hannah loved but feared her more severe, practical mother. She married a son of the lesser gentry and discovered even before the wedding that "we were *two* in the religion of the soul." Though he was kind and solicitous, "I never thought of telling him my sorrows or my feelings" but learned "to work out my salvation alone."

Most Mormon women of the time were too busy with survival to philosophize over relationships. Thus their memoirs give only hints and glimpses into their emotional lives. We know, however, that John Johnson Davies and Mariah Davies remained happy companions after marriage. For years after Mariah's death John fondly gleaned from his early diary those memories which he considered worth keeping. One of those reads: "My girl and myself used to go on excursions to the seashore in a steamer. And sometimes down to the seashore in a boat. England and Wales is a great country for enjoyments. Excuse me for saying so much about my girl, I can't help it for she was good company to me" (Mariah Davies).

Feelings were expressed more often in reminiscences than in contemporary accounts. One learns more about grandmother Sarah Hattersley Wells's temperament through the eyes of little Nellie's than through Wells's diaries. Grandmother Wells told Nellie stories about the early life in England because "I like to tell Thee things, Thee listens." Though bent and aged, Grandmother Wells had long brown hair only slightly greying, and one of her stories was about her husband Samuel Wells who had been a common laborer. "Thee Grandfather, just like a banty rooster, always ready, always got a chip on his shoulders," she would say.

The diaries are all but silent on the matter of sexual relationships between husband and wives—a predictable finding when dealing with Victorian ladies. My experience parallels sociologist Hulett's attempts to gather information about sexual habits in Mormon polygamous families. He could not get answers.[27]

Scholars say the Victorians were more delicate in sexual attitude than their Puritan ancestors: "A colonial lady or gentleman had no hesitation about using such words as 'legs' and 'belly' to describe those parts of the body; but their children and grandchildren preferred 'nether limbs' and 'lower portion'."[28] In the 1880s, according to domestic historian Mary Cable, "a squeamish female became the ideal."

Whether squeamishness about such matters was the British ideal, and whether this ideal was embraced by the working as well as genteel classes, cannot be determined from our histories. Only one woman permitted herself any frankness about her physical life: Hannah Tapfield King, the delicate, upper-middle-class English poetess, who probably referred to the onset of menopause with this statement: "I might have had children up to my 52nd year." Elsewhere in her journal she made one oblique comment on marital sex which is placed in fuller context with her story in chapter 9.

Cultural Roots: Church-schooled or Self-schooled

One aspect of Mormon stereotype was naivete bespeaking a lack of breeding and education. To approach the reality behind this image, we need to ask how much schooling the women attained. If we define education as formal schooling, the stereotype will be

27. James Edward Hulett, Jr., "The Sociological and Social Psychological Aspects of the Mormon Polygamous Family," Ph.D. diss., University of Wisconsin, 1939; cited by Jessie L. Embry, *Mormon Polygamous Families: Life in the Principle* (Salt Lake City: University of Utah Press, 1987), 50.

28. Mary Cable, "S*x Education," in *American Heritage* 25 (Oct. 1974), 6:41. For further discusion of Victorian mores, see *In Search of Victorian Values: Aspects of Nineteenth-Century Thought and Society* (Manchester, NY: Manchester University Press, 1988); and June Purvis, *Hard Lessons: The Lives and Education of Working-Class Women in Nineteenth-Century England* (Minneapolis: University of Minnesota Press, 1989).

verified, not only by the level of Mormon women but of Victorian women generally.

Even Mrs. King, seen as a poet and "lady" by her English and Utah associates, by her own admission received no more than two years of classroom training and none beyond the age of twelve. Probably Ellen Brooke Ferguson was the most highly educated. But while she was known as "Doctor" Ferguson, Ellen's education was not obtained in a preparatory school or college but under private tutors (some of them Cambridge dons) hired by her lawyer-father. Her medical training came largely from her husband, an Edinburgh graduate, since British society offered no outlets for a woman tutored in math and science.

A woman who impressed Wilford Woodruff with her educational accomplishments was Ellen Balfour Redman. Woodruff wrote proudly in his journal that Sister Redman, an enthusiastic member of the Whitechapel Branch, taught languages to daughters of the nobility.[29] However, I have been unable to find record of her anywhere but in his journal. Other Mormon women obtained degrees from American colleges, but this was in maturity and long after emigration.

Most women received at least some formal schooling. If nothing else, they attended day schools (also called circulating or scripture schools) taught by traveling preachers, where they learned to read through the Bible. Eliza Dorsey Ashworth, for instance, remembered attending (at an early age, before she went "out to service" [i.e., became a domestic help]) a Sunday school

29. Wilford Woodruff Journal cited in British Mission Manuscript History for 10 January 1842. Woodruff wrote, "She is a widow, a Scotch lady of the first rank and education. She formerly taught languages, French and Italian, as well as music, to some of the nobility in London. She has many acquaintances here and thinks the Lord has sent her here to do good . . . She is now visiting many persons of rank and preaching the fullness of the Gospel to them . . . She says she can get a Book of Mormon for us to the Queen . . . She has been a great traveler through the East Indies and other parts of the world, has been ship-wrecked several times, taken once by the Indians and once by Pirates." Sister Redman is mentioned several times over the next weeks in Woodruff's journal and then fades away. One wonders just what kind of a character she was.

that taught reading and writing. Even when a woman such as Mary Coslet Thomas left her mark rather than her signature on her marriage certificate, it did not mean she could not read. And though it is apparent that most Welsh women did not write other than by necessity, our histories testify that British women in general wrote as well as read. Most of the records, if not coming to us directly, were at least based on handwritten memoirs. Since the majority of the rememberers were of the working classes, we assume that people of all classes could write.

If we include informal education, then a good percentage of women acquired learning. Before and after age twelve, Hannah King was taught "by my mother" who "conversed a good deal" with her son and daughters, taught them the social graces, read to them, and listened to them read. In later years she recalled:

> I had been raised carefully as all our family had. My mother was a wise and judicious trainer of the young, and her mind was stored with much practical knowledge of character and circumstances. She was our daily, hourly Lexicon. If we spoke wrongly, she corrected us *there*, if ungrammatically, she made us repeat it *properly*. She talked knowledge and learning and good manners and morals and principles into us day by day, and so cultivated our minds and formed our characters. Still our lives were secluded and mine especially.

By the age of thirteen Hannah was perusing the Anglican *Whole Duty of Man* and the weekly preparation lessons for taking the sacrament.

Because self-education was so substantially a part of the Victorian tradition, the level of women's literacy varied as widely as the circumstances, ambitions, and tastes of the families and women themselves. Priscilla Merriman Evans began attending the National School at Tenby in Pembrokeshire, Wales, at an early age and continued until she was eleven. The school taught the Bible, sampling needlework for girls, and "other studies." She would have continued, but at eleven she was required to drop out to tend house for her ailing mother. An older sister should by rights have taken on this obligation, but she did not like housekeeping so Priscilla was commandeered into the assignment. Any further education she had to create herself, and she seems to have done so. When many years later her husband was called on another mission from Utah to Wales, leaving Priscilla pregnant with their eleventh child, she showed enough ability to manage the family store and support the family.

Vocational education had a larger role in nineteenth-century schooling than for today's children. Many were apprenticed to a trade through which they learned the skills necessary to earn a living. A liberal education came through family and social contacts rather than textbooks and classrooms. In Scottish families Robert Burns's poetry was an oral tradition, and recitations and singing took the place of television. In Wales choral music, hymn-writing, and poeticizing were a birthright. And for church-goers fortunate enough to have a cleric with high-church leanings, Sunday sermons could be an experience in literature, philosophy, and aesthetics.

For one Mormon girl, at least, her parents' conversion deprived her of formal schooling. Margaret McNeil Ballard, from a small coal village near the seashore of Scotland, told her children: "Because of being a Mormon I was not permitted to attend the schools and so I was entirely deprived of schooling while in the old country, and in pioneering there was little opportunity of education." This is further evidence that formal education in nineteenth-century Britain was tied to the churches, primarily motivated by the anti-papacy ethic of enabling common people to read the Bible for themselves. It also suggests that either the Ballards were too removed from a Mormon branch to send their children to Sunday school or that Mormon Sunday schools did not teach reading and writing.

A possibility is that Mormonism attracted readers because the illiterate depended completely on what other people said about the unpopular sect. There is corroboration of this in several memoirs and missionary journals. A common proselyting tool in the British mission was pamphlets distributed door-to-door and from street corners. Dan Jones, especially, used the printing press to spread his message in the Welsh language. Many converts reported encountering missionaries by reading a posted bill announcing the meeting. A few initially discovered Mormonism through printed literature. Two of the memoirs mention a specific book which converted them and which they then lent to friends and neighbors—*A Voice of Warning*, Elder Parley P. Pratt's discussion of millennial prophecies.

Moral Roots: Conventional Origins

Writers have tried to pinpoint what it was that predisposed 100,000 Britons, at least half of them women, to the doctrines of Mormonism. P. A. M. Taylor skirted the question when he posed several theories to explain the Mormon drive to emigrate. He considered millennial fever, contagion, economic depression and urban poverty, Zionism, and church financial assistance. He found too little proof for any one of these, concluding that those who proved susceptible to Mormon preaching "may have craved spiritual assurance at least as much as material betterment."[30]

Thorp studied 280 converts for prior religious affiliation and found that 70 percent of his subjects came from mainline churches: 25 percent were Methodist, 21 percent Church of England, 11 percent Baptist, 6 percent Independent, 5 percent Presbyterian, and almost 1 percent Catholic. A minority came from evangelical or splinter groups: 11 percent Primitive Methodist, 2 percent "teetotallers" and "infidels." Of the remainder, 1 percent were not religiously inclined and 15 percent were religiously inclined but not affiliated. Since the working class tended to belong to this latter group, Thorp's statistics may suggest that Mormon converts were more churched than their working-class peers. They were not culled from the religious fringe but from mainstream British culture.[31]

There were dramatic exceptions to this rule, Wilford Woodruff's 600-strong Herefordshire splinter group—the United Brethren—being one.[32] There were other instances of entire congrega-

30. Taylor, 269.
31. Thorp, 60.
32. Was this the Pennsylvania-born United Brethren, a Mennonite offshoot started in 1800 which baptized any way the recipient wished? If so, it might help to explain the mass conversion—the group was used to

tions joining the Mormon fold. In one village 90 percent of residents became Mormons. But these mass conversions did not occur within a mainline church.

Many of our histories tell of the woman's specific religious affiliation before her conversion. Susannah Albion's father was an Independent minister of London. Priscilla Evans's family was Baptist, a relatively rare but still acceptable commodity in Wales where Methodists predominated. Rachel Killian's parents were Catholic, also rare among Mormon converts and suggesting, along with their name, Irish background. The Thomas family's church affiliation is not stated, but the fact that they recorded their babies' christenings in the parish register identifies them as Church of Wales. Alice and Edward Horrocks's Welsh marriage was registered instead with the Society of Protestant Dissenters.

Other families whose religious affiliations are not given describe themselves as anything from "deeply religious" (a common phrase used by Thomas Bullock and others) to "almost Infidel to all Religion and did not belong to any therefore the children were not taught much about it" (statement by Mary Nixon Bate Buckley on her religious training). A number of other women, while also not reporting specific church membership, stated that as children they attended Sunday school and scripture class.

The phrase "deeply religious" could have applied to British society at large. The church was still pervasive in the private and public life of nineteenth-century England. Tithing was a tax exacted by the civil government from property owners and used to support the official church. When a man posted the banns to be married, it was not done at the courthouse but at the parish church—even if one was not Anglican.

The church was so ingrained in peoples' lives that probably only in a larger city could the Nixons have been "infidel to all religion." Elsewhere this course would have been more difficult if they wanted employment, education for their children, and acceptance into the community. Attending an alternate church had been a hard-fought and only 100-year-old right.

American preachers and was open to new ideas in doctrines.

{ 47 }

The level of mass religious fervor wavered, however. New and old sects bestirred themselves periodically to arouse the religious feeling inspired in the eighteenth century by Methodism. Probably to contrast low-church Methodism to Mormonism, the magazine of the LDS British Mission, the *Millennial Star*, reported in considerable detail one Irish revival, part of a series of Protestant revivals during the 1850s.[33]

It appears that in other ways Mormon proselytes mirrored the times and were conventional in their moral and social beliefs. This is an all-important claim which demands documentation. To begin with, lower-middle class girls like Priscilla Meredith Evans, who attended scripture classes as children, likely would have retained in adulthood the lessons of childhood. Upper-middle class girls like Hannah Tapfield King were taught by age two the limits of respectable behavior. As a toddler she was once severely flogged when her mother suspected she had lied about taking some honey from the parlor cupboard. Her Anglican mother "hated a lie with a perfect hatred."

The personal histories and branch minutes are replete with examples of Mormon intolerance of deviant moral behavior among members. The branches were quick to excommunicate not just for offenses deemed disloyal to the group or its leaders but for moral lapses. A girl would most certainly be cut off for fornication, probably for stealing or lying unless she repented or made amends, and often for swearing or missing meetings without cause.[34]

In the personal histories there is additional evidence of traditional mores. There is not one instance in our histories of abandonment or divorce due to infidelity—though there were a number of separations over religious differences. British Mormons believed in legal marriage, if one may judge from the case of Brother and Sister Booth of London. Reverend Albion, the once-Independent minister, charged Sister Booth with adultery because she had

33. For more on the *Star*'s report, see the chapter on women's activities in the branches.

34. Infractions and disciplining branch members are treated in detail in two later chapters.

never divorced her first husband. Branch leaders thought the accusation serious enough to convene two church hearings several years apart in which they ascertained that while she had been deserted as a teenage bride of only six weeks, Sister Booth had not been legally divorced from the young man. Her husband had taken another wife with whom he had lived for nineteen years, while the Booths had been together for ten or more years (no details given as to whether or how a second marriage was performed). The final church court forgave the couple and, while telling them to legalize Mrs. Booth's situation, then indicted James Albion "for maliciously putting charges against [Henry] Booth" as well as for slandering the character of an unnamed branch member.[35] Albion was eventually cut off from the London branch, though whether for stubbornness or a larger discontent is not known.

That the branch showed some leniency toward the Booths does not indicate condonment of common-law marriage. Some tolerance toward youthful indiscretions was typical of the times and its churches. Methodist Hannah Daniels of Carmarthenshire, Wales, was eighteen and pregnant when she wed Thomas Job, thirty-five, who was studying to be a minister. Obligations to parents and siblings resulted in many long and frustrating engagements, so there was no real scandal though, as Thomas put it, more was expected of a preacher than of others. His ambitions to the cloth were ended (Hannah Daniels Job).

In other ways the attitudes of British Mormons reflected the values of their culture. John Davies and his girl friend Mariah dated, as was common, and the branch kept tabs on them. Always concerned for the moral well-being of members, Amasa Lyman reported of the Whitechapel, London, Branch: "[It] is warm and friendly, holding social concerts to keep its members from other amusements."[36] A Mormon matron of 1875 looked respectably askance at violations of the work ethic:

35. London Conference Mission History, 1 Dec. 1841 and 8 Dec. 1844, LDS archives.
36. London Conference Manuscript History, spring 1871.

One of our sisters asked a fine grown, strong, healthy-look-
ing young woman, who came to the door begging, if it would
not be far better for her to try and get a situation at some
gentleman's house, than to go through the streets begging as she
was doing. The young girl replied, no indeed it wouldn't! . . .
There wasn't money enough in it. The sister opened her eyes in
astonishment, and asked her if she could get more money by
begging. She answered, "Oh yes! it is a very poor street that I
cannot get a penny in and I can visit sixty streets per day and at
least that will clear me five shillings, and I am my own mistress
into the bargain."[37]

The Critical Ingredient

But if Mormons were conventional, how were they attracted
to a sect which, after 1852, openly admitted the practice of plural
marriage? This was the question Fanny Stenhouse tried to answer
in 1870 as a fifty-year-old disaffected Mormon. She concluded
from her own experience and observation of others that "religious
tendencies and a devotional feeling were almost universally found
to be the causes which induced men and women to join the
Mormon Church." Most converts were like her, she claimed, in
being "religiously inclined . . . Evangelical Protestants of the Old
World." Even as a child she had been "disposed to religious
influences," trying with simplicity and enthusiasm to please God
by the life she lived. She contrasted this background to Roman
Catholicism, whose beliefs, she felt, emphasized dependence on
authority rather than personal piety. Converts were rarely "persons predisposed to infidelity" or little prior religious inclination.

Yet Stenhouse eventually left Mormonism, whereas many
stayed. Perhaps she exemplified those proselytes who brought to
Mormonism only half a disposition for it; who lacked a critical
ingredient which brought, for better or worse, staying power. This
quality has been given different names by different writers including church apologists, descendants, historians, and the women
themselves. Some called it prayerfulness or personal communion
with God; others described the proselytes as "religious seekers"

37. George L. Farrell to the *Women's Exponent* 4 (1 July 1875), 3:1.

who drifted from one church to another.[38] In contemporary Mormon meetings prayer-givers ask that missionaries will find "the honest in heart," and nineteenth-century Mormon women described themselves as "the blood of Ephraim."

Call it readiness. Many of our women were prepared for the Word when it came. They felt pre-selected, called, made ready. Fanny Stenhouse was not; her vulnerability to Mormonism came through familial loyalty. Yet there were facets to even her makeup which predisposed her to Mormon teachings. One was a tendency toward independence or at least mild dissatisfaction with the religions of her girlhood:

> In plainness of dress the Methodists and Baptists much resembled the Quakers. . . . I well remember one smooth-faced, pious, corpulent brother, who was old enough to be my father, saying to me one day: "My dear young sister, were it not for your love of dress, I have seriously thought that I would some day make you my wife." I wickedly resolved that if a few bright coloured ribbons would disgust my pious admirer, it should not be my fault if he still continued to think of me.

Another was a recognition that her family had improved under the new religion. A third was the desire to be spiritually united not only with her family, who had converted while she was away in Paris, but also with the young elder who taught her, baptized her, and, through the "magnetic currents" of his sensitive mind and her "excited state," produced what she came to believe was a false conversion experience. Perhaps she was right. She was an anomaly—that rare reality which resembled the stereotype of the too-impressionable young woman swayed by the dashing young missionary.

A few women had joined one church after another in quest of an institution which embodied the inner vision they possessed. Mary Nixon Bate Buckley, daughter of the "infidels," wrote:

> i had a great desire for Religion when i was quite [a] Small girl but could not get any Encouragement so it kind of laid dorment

38. Thorp, 61.

and after i got married and began to have a Family I commenced to go to church and then I began to wonder wich was the Right one but i could not tell[.] i went to the church of England [and] to the Methodist and thought i would give them a good trial[.] I prayed to the Lord in my weak way to know wich was the right the Lord gave me a dream or vision showing me they where none of them write . . .

This reminds one of Thorp's observation that some of the men drifted into as many as six churches before joining the Mormons. He found others who expressed disillusionment with all churches, in particular with the insensitivity of ministers, the constant cry for money, and the irreconcilability of orthodox doctrines with their own understandings of the Bible.[39]

The women of our histories say little about ministers, but they followed family members' discontent. John Powell reported that his mother was disillusioned with the religious "kant" and hypocrisy (Mary Powell). Alice Maw Poulter's father was one of those "not satisfied with his religion," and when he joined Mormonism his daughter went with him. Ann Killip Cowley's husband, for twenty years a Wesleyan Methodist on the Isle of Man, was at length disfellowshipped "because he did not think Wesleyan teachings fit the Bible." Since the Cowleys were together baptized into Mormonism, one presumes she was united with him in his earlier dissent. Other women said nothing about dissatisfaction but did report being "earnest Bible readers." They were certainly not disinterested bystanders.

Some women were prepared by dreams, visions, or other psychic experiences. Sixteen-year-old Priscilla Evans was promised by a gypsy that she would one day "cross the big waters." Lovable, 200-pound Eliza Dorsey Ashworth, who kept a garden and window boxes filled with flowers, had a dream about roses: "She dreamed she was dressed in white and was going on a long journey. On the way, she crossed a long bridge. She had two white roses in her hand, and while she stood on the bridge one of the roses fell in the stream. Soon the other one dropped in. She

39. Ibid.

watched them fall, and it made her feel so badly she awoke crying." Ashworth indeed made a long journey, settled the mouth of Millcreek Canyon in Salt Lake City, and lost two of her sons in the canyon stream.

Perhaps most poignant is the story of Martha Cumming Clark. She was a latecomer to the Mormon fold, the great-granddaughter of a Mrs. Low who with four sons emigrated to Zion in about 1860. A fifth son refused to go but stayed in England, raising his children as Presbyterians. He was Martha's grandfather.

Martha was destined from birth to be a Mormon. When two days old she was taken into the arms of her grandfather, who prophesied to her mother, "Maggie, this is your second child. You may have a dozen more, but remember from me, that this child will be The one in your family." As a girl Martha had dreams which, when told to her sisters as they gathered around the fire-place in their nightgowns, provoked them into calling her Joseph the Dreamer. "Do you mean to tell us that my father and mother and all us children have got to bow down to you some day?" they would taunt her. Her dreams told her that one day she would go to America and marry a widower. She had other mystical experi-ences which complicated family life but eased her physical suffer-ing while working in a mill to support her widowed mother.

Some of the histories contain no hints whatever about their subjects' spiritual lives prior to Mormonism. To all appearances Jane Graham Laidlaw Bell was a cheerful, gregarious girl who had few troubles until meeting up with the Mormons. Why would a twenty-six-year-old woman raised comfortably by an aunt and uncle in an intelligent, cultured home suddenly join a new sect, marry one of its preachers, and allow herself to be led to the wilds of Utah? Yet in her later years as a widow with three children "she never tired of talking over the principles of the gospel," testified a neighbor. A significant event is missing from her history, and it may well have been another spiritual catharsis.

For most women the way to conversion was not a spiritualist phenomenon but the kind of material hardship that needled them into seeking reasons for existence, such as the death of a father or sibling. For Mary Jane Ewer it was religious hunger but also the endless demands of her family's poverty. For Priscilla Evans it was a life of drudgery under a demanding father and as substitute mother to five brothers.

For lonely Hannah Tapfield King, living in her eight-room house in the midst of her husband's well-tended fields and no physical wants, the deaths of friends and family detached her from mundane life. But she also suffered from "triste" (sadness)—a lifelong if usually mild depression which she expunged through poetry, letters, and effusive confessions to her diaries. As a thirteen-year-old Hannah had been tortured by a sense of unworthiness mixed with skepticism at the preaching of the new curate, the "evangelical low-church" Mr. Williams. A visit to the bedside of a dying boy brought her overwrought sensitivities to a pique, and she became ill. Her mother found her crying one day, and though Hannah had dreaded this formidable person ever finding out her inner torment, she confessed how "the Lord had afflicted me." Her mother merely hugged her, assured her that "if the Lord had afflicted me, it must be for some fault of her and my father, for she considered me without a fault," and afterward spoke to the retired minister, a high-church soul whose plain, practical sermons spoken in a musical voice Hannah had loved. He wrote the girl a calming letter which assuaged her fears.

Hannah still suffered "a dark spirit for years." She was forty-two and had endured a year of "the breaking up of old associations" by death and disagreement, when her dressmaker introduced her to Mormonism.

> She told me that all other Churches were false! I had suffered so much in my early life for my religious feelings, and had by earnest prayer, and trying to walk consistently as became a Christian[,] gained a great degree of happiness in my religion, and I know the spirit of God has led and comforted me. And when she showed me that the last dispensation was opened and that there were but two Churches on earth—One God's and the rest the opposite power, I felt again stranded, and oh! how I trembled to think should I again have to "stumble upon the Dark Mountains" of doubt and uncertainty in which I had struggled and suffered for years? Oh! how she broke me up, how I wept "rivers of tears". She was shocked, and seemed to mourn over

me. I told her never to mention it to me again, etc. Under this wounded spirit came the letter from George D. announcing the death of his brother. I was already full of tears, and indeed were the "deep fountains" of my heart broken up. Truly I was "born in tears" unto the Church of Christ . . . (entry for Aug. 1849).

For other women, preparation meant circumstances which placed them in proximity to a Mormon branch. Several families moved from Ireland or south England to Scotland and the Midlands where the Mormon influence was more pronounced, just in time for the elders to find them. It seemed Martha Cumming Clark would spend her life as a drudge—six years in a textile mill, eight years caring for a retarded boy, three years as housemaid and nursemaid to an invalid woman—until her mother badgered her into the aid of a sister in Edinburgh. "You are the only one in the family who pretends to be a Christian," said her mother; "now I want you to show it." Despite her ailing stump of a foot and the harsh chores which had already driven other girls from the clergyman's household where her sister worked, Martha went—after praying and being told by the Lord to go. Within weeks she had been introduced to the missionaries in Edinburgh.

Chapter 3.

The Conversion Experience

Mormon missionaries were unanimously male, but then ministers of nearly all the churches were men. Mission and conference leaders tended to be American men, married and mature, while travelling elders were young converts like Mariah Davies's fiance—converted one week, made a priest the next, and soon called to travel with the full-time missionaries to bear testimony and sing.

Most missionaries were diplomatic, attempting to forestall antagonism by introducing themselves to town officials and even presenting a Book of Mormon to the Queen before beginning to proselyte in London. Others expected antagonism but went to work using any method that got results.

A typical tactic was to sell, door-to-door, copies of the Book of Mormon and other literature called tracts, hence the term tracting. George Cannon Lambert, whose parents accompanied him to the mission field, wrote that he spent most of his first month "walking about from one town or village to another, calling occasionally at the home of old church members." Under this routine, he and his companion would tract, each on a different side of the street, knocking on doors and "getting into conversation as often as possible . . . We met with a little encouragement occasionally but generally only indifference." This was in 1882 in Herefordshire, scene of Wilford Woodruff's baptisms-by-the-hundreds in the 1840s.[1]

If desperate in the early decades, when support from families in Utah was slim, elders asked for a meal and a bed. People willing to give an ear or comfort often proved receptive to the gospel message. Another common approach was to obtain a public hall, chapel, or private home, and advertise preaching through flyers, word of mouth, or the local newspaper.

If unsuccessful in these methods, elders would do as John Blythe in 1878 Scotland, who "Stood up on the north publick corner of the streets of Galston and Bare my testimony before the inhabitants." This was the first outdoor meeting of his mission. He and his companion had previously used the branch president's house for preaching. Public meetings occasionally turned into small riots, and young men must have felt like biblical prophets when forced from their podiums.[2]

Some young elders tried methods more imaginative than wise. James Kippen, a new convert turned missionary, "stood outside of the Kirks [church]" he had attended as a boy and bore testimony to the people leaving Sunday services. He was called "a Mormon delusion," and his old minister became "rather ankshus for him to leave."[3]

Fixed Friends

Overall, foot proselyting and preaching in advertised locations must have been successful, for many eventual converts encountered Mormonism through these elders traveling sometimes alone, often two by two, throughout Britain. Eliza Dorsey Ashworth was baptized in 1842 after a missionary (presumably Apostle Parley P. Pratt) came to her home. Felicia Astle "met the missionaries" in 1850 in Nottingham and was converted. In

1. Journal of George Cannon Lambert in Kate B. Carter, ed., *Our Pioneer Heritage* (Salt Lake City: Daughters of the Utah Pioneers, 1965), 9:269.

2. Journal of John L. Blyth, 14 July 1878, photocopy, Utah State Historical Society, Salt Lake City.

3. Ibid., 29 June 1878. Blyth cites a letter he received on that day from Elder James H. Kippen in Perthshire.

1854 Charles Penrose preached and fourteen-year-old Mary Jane Ewer Palmer "heard and believed." Sarah H. Wells "heard two missionaries preach shortly after her marriage" and was baptized. Sarah Isom, "with her parents, was converted to the Mormon religion by some of the early Mormon missionaries in England." Alice Horrocks Wood's descendants are told that "the LDS missionaries came into their [parents'] lives and they accepted the gospel."

Mary Ann Chapple Warner wrote, "Our home was always open to the missionaries, and seven years after the church was organized [in Britain] my parents joined." Mary Ann Weston Maughan, having learned of Mormonism through her employer, was alone the day Wilford Woodruff visited the Jenkins home and sang for her: "He looked peaceful and happy. I thought he was a good man and the Gospell he preached must be true." Hannah King described one elder almost in adoration:

> What were my first impressions with regard to him? I certainly felt directly that he meant to be kind to us. I next saw in his manner and something in his appearance that he bore a strong likeness to one in whom we had all been much interested, now gone to the spirit world, and he shone into my heart by reflection. Before two days he needed no borrowed pedestal to stand upon, for I found he had one of his own. Shall I attempt to describe him? I don't know that I could—but this I do know, that I liked him, for he possessed what I consider essential in a man, viz, he was manly, gentlemanly, self possessed and dignified, modest and retiring in his manner, gentle and kind to all, humble and unassuming, yet ever maintaining self respect and his own position . . . We spent the greater part of a week together, and by that time I had settled in my own mind that he had become one of the planetary bodies of our social system in the shape of a "fixed" friend.

The portrayal of Mormon elders in these histories stands in pointed contrast to the media image of vengeful Danites, kidnappers, and con men. Elizabeth Lewis defended mission leader Dan Jones against this image in her Utah letters to Welsh friends:

> Tell them and everyone who mentions Capt. Jones that he has

not been the evil man that they prophesied about him, rather until now his behavior has been the direct opposite. We all found him kind and benevolent, and his entire behavior is like a father toward his children . . . He has not received nor has he tried to get any of my money, and I have not heard that anyone of the company has been the loser of one penny because of him.

A story about eight-year-old Margaret R. Davis helps to explain converts' perceptions of the missionaries as friends and advocates. During a visit to her family's home, one of two missionaries asked her name. Confused, she answered, "Latter-day Saint." Thinking she was being insolent, her mother slapped her, whereupon the missionary said, "Never mind; she is the only one in the family who will have the privilege of going to the temple and doing work for the dead." Margaret McNeil Ballard was another girl who felt strong childhood loyalty to the missionaries: "Many times I went to bed hungry in order to give my meal to the visiting Elders."

Some women were unimpressed, however. John Blythe's niece wrote him a letter "Warming up my ears." But he forgave her, thinking it only "sho[w]s her warm impulsive nature." In another instance, Blythe tried to heal his sister-in-law, Agnes. As it happened, her leg got worse.

While the majority of proselytes came into the fold through the missionaries, others learned of the faith through hearsay or reading material. Sometimes the initial brush came accidentally. Mary Nixon Bate Buckley went by chance into a small meetinghouse, heard the elders preach, and was converted. In 1851 "the father and mother of the girl that [John Davies] kept company with were baptized into the Church of Jesus Christ of Latter-day Saints," so it was only through the happenstance of romance that John became a Mormon (Rachel Mariah Davies). Priscilla Merriman (Evans) was incidentally invited to a "cottage meeting" at the home of a friend where she was "impressed" by the Mormon elder who spoke. Alice Maw Poulter's father, not satisfied with his present religion, was on his way home from work one day when he noticed a large sign over the Temperance Hall. He went home, told his wife about it, attended the first meeting with her, afterwards investigated the church further, and was baptized.

Hearsay traveled from relatives and friends and ministers of other faiths, and it was often negative. Fanny Stenhouse had apparently "heard stories against Mormonism" even before being warned against it by her sister and brother-in-law, who had disaffected from the St. Heliers branch. Priscilla Merriman Evans's father told her, "I have heard of old Joe Smith and the golden Bible." He must have formed the opinion that Smith's followers were gullible, for he forbade his daughter going to their meetings by saying "the Mormons were too slow to associate with."

In those areas where Mormon baptisms were abundant, opposition stories were plentiful. The Welsh Mormon newspaper *Udgorn Seion* (Zion's Trumpet) alluded to a story that had "followed the Saints to every corner of the country ever since they first came to Wales, and before that in England, except that the name of the place is changed." The story was about a Newport man who pretended to be dead so that two Mormon "prophets" could resurrect him. The *Udgorn* spouted, "If anyone can name these three tricksters . . . they shall have the pleasure of hearing us deliver them to Satan."[4]

Few histories refer specifically to a printed work. Mary Nixon Bate Buckley's autobiography mentions Pratt's *A Voice of Warning.* About a meeting she had happened upon, she recorded:

> one old gentleman Spoke about the voice of warning Said it made the Scriptures plain to his understanding and i was very much taken with that title and with many things that was Spoken of in that meeting . . . [After the meeting] i bought the Voice of warning and Read it and Attended all the meetings[,] bought the book of mormon Doctrine and Covenents and all the books they had for sale at that Branch[.] i Read them and the Bible and found it was just the Kind of Religion i wanted.

One or two other diaries mention Pratt's book. But we know investigators must have been influenced by the *Udgorn* and its

---

4. Frontispiece of first issue (Jan. 1849). See the facsimile and translated facsimile in honor of the 140th anniversary of the January 1849 issue, prepared by Ronald D. Dennis, copy in my possession.

predecessor, as well as the church periodical in England, *The Latter-day Saints' Millennial Star*.

Another influence was correspondence from friends and relatives already baptized, such as letters from Elizabeth Lewis in Utah:

> I believe it is my duty to my Good Lord and His cause to send my witness back, for the sake of those who have not had this experience as I have had, and so they can take heart also to come here.[5]

> I promised to many of my dear friends, Saints and others, that I would write from here about the happenings and nature of the country, its inhabitants and the religion professed. Many promised to believe my testimony from here if I testified that Mormonism still seemed true.[6]

Of course there were anti-Mormon articles, books, and pamphlets to counteract the Mormon literature, but none are mentioned specifically in the women's histories. This is remarkable considering the popularity of Mormon-oriented literature. Mary Nixon Bate did tell of being taunted with such things by her husband and former friends. And Dan Jones, the Saint Paul of the Welsh mission, referred to two newspapers whose editors had apparently taken a stance against Mormonism: "The *Times* are frightfully against us and the *Stars* within Gomer's atmosphere foretell strange things about us."[7]

Jones also alluded to a pamphlet that claimed Joseph Smith and Brigham Young practiced polygamy. It is curious that he, who had contact with Smith in Nauvoo, should deny the Mormon practice of polygamy:

> There is some booklet called "Life in the Far West," which gives a story of polygamy among the Saints in America, and that one of them has forty wives! This, of course, is as true as that "old Joe Smith" walked on the water, or that he was seen by a relative of

5. 10 Apr. 1850 letter published in the *Ugdorn* and translated and cited by Dennis.

6. 1851 letter from Manti, Utah, in Dennis.

7. Dennis, facsimile ed., 5.

Job from Pantteg taking the form of a dove as big as a horse, to imitate the Holy Ghost descending on the baptized. What will be considered TOO untruthful for the publications and pulpits of our country?[8]

Yet the revelation on "celestial marriage" was kept from the church at large and was not publicly proclaimed until 1852.

In 1840 it was still possible for Mary Ann Maughan, and the Jenkins family with whom she resided as a well-treated apprentice, not to have heard of Mormonism until Mr. Jenkins, on a visit to Herefordshire, was baptized by Wilford Woodruff. "He came home and told us about it. This was the first we had heard of it." As the century progressed, Mary Ann's countrywomen were less and less likely to have encountered little of Mormonism before learning of it first-hand.

Fanny Stenhouse was told by her sister and others about the Mormons, and her feelings were tempered by her belief that Mormonism had had a benign influence in her father's house, evidenced by her sisters' changed manner of life, and a "peace, love, kindness, and charity seldom seen in households of religious people." But it was not until she heard "a certain young elder preach" that her antipathy melted and she was "converted."

Mormon Preaching

What did young Elder Stenhouse say that won Fanny's mind and heart?

> [She] was captivated by the picture which he drew of the marvellous latter-day work . . . The visions of by-gone ages were again vouchsafed to men; angels had visibly descended to earth; God had raised up in a mighty way a Prophet, as of old, to preach the dispensation of the last days; gifts of prophecy, healing, and the working of miracles were now, as in the days of the Apostles, witnesses to the power of God . . . All were freely invited to come and cast away their sins, ere it was too late.

A transcript of Dan Jones's farewell address to the Welsh conference comes to us through the *Udgorn*. It is more elated in

---

8. Ibid., backplate.

tone than Stenhouse's representation of an English sermon, possibly reflecting the more heated sectarian environment of south Wales and Ireland. Because there are elements in the speech which might be construed as paternalistic and condescending, but also because of its lyricism, it is cited at length, with paragraphing inserted where the theme shifts. This sermon was meant for standing members of the Welsh branches, people with whom Jones had worked for several years, but there would have been non-members and investigators in the audience as well:

> Since we have come to know each other, the period now at the door is the most important and the most sorrowful and joyful which has happened to us, namely my departure from your midst to a far away country . . . The Heavens know, and my conscience knows . . . I have not ceased or tired of working, night and day, for four years . . . and until now the pleasure of my heart has been to serve you, and my joy in the Lord is that he gave me a part in the restorative dispensation of the fulness of times to you, and instructed me in those principles which will bring you joy and which, if you observe them, will lead you to a fulness of pure joy . . .
>
> Great is your honor, yea, unspeakable is your own gift, dear Saints, in having been brought from the darkness of false traditions to the light of the gospel of the Son of God—in having grasped a religion with power in it and having become heirs of substance . . . Cling to this for your life—these things do continually; and thus I am assured that my labor will not be in vain in the Lord . . .
>
> You have heard and read much about God's deliverance of his children in Zion . . . and doubtless your longing for the deliverance of Zion will become much greater because of oppression and injustice, hunger and poverty in the coming years. But when God permits the doors of blight to open, the gates of hell to pour out their strongest armies to spill out their "vials" of destruction such as plagues, illnesses, and scourges to empty the kingdoms of the wicked who refuse the gospel of his Son, and who hate and persecute his children . . . at that time all will understand and confess the necessity for Zion as a place of deliverance for the Saints . . . [In the meantime] suffer all things patiently and . . . look forward to receiving your recompense . . .

It may be that even from your own midst there will be some selfish, jealous persons, who have lost the Spirit, who will rise up and try to lead unstable souls after them; but be particularly cautious and oppose those who oppose the authority which was placed according to the will of God to lead you and to nourish you . . .

Until I come back, keep reading, search the Scriptures, treasure the Book of Mormon in your memory, inscribe the "Doctrine and Covenants" on the slates of your hearts; keep yourselves spotless according to all I published in your midst . . . I am not claiming perfection for any of my writings or most holy things; but rather, my failings and my weaknesses, as compared to what I wish to be, form the subject of a constant prayer for strength from on high. I do not wish you to think that I am suggesting that the one or the other or all of the aforementioned books constitute a sufficient rule for the behavior of the Saints or for the work of the ministry; rather it is "the letter which killeth, but the Spirit giveth life." The Spirit is the PRIESTHOOD, through which God works, which has the right and the wisdom to end every argument . . .

Therefore obey your pastors as you would the Lord—pray for them constantly—do what you can to supply their physical needs so that they may devote themselves more to your service in spiritual things. Let not the enemy deceive you into believing that God Almighty who established his Kingdom this last time on the earth will allow all the priesthood in his kingdom or in Wales either to go astray so that there is no one to lead you in the paths of the Lord . . . The hills may leap like lambs, and the wild hills of Wales may jump like rams, and after that the priesthood will still not be stirred from its place. . . .

Its original source is the "order of the Son of God" from before the foundation of the world; its origin has been through all his servants in all the dispensations since the beginning of time . . . it has visited our dear nation, and the dawning of the great Jubilee has shone on the borders of our country . . . and there are nearly four thousand of the children of Gomer rejoicing because of it already! . . .

The greatest commandment of all, the last and most urgent to which I shall call your attention, and it is not a new one either, rather it is to love one another . . . Shun every occasion for contention . . . Be gracious, kind, gentle, and humble to one another as befitting the children of the same divine Father . . .

May your WALK preach to everyone that you are strangers and wanderers here, and may you prepare yourselves in everything for that day when your God will arrange your deliverance . . .

Dear brethren in the Priesthood . . . In love, patience, and gentleness, feed the dear flock . . .

You, Fathers—farewell to you. Love your wives, and keep an altar to God in your families . . .

You, dear Mothers . . . Obey your husbands as you obey the Lord . . .

You, the hopeful Youth . . . This is a time of harvest; shrink from serving the flesh and its lusts . . . instead of serving the Lord of this harvest . . .

And you, little Children . . . I expect you to obey your parents, and pray constantly for the Spirit of truth to lead you to usefulness.

May the grace of our Lord jesus Christ . . . be with you and remain with you all forever. Amen.[9]

Coming Home

How did women respond to this kind of preaching? Conversion images are few, which is puzzling considering how dramatic a step it was to join another church. This omission in the histories handicaps us in trying to understand what was operating in a woman's heart and mind as she made this monumental decision to join a strange new sect. What kind of experience was religious conversion? Was it emotional, intellectual, spiritual, or all three and more? Was it traumatic or joyful, a quick or lengthy process? We will have to read between the lines, and the lines are meager.

One might expect an exchange of one's religion to require time and adjustment. This proves to have been so for many women, although for others acceptance of Mormonism was almost imme-

9. Davies, facsimile ed., 5. Compare Robert Richards (pseud.), *The Californian Crusoe, or The Lost Treasure Found* (London: J. H. Parker, and New York: Stanford and Swords, 1854), 9-10.

diate. Some described the conversion experience as coming home. Fanny Stenhouse said of Elder Stenhouse's preaching:

> these [were] the self-same doctrines which my mother taught me, when I knelt beside her in childhood, and which I have so often heard—only in colder and less persuasive language— urged from the pulpits of those whom I have ever regarded in the light of true disciples of Jesus. Who can wonder that I listened with rapt attention, and that my heart was even then half won to the new faith?

Within two weeks Fanny was a Mormon. Mary Nixon Bate Buckley wrote: "I listened with great interest to the words that was spoken and they Sank deep into my Heart and I was satisfied in my own mind that it was from God . . . it seemed as though I had been acquainted with it before." Priscilla M. Evans showed a seemingly inherent predisposition toward Mormon teachings, for upon first hearing them she was "very interested in all the meetings and teachings." Hannah Settle Lapish at age seventeen heard the Mormon gospel and "I believed it implicitly." Mary Ann W. Maughan was like those women satirized by Maria Ward and Robert Richards who believed the elders could do no wrong.

Even so, most women took some time after their first encounter to decide. The conversion usually lasted several weeks to several months. For Mary Buckley, it was only "after going to meetings and Reading the Books for about three weaks" that she began "feeling it was just the thing I had been desiring to find." She then "went and gave my name in for Baptism and was Baptized on Sunday night . . . at Finsbury Branch London England." Although there were instant and mass conversions such as those wrought by the apostles in Herefordshire in 1848, generally on-the-spot conversion was discouraged. Said Joseph Smith:

> The elders or priests are to have a sufficient time to expound all things concerning the church of Christ to their understanding, previous to their partaking of the sacrament and being confirmed by the laying on of the hands of the elders, so that all things may be done in order.
> And the members shall manifest before the church, and also before the elders, by a godly walk and conversation, that they

are worthy of it, that there may be works and faith agreeable to the holy scriptures—walking in holiness before the Lord (D&C 20:68-69).

This policy was meant to discourage high pressure or impulsiveness. Emily Hart and her husband took their time, for Hart's "first reaction to Mormonism was opposition, but after much soul-searching and mature, prayerful contemplation, he was baptized in 1847."

Hannah King became convinced over a period of a few weeks. She wrote in her diary for 18 October 1849:

> My mind has been a good deal engrossed by what Miss Bailey has told me of the Latterday work—I asked her many questions and she was kind and gentle in telling me in what their principles consist. Certainly there is nothing in them but what I can test by the Bible, and I seem to gain strength from them—I feel to prove them all I can, for the Bible says, "Prove all things and hold fast to that which is good."

This was almost all she wrote, all she revealed about her thoughts and feelings between 18 October and her baptism three weeks later.

The Murdoch family history suggests what the process was for John Murray Murdoch, husband of Ann Steel. Ann's brother James had "received the gospel" from a friend, Elizabeth Wylie, while living in England. When James visited John's home village in Scotland, he gave him "his first impressions" of it. Murdoch was initially indifferent but piqued enough that he debated doctrines with James, who "could easily overcome John's arguments." Ann and John were baptized in November 1850.

A son-in-law of John's sister Mary Murdoch Main Todd McMillan described conversion as changing one's viewpoint and added that Mary was "handicapped" by her husband, who could not "see" the truth. John's mother, Wee Granny Murdoch, at the age of sixty-seven, "prayerfully investigated" until she was "convinced."

In later years Fanny Stenhouse, still trying to understand how she could ever have believed in Mormonism, called it "a mystery."

But she clearly remembered her "joyousness of heart" at the time of conversion and baptism and claimed "all proselytes have it."

Anxiety is evident in Hannah King's and Mary N. Buckley's diaries. But far more than fear, despair, fanaticism, or religious melancholia, these women were looking for something, though there is not enough detail to reveal precisely what. Presumably they found it. We have to be satisfied with information peripheral to the moment of conversion, attributes these women possessed. We know that they tended to be solid personalities—they had to, to surmount the disapproval of friends and associates and stick to a wayward course, though they were conservative in values, tended to view contemporary society as modern Babylon, and were literal in their interpretation of Bible prophecies.

Into the Waters

Again considering what a cataclysmic event baptism into the Mormon church was to a nineteenth-century life, it is surprising that only four record-keepers wrote in any detail about their baptisms. We know little about even the physical accoutrements of the baptism. Perhaps only the unusual was mentioned, leaving us to wonder what the usual was.

The unusual circumstances were ponds, rivers, and thin ice. Mary Ann Maughan was baptized in a pond in the center of town (as opposed to a font in a friendly Protestant or rented church), and the ordinance was performed at night "to avoid mobs." Some baptisms were at sea. While the ship *Olympus* floated between Liverpool and New Orleans in 1851, "50 persons were added to the church."[10] Mary Jane Ewer told her children that before she could be immersed, "thin ice had to be cut away." John Howell Price, husband of Rachel Jones Price, was baptized at night to avoid hecklers in a canal normally used for coal transport because no other site in town could be rented or borrowed. On a Saturday afternoon Fanny Stenhouse and several others "repaired to a bath-house on the banks of the Southampton river. This place was

10. Wilbur S. Shepperson, "The Place of the Mormons in the Religious Emigration of Great Britian, 1840-60," *Utah Historical Quarterly* 20 (1952): 207.

not perhaps the most convenient, and it certainly was devoid of the slightest tinge of romance; but it was the only one available to the saints at that time."

Then there was the somewhat sensational baptism of Sister Cartwright, who was angered because her husband had ignored her and joined the Mormon church. She gave the Chester branch trouble, taunting one family with "Damn you, I'll dip ye." Someone advised her to keep her peace, for who knew but that she might have a change of heart someday and be baptized herself. "I hope to God, if ever I am such a damn fool that I'll be drowned in the attempt," she retorted. Later, through a dream, her attitude indeed changed, and sure enough at her baptism a bank gave way, her arm slipped from her husband's grasp, and she drowned.[11]

Most baptisms were apparently done by day, often on Sunday, in borrowed baptismal fonts.[12] Nowhere in a diary or branch minutes between 1838 and 1888 is there record of a building fund for a local chapel. Meetings were held in rented halls, private homes, or the chapels of other sects.

Two aspects of Mormon baptisms were consistent: they were done by total immersion to symbolize rebirth, and the ceremony followed instructions given by Joseph Smith in Doctrine and Covenants 20:

> The person who is called of God and has authority from Jesus Christ to baptize, shall go down into the water with the person who has presented himself or herself for baptism, and shall say, calling him or her by name: Having been commissioned of Jesus Christ, I baptize you in the name of the Father, and of the Son, and of the Holy Ghost. Amen.

11. British Mission Manuscript History, 2 Jan. 1844, archives, Historical Department, Church of Jesus Christ of Latter-day Saints, Salt Lake City. Thomas Cartwright was tried for manslaughter in the accidental drowning of his wife during her baptism. He, Jonathan Pugmire, Sr., and Thomas Cargith were held in custody until the coroner's inquest, then acquitted.

12. Probably most evangelical sects, like Mormonism, baptized by immersion. Most, however, did not take Bible literalism so far as to reinstitute the Old Testament patriarchal tradition of taking plural wives.

Then shall he immerse him or her in the water, and come forth again out of the water.

Virtually all Mormon proselytes considered their baptisms a transcendent moment, though they did not express this as feelingly as Hannah Tapfield King:

Nov. 4, 1850. I formally changed my religion and was baptized by Elder Joseph W. Johnson buried in the waters of baptism according to the orders and example of our Savior, Jesus Christ, and ever dear Georgiana at the same time. 'Twas a most important and gran[d] epoch in our lives. Language is perfectly peurite [?] to describe my feelings but as I was *buried* in the womb of waters I *felt this is Baptism*! Oh! May this deed, this obeying literally the command of our Savior be registered in the records of heaven.

After baptism came confirmation. While Fanny Stenhouse was still investigating the church, she attended a Sunday afternoon meeting "held for the purpose of receiving the sacrament, and the confirmation of those who had been baptized during the week." Non-members were excluded from sacrament meetings, she said, indicating that proselyting meetings for non-members were kept separate from branch functions. After a song and prayer, Stenhouse recalled, the presiding elder asked all who had been baptized during the week to advance to the front seats. "Several ladies and gentlemen came forward, and also three little children." (Mormon children are baptized at age eight.) These people were "confirmed," or given an individualized blessing bestowing the Holy Ghost. Three elders gave the following blessing to a sister this day:

Martha; by virtue of the authority vested in us, we confirm you a member of the Church of Jesus Christ of Latter-day Saints; and as you have been obedient to the teachings of the Elders, and have gone down into the waters of baptism for the remission of your sins, we confer upon you the Gift of the Holy Ghost, that it may abide with you for ever, and be a lamp unto your feet, and a light upon your pathway, leading and guiding you into all truth. This blessing we confirm upon your head, in the name of the Father, and of the Son, and of the Holy Ghost. Amen.

{ 71 }

Stenhouse claimed that after one elder spoke these words, another proceeded to give a second blessing to the sister:

> He spoke for some time with extreme earnestness, when suddenly he was seized with a nervous trembling which was quite perceptible, and which evidently betokened intense mental or physical excitement. He began to prophecy great things for this sister in the future, and in solemn and mysterious language proclaimed the wonders which God would perform for her sake.

Stenhouse would later decide it was no wonder a convert believed she had received the Holy Ghost, what with the "magnetic currents" and "pressure of half a dozen human hands upon her head." By then Stenhouse could see nothing sacred about an ordinance which other converts considered a milestone in their lives.

The Aftermath of Baptism

The consequences of Mormon baptism were more than spiritual. I only partly quoted Mary N. Buckley on her baptism. To continue, "I was baptized in 1853 in Finsbury Branch London by John Mabien *then the warfare commenced . . . "* (italics mine). Most of the remainder of her story tells of emotional siege by husband, friend, neighbor. Where the diaries are mostly silent on the mode and circumstances of baptism, they tell again and again of the hostility which conversion inspired from co-workers, employers, and former ministers.

Mary Bate suffered more than most. Even before baptism she found that when she told her friends about it, "They where [sic] ready to fight it on every side told me i had better keep away from there." Her husband was "worse than the rest." He first enlisted their clergyman, then ordered her confined in the house to prevent her from attending church meetings. He continually "raged" at her, warning the children that she would "drag them into Hell where She was taking herself."

It is significant that in a day when wives had limited legal independence, and in spite of Mr. Bate's opposition, Mary was "able to get all my children baptized." Either she was wrong that he would stop at nothing to foil her or there were limits beyond which a righteously-indignant husband dared not go. In spite of the disruption of her once apparently happy home, Mary was able to make her own choice.

Besides her husband, Mary claimed, her "most Intimate" friend began to "act strange." One must consider the possibility that Mary tended to overstate things, for she and her husband continued connubial relations as evidenced by her becoming pregnant at this time. Or perhaps she had been accustomed to such harmony in her marriage and friendships that the disrupting influence of Mormonism seemed more severe. My own instinct is to take Mary at her word, to believe her when she says she wearied "after three years of this cruel treatment from my friends my life being threatend continualy . . . "

It is unclear whether Mary independently determined to emigrate or whether she came to this decision primarily in response to counsel. Priesthood leaders may have merely validated her own desires. She wrote:

> the president of our Branch told me i had better get some money out of the Bank and take my children and go to the vally[.] I invited Brother Dunbar with two Sisters to make me a visit[.] he my Husband came Home while they was there[,] a little conversation passed between them but not much[.] he my Husband acted very shy, when Brother Dunbar was about to leave i got up to accompany him to the door[.] when we got into the Hall i asked Brother dunbar what do you think of him[.] he Replied i would not baptize him nor council an Elder to do it[.] get your Famly to the Vally as soon as you can.

Richard Bate's attitude eventually softened so much so that, surprisingly, he emigrated with his family.

Mary Ann Maughan was not as fortunate as Bates. She lived in Gloucester at a time when opposition to Mormonism was militant. She was baptized at night to avoid the interference from "the mob."

> this summer [1840] I became Engaged to Mr John Davis . . . Dec 23d 1840 we were maried in Gloucester by a Clergyman of the Church of England[.] my husband had a home nicely furnished in Tirley and we went there to live imeaditialy. we both had good treads [trades] and pleasnty of work and were very happy. the

Elders soon called to see us. Brothers Willard Richards and Leivi richards, Woodruff, Rushton and others that I do not remember their names. there was no Saints in that place so Brother Richards counciled us to open our house for Meetings[.] we did so and [at] the first held in our house a lot of Roughs led by a Apostate Methodist came and made a disturbance [and] they threatened the Preacher with violence. but we surounded him [the preacher] and sliped him through a door upstairs[.] when the Preacher was gone the Mob dispersd, and we were left alone. notice was given for a Meeting in two weeks and the Mob came again. but we succeeded in hiding the Preacher and one of the Brethren took him away. the Mob then turned on my husband. knocked him down and kicked him. he was brused, Internaly and was never well afterwards.

After a later fall, John began to bleed at the lungs, consumption set in, and he "gradually failed from this time."

Throughout their four-month marriage "per[se]cutiors" would watch the Davis house, informing John's mother if the elders arrived so that she could disrupt any conversations between her son and the Mormons. "There was no Saints with in miles of us. we were alone most of the time. and this we prefered as it was better than having those who were not of our faith and would ridicule our Religion." By that winter John died and Mary Ann emigrated.

These two cases of antagonism pertain to women of lower-to-middle-class background. Mary Bate had property and some savings but a lack of schooling. Mary Ann Maughan's father was a farmer and orchard owner, and her husband owned a house. But she too enjoyed primarily a practical rather than liberal education, and she was associated with Methodists and the working class. One wonders if women of higher station experienced milder reaction toward Mormonism. Of the forty-nine histories which mention this period in a woman's life, eleven note hostility from family and associates, while seven women did not record it or actually reported the opposite. Of these seven, four came from circumstances of moderate or better education and financial stability. (The other thirty-one histories do not mention this topic, although they do cover this period in the women's lives.)

{ 74 }

Yet hostility experienced by working-class women can be characterized more often as intolerance than persecution. Sarah Jane Neat Ashley claimed that "due to religious persecution at the time, it was necessary for [her parents] to conduct their services in the home." The only evidence of persecution in her history is an incident at the circuit school she attended where the traveling superintendent criticized Joseph Smith as a false prophet. Young Sarah Jane defended Smith aloud and was then less afraid of the minister than of her father who she thought might punish her for speaking disrespectfully to an adult. Her fears were unfounded, for neither the minister nor her father reprimanded her.

Rachel Price's mother-in-law did not torment her son and his family but was embarrassed by their religious activities. When Rachel's husband, as presiding elder over the Merthyr Tydfill Branch, preached in street meetings, his mother refused to recognize him, saying he was bringing shame on the family (Rachel Price Jones).

The sense of anti-Mormon feeling is stronger in some histories while still not approaching a perception of outright mistreatment. Felicia Astle's history states that she and her family were "ridiculed and shunned by relatives and friends" in Nottingham. Susan Barker's husband's letters show that he was ostracized by his sisters, and that family division endured for many years. Margaret McNeil Ballard was not "permitted" to attend the local schools "because of being a Mormon," but this may have been predictable in circuit schools taught by travelling ministers.

Priscilla Evans encountered resistance from her family, but they also defended her. Her father at first forbade her to attend Mormon meetings. When she did so anyway, he would steal any church literature she brought home and destroy it. Yet his opposition was not as vehement as it seemed. When he heard the Mormon elders criticized he would come to their defense.

The letters of Elizabeth Lewis allude only to dubiousness from associates. When she and her children emigrated, Anna Evans Jenkins left "many loyal friends" in Wales, one of whom later wrote asking for a few shillings. These women did not emigrate to escape vicious opposition.

Mariah Davies's fiance described what was probably the most

common response to a Britisher's joining the Mormons: "Monday morning I went to my work; and when I entered the work shop they all made fun of me. But I did not care for I knew that what I had done was right." John's job was not at risk nor his reputation but merely the good opinion of his co-workers. So even though there were victims such as Mary Williams Rees, who was disowned by her parents, persecution was not a norm for British converts. Most proselytes did not flee their homeland in desperate search of religious freedom.

Once realizing this, it is possible to appreciate the variations on the conversion experience. In the Winner family, British transplants to Illinois who joined the Reorganized LDS church, it was the wife, Isabella Winner Burgess, who opposed her husband when he "lost interest in the Reorganized Church and wanted to move to Utah." He prevailed, for the family went to Zion where Isabella was eventually baptized and then sent back East by church leaders to study midwifery before establishing a long-lived practice on the Mormon frontier.

Rachel Killian's parents were each secretly baptized out of fear of the other's reaction. Hannah King expected a lecture when her sister visited, but the vacation proved friendly and restrained. Caroline Lloyd Corbett was the only member of her family to join the Mormon church, but her mother and most of her family emigrated with her to Pennsylvania. Later, when she prepared to continue west, her mother threatened to disown her but instead sewed twenty pieces of gold in a skirt for Caroline to wear to Utah. Elizabeth Steadman had a mostly fortunate experience. She, her family, and "many of our dear friends & neighbors" were converted together.

Many of the hardships attendant to Mormon affiliation were imposed by the organization itself. John, husband of Ruth Price, joined in September 1847 and in 1850 was serving a mission. He was unable to obtain work because of hostility from local people toward Mormon elders. He wrote: "They kept us so poor we were nearly starved for the want of food, living on a small piece of barley bread a day without anything with it except water. We lived in this way for many months and in this time my wife was with child."

Finally he approached the district president for permission to leave off missionarying for about a month "to work in the hay." The president

> promised to put my case before the Council and told a couple of the brethren to take their hats around the assembly and gather me a little means, so that I may be enabled to stop at home and not go away. The brethren gathered 1s 6 p [1 shilling sixpence] for me. . . . There were about sixty of the brethren present and not one of them asked me to come with them to sleep or offered me food to eat. It was 11:00 o'clock when the meeting was over and I had 22 miles to walk home.

Fortunately Price encountered a female member who kindly gave him "supper and a bed" and the next morning sent him on his way with another sixpence in his pocket. After an all-day trek he found his wife going into labor

> and no person with her except two little girls, and with nothing to eat but a little barley bread. Brother Isaac Evans came into the house and saw her and gave her two shillings and sixpence for pity sake, so by this time we had 5 shillings in all. This baby, Mary, was born 19 June, 1850. I went to Felintawa Mill to get flour and sister Jones gave me 17 pounds of flour without pay so I bought a little tea and sugar and butter and took it home and there was great rejocing [sic] with my dear wife and little children and myself.

Emily Ellingham Hart's is another family whose suffering was due to church responsibilities rather than outside opposition. She accompanied her husband during much of his seven-year mission to France but occasionally tried to catch her breath at home. During one such reprieve in 1854:

> Emily was very poorly. I told her I thought she had better not go. She was tolerably well enroute. I got her into the house and asked if she would excuse my absence for half an hour . . . On my return . . . I was met by [Elder Lamoreaux] and informed that during my absence my Beloved Wife had had a miscarriage. I waited with her for a few minutes and a doctor came who had been sent for . . . I shall not forget the sensation which came over me when I saw dear Emily suffering on the sofa where we formerly lived.

{ 77 }

I nearly fainted but by going into the air I recovered . . . I have expected this from the time I returned home, and consider it but a natural consequence of the worry, trouble, and excitement to which Emily has been subject.

Second Thoughts

After conversion and baptism, some women had doubts or even regrets. Hannah Job, of Abergwilly, Carmarthen, Wales, was one. She, her mother, and sister were persuaded by her husband Thomas whose uncle was Welsh mission president. Reports were coming back from Welsh emigrants that the streets in Salt Lake City were 130 feet wide and laborers there were earning three shillings a day, masons twelve shillings sixpence. "This is a better place for workers than Merthyr Tydfil is," wrote one laborer.

Hannah's father told other stories about Mormons in America and tried to prevent his wife from attending meetings. She remained firm, but Hannah and her sister wavered. Hannah "wondered if the stories were true." Although only eighteen and under pressure from her thirty-five-year-old husband, she would later decide not to emigrate with him.

Conclusions

For most people the elders were their first encounter with the new church, which may be one reason for outside resentment toward missionaries and development of their image as skillful deceptors. The majority of the members in the little Mormon branches loved the elders to the point of adoration, another possible inspiration for the stereotype. The woman whose diary reveals the most obsessiveness with missionaries, however, was not a poor shop girl or an illiterate, though she could have inspired Maria Ward's stereotype of the well-kept wife who leaves a prosperous and devoted family behind in joining the Mormons. But there is little evidence of an elder taking advantage of the Kings or other converts while proselyting. Many elders were local converts whose friends and families knew their characters well.

Not much is said in the histories about the women's conversions. Those who did refer to it often described it as something like coming home. It was what they had been looking for. Others, however, reveal being initially repulsed by Mormon preaching and only gradually persuaded through intellectual study, soul-searching, and prayer.

Baptisms took place anywhere a body of water could be found, in daylight on weekdays or Sundays if necessary, and by immersion. The aftermath of baptism was, in many cases, trouble with family and associates. Persecution may have been more pronounced in the lower classes. But the persecution motif has also been overdone in pro-Mormon history, perhaps in retrospect as converts, relocated in Utah, came to see it as an initiation rite. Persecution does not seem to have been the motivation for most converts to leave Britain. The women in our histories were not religious refugees.

When opposition did occur, it was usually not in the form of physical abuse or the loss of a proselyte's job or housing (except possibly in Ireland). More often it came in the form of strained family relations, comments from co-workers, or ostracism from friends and family members. In fact, there seems to have been no predictable pattern. Converts expected more trouble than they actually faced. There was a lot of talk against Mormonism, but it remained mostly talk.

Missionaries were more on the battlefront than other members, along with their wives and families. But there is evidence that they suffered from organizational lethargy as much as from outside opposition.

One might theorize that conversion alienated Mormon proselytes from their cultures, but the histories do not show this. Mary Ann Maughan and Mary Nixon Bate are exceptions against surprisingly few others. And even Mary Ann Maughan hints at a different motivation for emigrating: "My relatives did not obey the Gospell (but they did not oppose me) and this made me sorrowfull and lonely. I attended all the meetings I could often walking many miles alone . . . One ship load of Saints has gone to Nauvoo from Gloucester and another will go soon." While she believed passionately in Mormonism, her friends and loved ones could not see it. She was alone among company and longed to find kindred souls.

Chapter 4.

The Branches

Baptized in 1850, Ann Jones Rosser was a stalwart in three Mormon branches during her life: Llandysfod, Newport, and Bristol. In one day she personally distributed fifty tracts and seven copies of the Book of Mormon, an effort which reportedly led to twelve baptisms. Over the years she assisted scores of converts in emigrating to Utah. Yet she herself never followed them, fortunately for the several hundred church dignitaries and missionaries housed and fed in her home over a period of sixty-six years.[1]

It was of no apparent concern to Ann Rosser that her contributions remained unacknowledged except as she became a legend in the hearts of local members. Yet one wonders why she was eighty-two before someone thought to honor her with a short biography in the *Millennial Star*.

Perhaps the tardiness was due not so much to a lack of appreciation for women's work as to the simple failure of clerks to report much of what went on in the branches. History was not of the

---

1. Report by Elmer Edwards of Bristol Branch, *Millennial Star* 78 (1916): 278. Born in Monmouthshire in 1834, Ann Sophia Jones Rosser was baptized at age seventeen in South Wales. At nineteen she married Charles Rosser, who died in 1909. According to Edwards, she related that in 1857, while living in Newport, only one of 350 members died during the cholera plague there.

people, female or male, but about people of note—apostles, mission leaders, prominent elders, sometimes branch officers. Taken for granted was the quiet life well-lived.

Still one must ask why spiritual achievement should remain uncelebrated in a church which set itself apart from the world as accessible to all regardless of rank. In this regard at least—status accorded women—Mormons were like their contemporaries. It should be admitted that women themselves colluded in this negligence. Like Ann Rosser, most sisters did not leave records of their lives or works. Their own histories slight their youths, conversions, and branch experiences in their homeland. Were it not for reports to the *Women's Exponent*, we would know nothing about the Whitechapel Relief Society, one of the earliest and the longest-lived of women's organizations in the early British church.

Ironically then it is to clerks we turn for details about the British sisters: sporadic references in branch, conference and mission histories supplemented by obituaries in the *Millennial Star* and the sometimes richly-detailed journals of male missionaries.

1838-58: Individual Initiative

In the early decades women's contributions were usually private and *ad hoc*. In the first quarter-century, wherever the church was small and more personal than institutional, individual initiative seems to have been the pattern of female activity.

A woman was frequently the first in a town to listen to the Mormon message. In important locales, according to early journals, a woman, often a widow, housed and fed the missionaries. Other women were cash subsidizers of the elders and generous donors to mission funds. Women not only succored but sometimes married the elders. It was women as often as not who maintained the meeting houses and furnished wine for the sacrament.[2] They orchestrated the "tea parties" (socials) which followed mission conferences. They helped one another by nursing and, in two documented cases, anointing with oil during illness. There are two

2. Liverpool Branch Manuscript History, 19 Aug. 1842, archives, Historical Department, Church of Jesus Christ of Latter-day Saints, Salt Lake City, Utah (hereafter LDS archives).

instances of women proselytizing. Others set examples of Christian character, especially of faith to be healed. Finally, women were spiritual leaders and prophetesses, occasionally showing more enthusiasm than mission leaders thought appropriate.

Notice that all but two of the gifts seem on the surface to be supportive rather than inventive. That Ann Rosser's tracting was exceptional, even unorthodox, may give a clue as to why her recognition was so belated. Perhaps at eighty-two she posed no menace to masculine ego. Young Priscilla Evans (Merriman), converted in the 1840s in Wales, also "would go around and help the elders sing," but she did not go by her own initiative and she did not proselyte. Generally, the women's role was to help the effort indirectly by helping the men.

There is another outstanding exception. We are not told the age of Mary Powel, an early member of the Manchester Branch who took it upon herself to journey "to Burslem on a mission." According to Alfred Cordon, her preaching drew enough attention that the Aitkenites (a group related to the United Brethren) formally denounced her as "a deluded woman" so as to warn off any who might be influenced by her. Cordon himself was one. After hearing her, he walked to Manchester where he was baptized by David Wilding.[3]

But if the sisters' work was ancillary, it should not be underrated. Joseph Fielding's journal provides examples of notable sacrifices by female converts. Elizabeth Cottam and her husband, of "Burly" (Burleigh), vacated their own house so that a group of missionaries could use it for a two-day conference.[4] And it was Cottam's mother, Ann Dawson of Preston, who figures most enduringly as an early nurturer. "Sister Dawson, a Widow in whose House we are lodging, is exceedingly attentive and kind to us. A very diligent woman," Fielding first wrote in 1837. When Fielding married a year after arriving in the mission, Dawson

3. Alfred Cordon Journals, LDS archives, as cited in John Cotterill, "Midland Saints: The Mormon Mission in the West Midlands, 1837-77," Ph.D. diss., University of Keele, 1985.

4. Diary of Joseph Fielding, 24 Mar. 1841, photocopy of typescript, LDS archives.

housed the couple, along with Willard Richards and wife, charging them less than she should and throwing in her family's support of the local branch in the bargain. A full three years later, upon returning to Preston, Fielding found missionaries still boarding at "Sister Dawson's, our old Mother."[5] Things did not always go smoothly between Mother Dawson and her dependents, as we will show later, but her support was steady and sustained during a time of fragile success for the church in England.

In Greenland, Scotland, it was a wealthy widow who first stepped forward to offer herself for baptism despite "much opposition to the truth in this part" and "many false tales against the Saints."[6] In Blackburn it was again a woman who told Fielding "she would be baptized if any others would." Fielding added that "since then there has been preaching there regularly."[7]

Judging by the limited records, women joined the Mormon church in greater numbers than men. An example is the Liverpool Branch, which at the end of 1840 had 150 members. Of sixty-eight listed by name in the branch minutes for this period, forty were women. (Interestingly, only eight of the forty had husbands also mentioned.[8]) In 1846 the ruling elder of Vinehill Branch, Dean Forest Conference, had to make do with one elder and two priests among thirty members. He told superiors that "The members in this branch were mostly females, but good Saints, and almost wished that they were males, that they might go and preach the word of the Lord."[9] In 1881 in "Herts and Beds" (Hertfordshire and Bedfordshire) "the whole district [had] only fifty members, mostly females."[10] Statistics from Glasgow show a few more women than men were baptized in 1840.[11]

5. Ibid., 9 Apr. 1840.
6. Manuscript History of the British Mission, 10 Jan. 1844, LDS archives.
7. Fielding Journal, 22 Sept. 1838.
8. Liverpool Branch Manuscript History, 31 Dec. 1840, LDS archives.
9. British Mission Manuscript History, 1 Feb 1846.
10. London Conference Manuscript History, 3 Apr. 1881, LDS archives.
11. Glasgow Branch Manuscript History, 31 Dec. 1840, LDS archives.

Despite their predominance, women were neglected in early statistical reports. While priesthood enrollment (tallied by office) was faithfully compiled for every quarterly conference, women were lumped with total branch membership. Except for the fact that this practice continues today, one might assume it to have been less sexist than elitist, for neither were children and non-priesthood males separately monitored at a time when Mormon men were not routinely ordained as they are today.

Women influenced the church not only through numbers but through force of character. Wilford Woodruff's London journal bequeaths us images of two colorful personalities. In the fall of 1840 Woodruff was a tired laborer. He had spent "23 days in the great Babylon of modern times, and . . . found it harder to establish the Church there than in any other place we had ever been."[12]

But then Susannah Albion and Ellen Balfour Redman swept into his life. First Susannah, daughter of an Independent minister, was baptized, drawing her mother, sister, and father into the church as well. And two days after Woodruff's dejected diary note, Ellen Redman made a dramatic entrance as the tiny London branch took sacrament. Woodruff knew her from the New York City branch, having met her briefly before sailing to England, and he now recounted her story:

> There is something singular about her coming to London. She was taken sick nigh unto death, and counseled to take a sea voyage for her health. [She was anointed and] carried on board of a ship to come to London, and a ship was never known to live through such a rough passage, 35 days and only 12 hours of fair weather. They were driven to the Cape of Good Hope under bare poles, constant thunder & lightening, for 16 nights in succession. The cook jumped overboard because he said the ship was covered with devils. But Sister Redman arrived safe in London Dock and has spent a fortnight in this city trying to find us. She found me yesterday by a dream that she had Saturday nite and we were happy to meet . . . She . . . thinks the Lord has sent her here to do good.[13]

12. London Conference Manuscript History, 20 Sept. 1840.
13. Ibid., 10 Jan. 1840.

Woodruff accepted the Widow Redman's self-characterization as a woman of connections. She claimed to have made acquaintances through tutoring gentlemen's children in languages, and Woodruff thought she could thus be of great help in winning respectability for Mormonism. And indeed Redman and the Albions fulfilled his hopes by brightening the elders' spirits, providing companionship, and enlarging the fledgling London congregation so that within two weeks Woodruff was writing, "The Lord is beginning to bless us here in London. We have baptized 16 . . . Our little room is almost getting full of Saints."[14] Yet the lively Sister Redman, whose flair for the dramatic promises an interesting story, fades from the record. Only once or twice more does Woodruff mention her in letters and journal, and no record of her or her children can be surely identified in branch or mission books.

Given Reuben Hedlock's later reputation for womanizing (which may or may not have been warranted), one does not know whether to take at face value his depiction of yet another lady, one of "a respectable Yorkshire family soon a going to remove to France," who relieved him from the Woodruff-like doldrums. He reported to mission leaders that, upon being baptized, the woman had invited him to her vacation home in Bologna from which he hoped to begin proselyting in France.[15]

Whatever infatuation occasionally existed between missionaries and female converts, it was spiritual longing that proved lasting. There is an account of a seventy-year-old Welsh woman who walked forty-two miles to attend a church conference in Merthyr Tydfill. With such devotion, the meeting was "the best Conference held in South Wales; it lasted two days, and truly it was a time of rejoicing."[16]

Women gave economic as well as moral support to missionaries. Fielding and Richards received such generous donations from a Sister Chandler that they "rather checked her, but she said the Lord always makes it up to her and more, whatever

14. Ibid., 25 Jan. 1841.
15. British Mission Manuscript History, 25 Feb. 1844.
16. Ibid., 21 June 1845.

she gives us."[17] Elder Lyon, working in one of the Scottish branches and unable to repay money loaned him by Lucy Martin, repaid her in verse: "I your brother, thanks expressing,/ ought [sic] can give you, but his blessing."[18]

Interestingly, two women worked outside the home to underwrite their husbands' missions. Elder and Sister Henry Cuerden arrived in Bradford in April 1842 without a sixpence between them. While walking through town their first evening, they came upon a mill where she obtained employment to support her husband for the next year.[19] Hannah Greenwood, Joseph Fielding's English bride, supported herself and husband so as not to depend on donations, although within a few weeks pregnancy forced her to quit factory work.[20] Repeatedly, improvisation characterized the early Mormon work in Britain, and traditional gender roles were set aside when the cause required it.

Missionaries were not the only beneficiaries of women's generosity. Upon receiving an inheritance, Caroline Rogers Taylor bought not only her own family's passage to America but "assisted 124 persons who could not emigrate without assistance, many of whom are now in [Utah's] valleys, with good and comfortable homes."[21]

An Interval of Female Organization

For a brief period in the British church women had their own organization. But like the fate of women's groups in the Utah

17. Fielding Journal, 16 June 1840.

18. John Lyon, *Harp of Zion* (Glasgow, 1852), 133. In 1991 I found a copy of this volume of poems lying on the ground of the Sanpete County Landfill. It was missing the title page, but I first surmised the author from a short biography in Edward W. Tullidge's *History of Salt Lake City* (Salt Lake City, 1886). Tullidge dedicated page 806 to a John Lyon, "veteran poet" of Scotland, who "came into the Mormon Church as an author." According to Tullidge, Lyon's best writings were his Scottish stories and depictions of Scottish scenery. See also Ted Lyon, "John Lyon, Early Mormon Poet," in *Latter-day Digest* 2 (Nov. 1993), 7:48.

19. Bradford Manuscript History, 1 Apr. 1842, LDS archives.

20. Fielding Journal, 15 Dec. 1838.

21. London Conference Manuscript History, 7 Sept. 1873.

church, although instigated, developed, and managed by women, they would eventually be appropriated by male priesthood organizations at which time women would become excluded from most planning and decision-making.

Inspiration for the Nauvoo Temple Fund of the 1840s is not known, though women's contributions to the funds are legendary. It is known that the Penny Fund in England was inspired by sisters who had emigrated to Nauvoo, where they joined the Female Relief Society managed by Emma Smith. Just before the martyrdom of Emma's husband Joseph the *Millennial Star* published a letter from the former Britons:

> To the Sisters . . . in England: Greeting:
>
> Dear Sisters—This is to inform you that we have here entered into a small weekly subscription for the benefit of the Temple Funds. One thousand have already joined it, while many more are expected, by which we trust to help forward the great work very much. The amount is only one cent or a halfpenny per week. As brother Amos Fielding is waiting for this, I cannot enlarge more than to say that myself and sister Thompson are engaged in collecting the same.
>
> We remain your affectionate sisters in Christ,
>
> Mary [Fielding] Smith.
>
> M[ercy]. R. Thompson[22]

Mission leaders endorsed the proposal and added a request that "strictest accuracy" be respected in collecting the Temple Fund by preserving the name of each donor and the amount. "The sisters or others who may collect the subscriptions, will please be very particular on this point."[23]

A year later Apostle Woodruff was still promoting the temple subscription, but in a letter to *brethren* throughout the missions he wrote:

> I wish the Female Society, in all the branches, to continue their

22. Mary Fielding Smith was sister to Joseph Fielding and a convert originally from the Preston Branch. *Latter-day Saints' Millennial Star*, 1 June 1844, as cited in British Mission Manuscript History, 1 June 1844.

23. Ibid.

subscriptions for the temple until it is finished; let their money and means be brought together the same as all other tithes and offerings, that, when the temple is finished, the whole amount they have paid may stand opposite their names in the Book of the Law of the Lord, that it may be known who are the owners of the house.[24]

Without making too much of a slight change in tone, Woodruff assumed closer direction of the fund while at the same time noting the existence of a Female Society previously unrecognized in Great Britain. Woodruff followed his statement with a comment on the prophet's last speech to the Female Relief Society of Nauvoo, acknowledging that the Nauvoo Temple Fund was a program of the Relief Society.

Little mention of female societies appears in Britain apart from the Temple Fund. And from the beginning men were active in the fund drive, as in London where President Hedlock "urged *Brethren* to introduce the Female subscription for the Nauvoo Temple," and *Brother* Cope was appointed collector for the same.[25] This was quickly amended by the branch council, who voted that a treasurer, secretary, and four *female* collectors be appointed for the fund.[26] A year later Woodruff was particular on the point that all donations to the temple, "whether from churches, individuals, or the Female Society," be sent to Liverpool, "that it may go through the proper channel." This implies both that female societies were distinct from branch and individual efforts and that they were kept under the priesthood wing.[27]

This female subscription of 1844-45 became a broad effort. Hiram Clark, proselyting near the Staffordshire Potteries, wrote, "I have organized the sisters in Hanley, Bruslem and Lane Ends [sic], so that they are contributing their penny a week towards the Temple."[28] By December 1845, 220 pounds had been donated by

24. British Mission Manuscript History, 2 Feb. 1845.
25. London Conference Manuscript History, 17 June 1844, emphasis mine.
26. Ibid., 1 July 1844.
27. *Latter-day Saints' Millennial Star* 5:134
28. Ibid., 15 Aug. 1845.

the women of those areas.[29] The Newcastle-on-Tyne Branch collected 14 pounds 8 schillings by January.[30] All these temple contributions were in addition to tithes and emigration donations.

There is other evidence of organized, officially-sanctioned activity by women during these early decades. The poor of the entire mission were helped at the anniversary of the prophet's martyrdom when the British sisters fasted as a group then contributed their savings to the needy.[31] Men called for the fast, but women were solicited as a group. As another instance, on the birth of Joseph and Hannah Fielding's daughter when two women "who regularly wait on the Sisters in such Cases" happened upon the Fielding household, they promptly gathered up the laundry to bring it back clean along with a meal.[32]

Spiritual Gifts

The Temple Fund shows that, if self-motivation characterized women's church efforts, the sisters did not act autonomously. This is illustrated in the case of Ann Dawson, Joseph Fielding's "Old Mother" of Preston:

> Sunday December 16, 1838 - Offended Sister [Ann] Dawson by refusing to give her my blessing, she had a pain in her Head and wished to receive a Blessing to go to anoint a Sister that was sick. She had spoken some things about us and given way to a bad Spirit and I told her I could not do it. This was a new thing for she had always received blessings from us for asking . . . She endeavoured to make it out that I had refused to pray for it but I told her I would do that readily, she said she would be well without it, and said it was so, this was Sunday. She went to Meeting in the Evening and was too ill to abide in and almost too ill [to] get out, but afterwards went and anointed the sick sister who was much better . . . [33]

Fielding's words suggest that Dawson was accustomed to receiv-

29. British Mission Manuscript History, 14 Dec. 1845.
30. Newcastle-on-Tyne Branch Manuscript History, 29 Jan. 1846.
31. British Mission Manuscript History, 27 June 1845.
32. Fielding Journal, 20 Feb. 1841.
33. Fielding Journal, 14 Dec. 1838.

ing two kinds of blessings: healing blessings for herself and authority to anoint other women. In acknowledging that Dawson's blessing was effectual even while she was at odds with her priesthood superior, Fielding indicates respect for her power. The incident further demonstrates the improvisational nature of early Mormonism. That Dawson was permitted to exercise a priesthood gift later restricted to men hints at a relative freedom enjoyed by the Saints under Joseph Smith's administration.

Besides pointing up discords which so often erupted in the branches, the Dawson incident reveals the high spiritual standing of women in the early mission. British sisters were frequent recipients of healing miracles. "A woman at Water," wrote Fielding, "thought we were men of God and if she could touch us she would be better." Upon shaking hands with the elders "she was instantly better" and, as Fielding characteristically thought to add, her doctor testified she stayed better.[34]

Another sister, Harriet Beresford, told the *Millennial Star* that after enduring a tumor for five years she was directed by "a glorified messenger" how to regain her health. She received a healing blessing "by oil and prayer of the elders."[35] A blind Welsh Sister Evans, too weak to get out of bed and pronounced incurable by her doctors, was also healed through a blessing from the missionaries, as was Margaret Jenkins, cured "almost instantly" from her deathbed.[36]

Female spirituality was not just a passive manifestation of faith. Early elders greatly trusted the dreams and intuitions of Katharine Bates, whom they called the Prophetess of Manchester. In October 1840 she prophesied that America would rise up against the Mormons and drive them from Illinois. Wilford Woodruff

> had a long conversation with Catharine the Prophetess upon these things . . . She spoke of many things past and to come, and among the many things she says Brother Joseph Smith jr with his

34. Ibid., 5 Feb. 1840.
35. Birmingham Branch Manuscript History, 16 Apr. 1853.
36. Cardiff Branch Manuscript History, summer 1848.

Councillors are on their way to England will be here soon. She says my family suffer the most for clothing of any thing at present. She says my wife has many sorrowful hours and sighs much in my absens.[37]

Woodruff believed these pronouncements enough to become "depressed in spirits over the trials soon to come to the saints in Europe and America." (The prediction that the prophet was coming to England was partially fulfilled when several of the apostles arrived later in 1840.)

Other women reported dreams and visions. Within a few days after Sister How of the Cardiff Branch prophesied "that a great many accidents should take place shortly . . . 13 accidental deaths were recorded."[38] Sister Bates of London saw in vision the spirit of a recently-deceased woman with whom the elders had first found a home in the city.[39] This seems to have assured her mourners that she was in a gentler world, important in this case because officials arraigned her husband for not calling in a physician during the woman's illness.

Respect for women's spiritual identity underlay these reports. It was when they created disunity in the branches or trespassed too far into priesthood domain that disapproval emerged. A tantalizing hint of such tension appeared in a letter from Reuben Hedlock: "I do not hear much of late of the prophetesses in the Isle of Man; however, there are some difficulties among them. I shall visit . . . as soon as possible."[40]

Joseph Fielding also mentioned trouble between women of the Preston Branch caused by what he determined to be overzealous spiritualism. Returning there, he found "a group of Prophetesses having visions" through which they learned "who is going to die and who a female is going to become an elder's wife instead and who will be companions in the next world and who will not." He told them that God's will was that "all should stand" and warned

---

37. Mentioned in Wilford Woodruff Journal as cited in London Branch Manuscript History, entries beginning 10 Jan. 1840.
38. British Mission Manuscript History, 10 Jan. 1850.
39. London Conference Manuscript History, 28 Oct. 1841.
40. British Mission Manuscript History, 10 Jan. 1844.

them against considering themselves "a select little Company . . . better than the rest."[41]

In a farewell address at the end of his second mission, Wilford Woodruff warned the membership generally about spiritualism: "Let them take heed then that they be not ensnared; or because some women had got a peep stone, and was picturing some great wonders, or maybe a priest had healed one that was sick here and another there. [They] must seek to be fed through the head and not through the feet."[42] Six years later, while preaching in Bromley Branch, President Eli Kelsey chastised "an old sister" who had "jumped upon her feet, thrown herself into a theatrical attitude, and broke forth in tongues":

> I immediately rebuked her and commanded her to sit down. I found that the young Elder in charge of the branch had, in his inexperience, suffered such things, feeling a great delicacy in checking the gifts in the branch. If a bombshell had fallen, it could not have caused a greater surprise among some of the young members than did the sudden and peremptory check being put to such a glorious manifestation of the power of God. I was soon enabled to show them the impropriety of such conduct and I feel sure they will be more careful in the future.[43]

Because charismatic gifts were most often displayed by women, and the pruning was usually done by men, one wonders if spiritualism was a masked attempt at influence, identity, perhaps self-esteem. Studies of other cultures and times suggest that ecstatic religion is the property of the disinherited, "a struggle against some illness in the larger society."[44] Most of the women were part of an oppressed working class and further rejected by English society as members of an unpopular sect. In their own subculture they were continually advised to yield to males. Perhaps some women found refuge in spiritual outlets, in the hope of worth and status in another world.

41. Fielding Journal, 1 Sept. 1841.
42. British Mission Manuscript History, 15 Dec. 1845.
43. London Conference Manuscript History, 19 Mar. 1851.
44. Robert M. Anderson, *Vision of the Disinherited: The Making of American Pentecostalism* (Oxford: Oxford University Press, 1979), 15.

Religious groups besides Mormons evinced such spiritual outpourings. Mid-century Britain saw several waves of revivals which originated among evangelical sects and dismayed high-church exemplars. One such Irish revival caught the attention of an Archdeacon Stopford and the editors of the *Millennial Star* who cited his report at length. It begins with realistic detail which began many an eye-witness narrative about Mormons:

> One hundred fifty [Methodists] were present in the schoolroom. All were invited to declare what the Lord had done for their souls. Many did so, some with feeling. A young girl, evidently still in the state of excitement which follows the actual prostration, rose up and spoke at much greater length than the others. Her whole demeanor in that trying ordeal was the perfection of modesty, humility, and gracefulness.

But Archdeacon Stopford was a conformist, and he worried about the girl's mixed calm and fervor, thinking that her excitement must be diseased in nature. "Deeply grieved and sad" were his feelings "when a gross specimen of self-glorification was then set before that young creature as a pattern of what she might hope to attain to."[45]

Women seem to have been particularly prominent in these revivals. At another meeting, this time Presbyterian, Deacon Stopford's attention was again drawn to a female member of the choir: "[She] was the very type of all that was impressionable in woman ... I marked her slight figure, the hollow cheeks, the muddy colour under a clear skin, the intelligent face, the unnatural calm of the brilliant eyes under the dark lashes of singular length, and the fearful energy with which she sang." This girl was typical of "hundreds of mill girls in Belfast [who] have prayed and are praying to be 'struck.'" Stopford thought the situation "notorious."

Of interest is what Mormon women, reading their own newspaper, might have thought of Stopford's report. One can only speculate on the editors' intention in reprinting it. Primitive Methodism and evangelical Presbyterianism competed actively

45. *Latter-day Saints' Millennial Star* 21 (1859): 624.

against Mormonism. But the *Star* may have wanted to make a point among its own women. Mission leaders were apparently as discomfited as Stopford by the "groans, cries, and amens" of those who were "struck" by the Spirit. They publicly denounced such excessive spirituality and now backed their position editorially.

Equal Partners in Mischief

Spiritualism was only one point of tension in the branches. It is surprising to discover a good deal of open squabbling among members evidenced in the frequency of excommunications, disfellowships, and complaints by missionaries about disunity. Contentions steeped and stewed, and women as often as men stirred the kettles.

Consider Mother Dawson, of whom Fielding spoke so highly. In December 1838 he confided to his journal: "Things look very dark. Have been at Sister Dawson's in Preston, but it appears that Satan [is] getting Advantage of her and her Family. She is thinking of taking a less House, we suppose to get rid of us . . . "[46] Apparently the difficulty was not so much nursing the ailing Richardses as concern for one of her daughters (not Elizabeth Cottam) who had been accused of some offense: "Sister . . . Dawson said at Brother Burrow's a short time ago that if we did not place her Daughter Jane in the Church she herself would transgress on purpose to be cut off, and then she would tell some thing as that we should not like to be told, in a very threatening tone."[47]

Dawson was not the only temperamental sister. Elder James Whitehead's wife tore up his preaching papers and threatened to report him for abandonment if he went missionarying again. Fielding and Richards "therefore advised him to submit and remain as he is."[48] Elder Sloan wrote from Ireland that he and his wife were doing all they could to further the truth—but when might they go home, as his wife "would rather be in Nauvoo."[49]

46. Fielding Journal, 15 Dec. 1838.
47. Ibid., 12 Mar. 1839.
48. Ibid., 20 Apr. 1840.
49. British Mission Manuscript History, 10 Jan. 1844.

In 1842 Sister Parr and her husband were charged with "returning from America in defiance of the Lord, speaking evil, giving false report of the Church at Nauvoo, giving heed to statements of enemies, [and] not conferring with members of the Church."[50]

Similarly, in London, Susannah Albion and her mother left the church when her father was disfellowshipped for harassing the Booths.[51] Matilda Redmund was cut off for "absenting herself from the church without cause."[52] Harriet Heath, cut off from the Bristol Branch for "contempt," was rebaptized a year later, and Hannah Heath, probably a relation, was cut off "for cursing and swearing." An unidentified Sister Redman (not Ellen Balfour?) was disfellowshipped by the London Branch "for stealing and failing to acknowledge her fault as agreed upon." Other sisters were disciplined for failing to attend meetings, neglecting their duty, and making threats against mission leaders.[53]

During the 1840s and 1850s excommunications became so frequent that two mission presidents chastised the elders for over-zealousness. Reuben Hedlock complained that "In London people were cut off for trifling offenses," some merely because "they would not come before the Church and confess that the Elders were right in cutting their husbands off."[54] A decade later James Marsden advised branch councils "not to excommunicate people for not attending meetings."[55]

Ironically, both Hedlock and Marsden were themselves disciplined. Two years after Hedlock's plea for restraint, Apostle Orson Hyde accused Hedlock of "fleeing at our approach," leaving debts unpaid, and "finally living incognito in London with a vile woman." Hyde opined that Woodruff, "while a good man ... erred

50. Liverpool Branch Manuscript History, 9 Sept. 1842.
51. London Conference Manuscript History, 22 Dec. 1841.
52. Ibid., 9 Mar. 1842. Maria Dean was excommunicated for a more serious charge, "bearing the child of a man not her husband" (ibid., 28 May 1846).
53. Mini Margetts card file, British emigration index compiled by an early LDS Genealogical Library employee from ship and emigration office records, Film #415,443.
54. British Mission Manuscript History, 10 Jan. 1844.
55. Liverpool Branch Manuscript History, 8 Dec. 1856.

in appointing Hedlock, in whose heart the spirit of God did not dwell."[56] Three months after urging others to be slower to discipline, Marsden was excommunicated for "not emigrating by Brigham Young's counsel and general apostasy."[57]

No wonder Joseph Fielding and later elders sometimes became discouraged. "We are endeavouring to [make] the Church pure and in order, but it is difficult. We have diversity [of] Spirits to deal with."[58] Yet both Fielding and Richards were criticized for marrying (both to first wives) while on their missions and burdening the branch members who supported them. Perhaps it was the stress of close living quarters that resulted in Richards blaming Fielding's wife for her husband's preaching schedule. Later Richards, weary from criticism and in poor health, accused Sister Walmsley of saying "hard things" against his own wife. Asked to referee, Fielding declined, saying that "none are perfect" and that perhaps Richards was trying to get even. Walmsley sometimes let her tongue go at random, Fielding confided to his journal, and perhaps she was unused to polite company, but she was not one to bear grudges and possessed "a certain honesty" along with so much commitment that "she could not be whipt out of the Kingdom."[59]

What can be said about the disputes among these early Mormons is that, although not the happiest of proofs, they reveal that women were more than passive members of the church. They were an integral part of its progress and problems.

Hard Times or Sublimated Anger?

One approach to understanding dissension is to speculate on the origins of contention generally. One could argue that contention is normal, that had there been none we would be surprised. But disturbed feelings have causes. One can surmise several sources of tension in the British branches.

56. London Conference Manuscript History, 18 Oct. 1846.
57. Liverpool Branch Manuscript History, 29 Mar. 1857.
58. Fielding Journal, 27 Aug. 1838.
59. Ibid., 5 and 27 Feb. 1840.

There was the obvious stress of belonging to an unpopular sect. Fielding voiced this frustration:

> The Church is at this time in a State of depression almost throughout ... [There is] no lack of lies emigrating from America. Besides many native ones, they are all over the Country in the 43 NewsPapers etc. The Priests every where are fortifying their hearers against us. A strong tide of Prejudice is flowing. Which ever way I go, trouble in the Church meets me.[60]

Doctrinal strain was another source of tension. Elders defused suspicions of polygamy by members and outsiders. Reuben Hedlock, for instance, apologized to Richards for having to mention that "delicate matter":

> I have much trouble with the spiritual wife system, as it is termed here. It has caused much confusion among some of the branches and I have opposed it with all my power, and it is thrown in my face both by Saints and worldly people, that we do actually uphold such things, because they say Brother Hiram Clarke has made free with some of the sisters, so much so that in Macclesfield it is currently reported that he used, when there, to sleep with a certain sister, and also in Manchester . . . [61]

Spiritual wifery was a contributing issue in the Preston spiritualist episodes, for Fielding found along with too many visions "too great familiarity between the Brethren and Sisters in this Land." One elder was said to be assuring Preston sisters that bedding together was no evil unless they actually fornicated. The trouble was that occasionally he and a sister would be "overcome" and now one woman was pregnant.[62]

An organizational difficulty in the church itself was the scattered condition of the branches. Many drew membership from areas 900 miles square. Urban mill workers had an easier time

---

60. Ibid., 31 Oct. 1838.

61. Hedlock's letter indicates that the secret practice by some Mormon leaders of spiritual wifery was common knowledge in at least some of the British branches by roughly the time of Hedlock's letter (i.e., mid-1844).

62. Fielding Journal, 1 Sept. 1841. Fielding does not mention spiritual wifery. Apparently, it was not common knowledge in 1841.

getting to meetings than rural members, since missionaries tended to work the towns where public halls were available, but neither workers nor farmers nor miners could be easily reached when needed. The most common disappointment among missionaries was poor attendance, and logistics were more the culprit than apathy.

Primitive transportation and communication, and a sense of isolation and neglect, led to the disintegration of The Potteries branches in Staffordshire. Initially a strong conversion center, the area declined after 1844 when elders began to report increased apathy in attending meetings. The problems in Staffordshire were similar to those plaguing branches throughout the mission.[63]

The cyclical flowering and waning of numbers and activity was also influenced by events in the American church. During up times, such as the Reformation of 1856 or whenever members of the Quorum of Twelve Apostles could be dispatched, the British branches flourished. During hard times, such as the late 1850s when Utah was preoccupied with famine and invasion by federal troops, attendance and activism in the British branches flagged. An example is the London conference of early 1857 at the height of the Mormon Reformation in Britain when the Saints were paying tithing, saving their emigration money, distributing tracts, preaching out of doors, and accepting rebaptism as a sign of their recommitment to the church.[64] On the other hand, much lower activity is evident for 1858, 1859, and 1860, years of the lag effect of the Utah War.

Yet an American event which might have created chaos and did not was the martyrdom of Joseph Smith. Elders and leaders unanimously reported renewal. Liverpool Saints draped the chapel podium in black and, for some time after news of the assassination reached Britain, enjoyed very large congregations.[65]

63. Sherry Dew, "Mormonism in the Staffordshire Potteries," photocopy, LDS archives.

64. London Conference Manuscript History, 10 Feb., 5 Apr., and 28 June 1857.

65. British Mission Manuscript History, 5 Aug. 1844.

The 116 Saints of Chalford "generally manifested an increase of faith in the work."[66] When the news was announced in Birmingham, there followed

> an universal burst of tears and four sisters fainted away. It has produced a great change in the feelings of the Saints. It seems to have settled many petty disputes. I have heard it remarked by some that the Church in Britain never was in so flourishing a condition before. It would do you good to hear the English sisters talk of fighting the mob.[67]

Some periods of reduced activity had another cause entirely. Almost everyone had emigrated. Emigration was a prime motivator and chief exhaustor of the branches. It was the goal of nearly every dedicated Mormon and the bane of mission leaders who wrote after one wave of depletion: "We have lately made what provisions we can to supply the lack of offices in different branches, caused by emigration, and shall continue to do our utmost to keep all things in order."[68] Those left were stretched to carry full work loads with fewer and untrained people. Consider the Brierleyhill Branch, which by 1841-42 had only of forty-three members the Thomas Bullock family, his in-laws, a few single members, and three other families trying to staff an entire branch.

Emigration was costly in pounds as well as leadership. Even temple funds were sometimes diverted to helping the poor with sea passage. Year-end reports give examples of branches of 150 or 200 members which saw sixty baptisms in a year offset by seventy emigrations and three or four excommunications. Rarely did baptisms keep pace with emigration, and branches continually sent away their most devoted supporters.

Conclusion

Perhaps I have sidestepped the issue of female discontent. Not until the 1860s did anyone address the problem of female subordination (much less insubordination) openly through letters to the *Millennial Star*. These letters intimated for the first time resentment

66. Ibid., 20 Aug. 1844.
67. Reuben Hedlock to Willard Richards, ibid., 3 Sept. 1844.
68. Ibid., May 1843.

over women's restricted role in the kingdom, as discussed in greater detail in the next chapter.

For the first quarter-century of the British Mission, women's relationship to the church could best be described in terms of their relationship to local elders. Missionaries *were* the church during this period, and members related less to an institution than to their personal ministers of the gospel. The quality of that relationship may well have determined the loyalty of many female converts.

Elder John Lyon was a Scottish convert and missionary to Glasgow when he published his 1852 volume of poems. These tell more in verse than could several historians writing in prose about women's relationships with leaders in the little British churches. One poem in particular testifies to the affection that existed between missionary and convert, elder and sister. The poem reminds the hindsight-observer to expand her focus beyond the little troubles in the branches. Good will and common purpose overrode many a difference, so that members' faults became "a' virtues."

Furthermore, the poem confirms the independence of at least some Victorian women. Old Mrs. Beard, probably a widow with autonomy over her household and finances, could lodge and feed the elders without fee "nor tell it to others." Here is Lyon's tribute to "Auld Mrs. Beard":

There's auld Mrs. Beard who lives at Shrubhill,
I've lived wi' her lang, and had her good will,
Yet she never grew tired, nor lost her regard;
A kind-hearted Saint was auld Mrs. Beard!

CHORUS—
Auld Mrs. Beard, auld Mrs. Beard,
May thy fortune be great, and thy life be long spared,
Till thy children's children, thou seest them all paired
To raise up a kingdom for Mrs. Beard.

Sometimes she was cruse [cross], sometimes she was shy,
Sometimes she was douce [sweet], sometimes she was dry;
But her faults were a' virtues, with others compared,

For a thrifty guid wife was auld Mrs. Beard.

Auld Mrs. Beard &c.

When the Elders came roun', none more friendly could be;
She lodged them, and fed them, and welcomed them free;
In health or in sickness, her fortune she shared!
Nor told it to others, did auld Mrs. Beard.

Auld Mrs. Beard &c.

O had I the power to reward her past toil,
I'd make her my lady, tho' lord o' an isle,
But my proffers are vain, wi' a guid wife I'm saired,
To speak sic-like nonsense to auld Mrs. Beard.

Auld Mrs. Beard &c.[69]

Thanks be for the missionary writings which reveal like no other source the spirit of these early Mormon women's lives. No wonder Fanny Stenhouse, even deep into her career as an anti-Mormon, retained that sense of nostalgia toward her early years in the British church.

69. *Harp of Zion*, 182 (see n16). Some of these poems were previously published in the *Millennial Star*. Lyon, whom Edward Tullidge says became a poet in the 1820s, joined the church in Scotland in the 1840s and knew the Stenhouses, incorporating one of Fanny's poems in this volume.

Chapter 5.

Women Organize

Victorian women were oppressed. They shared the official status of the insane and mentally deficient. Upon marriage they relinquished property rights to their husbands, and divorce laws were so punitive as to make prisoners of women in abusive marriages. Only in a few towns and an American state or two did businesswomen enjoy citizenship rights. Enfranchisement of the common man was a recent innovation. The idea of females deserving equal rights was counter to biblical law in the minds of most church and civil leaders.

Mormon women enjoyed this sub-status plus additional insults reserved for members of their religion. Certainly polygamy implied subjection of women. Moreover, church offered faithful female members few official outlets for their energies during the first quarter-century. Yet there is considerable evidence that Mormon women insisted on a good deal of latitude of action in personal and many church arenas. Their histories prove that some women enjoyed considerable autonomy in their economic lives. Family bonds and social attitudes worked against legalities to enable many a convert to do just as she wished (though sometimes with battle) even to the point of abandoning a spouse and taking his children to America.

Within the church sisters counseled and argued with elders,

anointed each other in sickness, and financed proselyting endeavors (surely she who held the purse strings held sway over some decisions). A number of sisters married elders, putting themselves in the better position to give counsel. Many prophesied and spiritually advised both men and women, and all looked forward to the time when they could meet in Zion's temple, where women were ordained and officiated in ordinances.

What British sisters could not do was perform non-temple ordinances such as administering the sacrament, baptizing, confirming, blessing infants, and anointing men in illness. They also could not serve in higher offices, be ordained missionaries or mission leaders, be counted by priesthood office in church meetings, or act as the designated decision-makers in two-parent families (even many single women relied on "the elders" to make family decisions for them). They could proselyte as unordained missionaries, but those who assumed this duty apparently confined themselves to handing out tracts to neighbors and associates. It is not clear from the histories and minutes whether women helped to "sustain" branch, mission, and church appointees through consensus vote or if this was reserved for men.

Yet most sisters do not appear to have chafed unduly in the shadow of the elders. This may well have been because Mormon men took the brunt of the social disapproval gratuitously offered by British society. It was not a coveted status having doors slammed in your nose, enduring criticism from pulpit and editorial, being expelled backside first from a neighborhood, or, in a few cases, being tarred and feathered or arraigned before a magistrate.

There was a balancing ethic that discouraged oppressive male authority. Elders were expected to lead in tactful, even democratic tones. When they did not, it was attributed to a lapse in character. Early in her church career Hannah Tapfield King was irritated at her son-in-law Elder Claudius V. Spencer's dictatorial behavior. She wrote drolly, "He seemed to have made up his mind and when that is the case, 'It is no compulsion—but you must!!!' So we arose with all obedience . . ." Only much later, while crossing the plains, did her feelings strain towards him, and then not because of his overbearing manner but because of his coolness toward her. The issue for her was courtesy and love.

Intimations of Raised Consciousness

The mid-nineteenth century saw the beginnings of the Women's Suffrage movement in Great Britain, with considerable discussion of women's rights by social reformers. There was new militancy by a few and a new awareness by many on both sides of the Atlantic that women continued to lag in the progress toward popular rights. Perhaps younger British sisters caught this perception, or perhaps it was the now-unavoidable fact of Mormon plural marriage that set wives to self-examination, leading to a new, philosophical discontent.

In 1859 the *Millennial Star* published its first comment on "Woman's Sphere and Duties" in an editorial by Emily Teasdale. Although woman's focus should be on "the rising generation," this British woman wrote, with love and intelligence she could enlarge her scope to include the sick and afflicted outside her walls. And, she tactfully added, while feminine influence presently flowed only as an undercurrent, "its influence will be felt, and in the kingdom of God appreciated and ultimately placed in its proper position."[1]

It was three years before another letter to the *Millennial Star* ever-so-gently expanded the theme. Elicia Grist, a Liverpool convert of six years, wanted British sisters to exert "more lively interest in each other's society." "Some feel," the young matron wrote with contempt, "that women shouldn't interfere in the least in the Kingdom of God" and that women, being the weaker vessels, "cannot carry the higher responsibility as oracles of God." She urged women to step forward and "perform acts . . . nearly allied to the brethren." Women were not vocal enough in the branches. They should at least bear testimony in "fellowship meetings" to help listeners "reflect more deeply and closely on what has been said."

She next proposed an Ann Rosser-like model of feminine action: Those who could not meet with the Saints could individu-

---

1. *Millennial Star* 21:2-7.

ally encourage family and friends, converse on gospel principles with neighbors, disseminate literature, invite others to meeting, and cherish "a loving, kindred spirit to each other."[2] Her letter ended with an idea of how to fund the emigration. Mothers could teach their children to save pennies in a box, remembering that every penny would bring them three miles closer to Salt Lake City. Elicia herself, with her husband and daughters, emigrated two years later, costing the mission another female activist.

The Era of the Auxiliaries

The action now changes under the sway of two developments: normalization of Utah Mormonism so that by 1860 it could afford more consistent support of its foreign missions, and growing social consciousness expressed in auxiliary organizations such as the Young Ladies Improvement Association, the children's Primary, and the women's movement of the 1870s.

If the 1850s were a time of continued upheaval in the Utah church, the 1860s were relatively stable. Settlers had time to put down roots, build more permanent homes, and establish productive farms, towns, and trades. The Utah church entered a phase of discretionary energy. As early as 1854 attempts were made to reinvent the Nauvoo Female Relief Society as well as the Salt Lake Thirteenth Ward Indian Relief Society. The latter was organized to manufacture clothing for Native Americans, make rag carpets for the new Tabernacle, and monitor the needs of the poor for Bishop Edwin Woolley.[3]

This society dissolved in 1858 during the Utah War and temporary abandonment of Salt Lake City, but the following decade saw the permanent reestablishment of female Relief Societies throughout the territory. In the 1870s feminine collaboration flowered. A magazine founded in 1872, with women as editors and correspondents, promoted the cultural, political, and economic advancement of Mormon sisters. Utah women became involved in the suffrage movement, sending delegates to the

2. Ibid. 23:277.

3. Leonard J. Arrington, *From Quaker to Latter-day Saint: Bishop Edwin D. Woolley* (Salt Lake City: Deseret Book Co., 1986).

newly-emboldened suffrage conventions in the East and Europe.

All of these events affected the British mission. During the three-year retreat of 1856-59, when the church was preoccupied with troubles at home, the mission fell into a state of neglect. When sent there in 1860, Jacob Gates was surprised to find Preston members of twenty-plus years standing with no plans to emigrate.[4] In the mining district of Newcastle, branches had dissipated never to regroup as miners moved to new areas.[5] In 1860 John Cook noticed a "coolness among the Saints in London unlike any other conference."[6] Another elder wrote that, while he had located isolated Saints on the Isle of Man, they "didn't know whether they were in the Church or not."[7] Everywhere branches were still small and members so sparsely strewn that it was hard to gather many together at any one place. A scarcity of officers meant that "the meetings [were] not as interesting and efficient as we would wish."[8]

This new corps of elders attacked the perceived lethargy with enthusiasm. Gates became a popular elder, addressing mixed congregations as "Brothers and Sisters" rather than just "Brethren." Thomas Wallace steadily organized and reorganized branches in Newcastle to align with relocations of members. He reported few baptisms but said the people had "a good spirit." Cook gave the work in London "a fresh start" and was soon reassured by a new "liberality" among members there. And the missionary to the Isle of Man decided that the poor Saints there were, after all, "glad to be collected to hear the word of life."

Once again they stressed emigration. The *Millennial Star* reprinted Eliza R. Snow's rhymed address to the young sisters of the church, the closing lines of which read: "That scatter'd sisters may be gather'd home/ To Zion, where the best from worlds will come."[9] Elsewhere people were told, "This work, this king-

4. *Millennial Star* 22:411.
5. Ibid.
6. Ibid., 428.
7. Ibid.
8. Ibid., 44.
9. Ibid. 23:254.

dom, is not represented here, or in Liverpool . . . but in the Mountains." Members could not expect the church to blossom in Britain but should look for its maturing power "in the west."[10]

These entreaties proved effective. While little activity was reported in the London Conference for the late 1850s, by 1861 eighty-one members had emigrated, delinquent members were "rallying," and the halls were "replenished."[11] In May 1862 the Liverpool Conference reported that one-fourth of its members had emigrated already that year with others to follow, while many additions had been received through baptism.[12]

In 1864 George Reynolds noted in his journal, "Last season [saw a] remarkably large emigration" of 160 members.[13] In 1866 Birmingham branches emigrated sixty-five members, the next year 134 out of a total membership of 848. (Uncharacteristically, 137 were baptized, more than replacing those who emigrated.[14]) In 1862 the Preston and Liverpool conferences together emigrated 150 and baptized 249. These are high numbers when one considers that during the previous three years a total of only 1074 emigrated from all of Great Britain.[15]

The Utah Connection

It was ten years into the second quarter of the mission when by both design and circumstance Eliza R. Snow, churchwide president of the Relief Society and editor of *Woman's Exponent*, became a motivating force for the advancement of British Mormon women. Her world tour of 1872-73 was largely personal, but during stopovers in Liverpool and London she made quasi-official ventures into British conferences. One aspect of this tour indicates that Snow had adopted American middle-class condescension

10. Ibid., 490.
11. Ibid.
12. Liverpool Conference Manuscript History, 27 May 1862, archives, Historical Department, Church of Jesus Christ of Latter-day Saints, Salt Lake City, Utah (hereafter LDS archives).
13. Ibid., 1 Jan. 1864.
14. *Millennial Star* 29:149.
15. Ibid. 21:638.

toward the Old World with her concern for the condition of women there. In November 1872, during her nine-day stopover in London, she used a day in "making calls among the Saints." Because she had asked to be shown "the poorest Saints in London," the conference president obliged, although he advised her that the even-more destitute might be found outside the city. Snow found the members to be "cheerful and happy," although one family was living in a one-room flat reached by "a narrow, winding stairway." This mother and two daughters earned their living with seasonal employment, making Christmas baskets out of trimmings and ribbons provided by a London merchant who "paid them at a very low figure for their work."[16]

On her return from Palestine Snow visited the London Conference again. Although she had little to say about this second stopover, the president of the mission said that the congregation that Sunday contained "the best numbers [he] had ever seen."[17]

Both visits inspired the Manchester Saints. A. J. Scofield subsequently wrote to the *Woman's Exponent*:

> I was one of the few to whom was granted the pleasure of an introduction to our mutual sister, Miss Eliza R. Snow. It was a privilege that I greatly appreciate, and though I only saw her during her short visit in Liverpool, I should, did I never see her again, always remember her with love and veneration. I went with President Carrington and a few others to the station, and when I saw her and party leave en route to London, I felt as lonely as if I had known her for years.[18]

This visit had the effect of kindling the first full-fledged Relief Society in Great Britain. Although never mentioned in the *Woman's Exponent*, which identified the Whitechapel Relief Society organized a year later as the first women's auxiliary in the British mission, the Manuscript History for the Nottingham Branch states: "There was a Relief Society in existence in Nottingham as early as January 1873, which had a continued existence until October,

16. *Woman's Exponent* 1:139.
17. Ibid. 2:22.
18. Ibid. 2 (15 June 1873): 2.

1875."[19] The timing—a month after Snow's visit—suggests a connection.

It is puzzling that the Nottingham sisters did not publicize their accomplishment. Curiously, their only communication to the *Woman's Exponent* was through a Utah missionary, George L. Farrell, stationed in the city. While his intent was merely to report on life in England, we learn something about the Nottingham Branch sisters from his May 1875 letter. The missionary worried about 120,000 habitual criminals and 33,000 drunkards among London's four million people. London's liquor houses, "if their fronts were placed side by side, [would] reach from Charing Cross to Portsmouth," and "above a million people [who were] practically heathen, wholly neglecting their religion," he wrote.[20] Farrell's perspective was not feminist. He was not anxious for the sisters to unify or enlarge their scope of influence, merely for them to "break off from their old habits of drinking beer, tea, coffee, etc." and put their means into the Perpetual Emigration Fund.

Another visitor, Elizabeth H. Goddard, was proof that a woman from Utah could exert very little influence if she put her mind to it. Her 1879 extended stay in her birthland had no discernible effect on the branches she attended. Granted, the purpose of her tour was truly private—to escort her son to the mission field and visit relatives in Leicester—and she did not enjoy the prestigious reception given Eliza Snow, Brigham Young's polygamous wife. But Goddard's letters to the *Woman's Exponent* were not marked by curiosity, enthusiasm, or awareness of a cause—simply by homesickness: "My brother has a beautiful home and lovely surroundings, with every comfort, but I would not exchange for my dear home in Utah . . . there is something wanting, that is only to be found in the society of the Saints of God, of which there are but few in Leicester, and those few most of them are intending to emigrate this Fall."[21] It was some time, she complained, before her son could locate an LDS branch at all, and when he did it consisted

19. A. J. Field notes in Nottingham Branch Mission History, 1873, LDS archives.
20. Letter to *Woman's Exponent*, July 1875.
21. *Woman's Exponent* 8:38.

of seven members who met only on Sunday afternoons to take the sacrament and bear testimony. "They did not have any singing because it annoyed their neighbors." Her son was finding it impossible to attract audiences to indoor meetings so had resorted to outdoor preaching "which . . . was rather tough on him at first." Her conclusion: the work in Britain was "like the gathering of grapes when the vintage is over."

To Goddard's credit, she did visit isolated sisters in the Leicester Branch and also attended meetings in Nottingham, Lincoln, and Derby, although she "did not stay long to visit the Saints in those places." In one town she found sixty-two Saints meeting "in a small house on a quiet street." The work there, too, she said, was "at low ebb."[22]

Perhaps this is harsh commentary when Goddard's frank impressions tell at least the extent to which one British emigrant had transferred her loyalties to her new home. And her insight may have been valid that "the gathering" was waning in Britain, or at least that the British Mission was fading as the once-foremost vineyard. Dwindling numbers of baptisms and emigrations from the late 1860s on confirm Goddard's impression.

A year later Georgine Bird was on the Tyne River on a protracted visit and did not find a Relief Society in Newcastle, although the branch there had had a society for a brief while in 1877. If she was concerned at this lack, however, Bird's long letter published in the *Woman's Exponent* voiced a call to wagons, not to arms. Think, she pleaded, of "the hundreds of anxious hearts and ears that are waiting to hear a word from the mountains.

> Remember the condition of the honest poor woman in this part of England? The pitman's wife is a drudge; the agriculturist's a slave. Do they know that women still work in brickyards, bind the wheat, pitch and stack the hay, drive farm-carts, fill the carts and spread manure on the land, and that in a wet, cold climate?[23]

Without a chance to emigrate, girls would "naturally drift into

22. Ibid., 93, 101.
23. Georgine A. Bird, "A Voice From the Tyne," *Woman's Exponent* 8 (15 Jan. 1880): 123.

marriage, at best, and thus become fettered to a man who knows not the way of the Lord." Utah sisters should think of assistance "not as a donation, but as a duty to anxious ones who have been born in the Church."

This is further indication that British sisters who were concerned about women's advancement saw the doctrine of gathering as a means to this end. Bird was an activist for her sex, but she, like Snow, Grist, and others, either subordinated the immediate cause to The Gathering or—as is more likely—equated the two.

Prodding from Men

Through the impetus of a few local sisters, and with a further boost from these Utah women, the British church began to show an interest in organizing. Apparently another ingredient was needed to turn interest to action. Not enough information exists on how each of the branch Relief Societies was formed, but the few facts that have survived reveal a pattern of male initiative and patronage to bring this change about. The most dedicated to the creation of women's societies in the mission seems to have been young Utah elders who had seen their mothers involved in the society back home and were convinced of the good it could do.

The first British Relief Society to announce itself to Utah and thereby put itself into mission consciousness was in the Whitechapel Branch of east London. A good deal of information exists about this society because its officers bothered to report their activities to the *Woman's Exponent*.[24] By 1871 the Whitechapel Branch was described by missionaries as friendly and protecting its members from city lures through social concerts.[25] Yet Eliza Snow's 1872 and 1873 appearances did not spark an immediate response as in Nottingham. It was over a year later, in March 1874, that an organizational meeting was held, dominated by men:

> This branch [society] was organized by Pres. R. T. Burton of the London Conference, assisted by the branch Pres. Peter Romerell and others of the Priesthood. The nominations were carried by

24. *Millennial Star* 40:203.
25. London Conference Manuscript History, 1871.

all the members present at the meeting.

Elder Romerell encouraged the sisters to faithfully carry out the duties connected with the Society and a great amount of good would be the result. Elder R. T. Burton followed with good instructions and an interesting account of the Relief Society in his ward at home in Zion. The teachers received by donations, the amount of six shillings and sixpence at the close of the meeting. Adjourned to next Wednesday evening. Benediction by Elder R. T. Burton.

H. H. Edenboroungh, Sec'y[26]

The Whitechapel Relief Society would offset its initial sluggishness by lasting more than a decade, an apparent record.

By 1875 a second Relief Society was operating in the conference in north London. It was organized in February 1875 among an "energetic and liberal" membership of ten ladies led by the Cross family. They outdid the east branch in charity collections and disbursements. In 1877 a third conference society, attached to the London-Lambeth Branch, was organized along with a Sunday school. With the Whitechapel society, these organizations were later reported to be "in good condition and doing much good."[27]

At church headquarters in Liverpool one might expect to find evidence of a thriving women's organization, but this was not so. A society was not organized until 1878, five years after Nottingham. An organizational meeting attended by "a number of sisters" was held at the home of branch president Scott Anderson apparently at the initiative of conference president James L. Bunting:

President Bunting opened the meeting with prayer, after which President [of the European Mission William] Budge delivered a very interesting and instructive address, fully explaining the work done by Relief Societies in Zion, and their incalculable value as an auxiliary agency in advancing the work of God.

Elder Bunting said he would be delighted if the sisters could see their way to form such a society; after which, on the motion of Elder Anderson, the Society was duly formed.[28]

26. *Woman's Exponent* 9 (1 Jan. 1881): 118.
27. London Conference Manuscript History, 2 Jan. 1876.
28. "R.S., Y.L.M.I.A. and Primary Reports—Liverpool," *Woman's*

A presidency was then appointed and resolutions passed to hold weekly meetings and begin at once a campaign to visit every sister in the branch.

At the end of a year the Liverpool society reported to the *Woman's Exponent* that they had added five members to their original eight but lost five to emigration, relocation, and apostasy. "Most of the members have pressing household duties to perform," and members had encountered "many difficulties" during the year. Still, they had been able to afford "some little relief" to the poor.

The second year of the Liverpool Relief Society went more smoothly. Beginning with nine members, the society gained four while emigrating four, but twenty-one meetings were held during the year with "good attendance indeed," and 134 visits were made to branch members. Only 4 pounds 9 shillings 2 pence was collected, but "even with this small sum every pressing need [was] relieved." Again, mention is made of an elder (C. W. Stayner and wife) who attended meetings regularly and supported the society "with loving words and wise counsels."[29]

All told, between 1873 and 1881 at least fifteen societies were founded in the mission, some tenuously, as in the Newcastle-on-Tyne Branch on the northeast coast of England. In 1877, at the conclusion of a Wednesday evening meeting, a women's presidency was appointed who were to call a meeting of the sisters and appoint a secretary. A few months afterward, at another branch meeting, "it was moved, seconded and carried that the Relief Society be disorganized." There is no record of its reorganization in the nineteenth century, although a Mutual Improvement Society and a Tract Society operated in Newcastle in 1880 and were supported by women as well as men.[30]

The Flavor of a Victorian Relief Society

The Glasgow-Parkhead society of Scotland was one of the more successful. In the minutes collection of the Glasgow Branch

Exponent 18 (1881): 183.

29. *Woman's Exponent* 10 (15 Mar. 1883): 158.

30. Newcastle-on-Tyne Branch Manuscript History, LDS archives.

is the only British Relief Society minute book to survive in LDS church archives. Supplementing this record with details from other branches, we discover the flavor of a British Relief Society— its purpose, structure, problems, significance in the lives of branch sisters, and influence in the mission.

Using Utah societies as a pattern, the purpose of a British Relief Society was to relieve the poor and ill and "do much good." Between 1881 and 1887 the Glasgow Relief Society held monthly meetings. Its agenda usually included a prayer followed by a hymn (often the same one from month to month), a reading of the previous month's minutes, and reports by the society's six or seven visiting teachers who made housecalls to branch women. In one early meeting, responding to a teacher's report, the sisters agreed to give three shillings to Sister Neilson "in poor circumstances." At another meeting, when Brother Cooper of Tollcross was re-ported in poor circumstances, President Flora Crawford moved, her counselor seconded, and the members unanimously approved a loan of ten shillings to the branch president for the benefit of the ailing brother.[31]

Records of other societies show that they too assisted the needy and sent out teachers to "visit every sister in the branch." Virtually all charitable donations came from the sisters them-selves. The Liverpool society used 2 of 6 pounds collected to purchase tracts which were then "carefully distributed from house to house."

In April of the first year of the Glasgow society there was an attempt, perhaps inspired by Brother Burt, the presiding elder of the area, to meet weekly and expand the society into an educa-tional forum. At one of the new meetings President Crawford and her counselor read from the *Woman's Exponent* discourses by Parley P. Pratt and Eliza R. Snow. But weekly meetings apparently proved unfeasible, for in May the sisters resumed a monthly schedule.

---

31. Glasgow Branch, Scottish Conference, Relief Society Minute Book, 1881-87; entries for 1 Feb., 13 Mar., and 11 Apr. 1881, LDS archives. That the society "loaned" the funds to the branch president indicates the society's degree of financial independence.

The Liverpool society succeeded in holding twenty-one weekly meetings during its second year, and Whitechapel sisters consistently met bi-weekly during the 1880s, no doubt helped by the circumstance of all living within relatively convenient distance to the meeting house. When conditions dictated monthly gatherings, meetings were taken up largely with business, reports of visits, and occasional "loving words and wise counsels" from branch leaders and missionaries. Instead of lessons, sisters were invited to bear testimony, something many were reluctant to do in the Sunday sacrament meetings dominated by brethren.

The little Relief Societies encountered "many difficulties," some unnamed. Not the least problem was instability as women relocated to Utah. Most societies were founded by fewer than ten women, and attendance seldom exceeded this. It appears that younger women were less enthusiastic than mature sisters, for a July 1887 entry in the Glasgow minutes reports that the president would be "glad to see the young sisters turn out as well as they could for there were places for them all." She proposed asking some younger women to sing for the group "to make the meetings interesting."

Few of the British societies lasted six years. Most seem to have met the fate of the Bradford Branch in Leeds District. It was organized in October 1881 but not mentioned again in the branch records. By 1885 the entire branch was in arrears on chapel rent, a dilemma which someone tried to remedy by renting another room in nearby Clayton and entrusting branch benches, hymnbooks, manuals, and records to a sister there. But the sister was planning to emigrate, and, besides, the members in Bradford demanded that the items be returned. So someone paid the shipping fee and the belongings were sent back to Bradford. In 1887-88 no activities were reported for the branch. How could a women's auxiliary function when the main body was dying?[32]

The limited appeal and short lives of the fifteen original British Relief Societies lead one to ask how significant they were. Charitable talents varied greatly from group to group, but during one

32. Bradford Branch Mission History, 29 Oct. 1881-88, LDS archives.

year four of the societies collected a total of 52 pounds and disbursed over 43 pounds to the poor. These are worthy sums considering that a worker's annual income seldom exceeded 15 pounds. And the Liverpool society, which apologized for doing so little, one year visited a total of 134 homes, meaning at least two visits per sister, and claimed that it had alleviated "every pressing need." Such efforts relieved the branch president of much of the burden of assisting members in misfortune.

While the 1870s and 1880s began a golden era of women's activities in Utah, in Britain the auxiliary had rough going. Women were increasingly requested to serve in other areas of church organizations. In 1916 the Leeds Branch Young *Men*'s Mutual Improvement Association had a male president with two *female* counselors. Women served as Sunday school teachers. The Leeds Branch went without male priesthood leadership in 1892 and then ceased entirely for the decade because its most active members had all gone to Utah. Not until 1916 would the branch reawaken and a Relief Society again be established.[33]

When Romania Penrose accompanied her mission president-husband to England in 1907, she found female Relief Societies functioning only in Leicester, Norwich, and Liverpool. In one year she reorganized thirty-six societies, followed by another fourteen by the time she left in 1911. But less than five years later Ida Smith arrived to find that "the splendid work done by Dr. Penrose had fallen off materially for lack of a directing head." Within a year of her own arrival Sister Smith had forty-two societies again functioning. It seems clear that organized female effort seldom survived unless sustained by a Utah leader.[34]

Conclusion

British women proved themselves able to fill nearly every role performed by men, including ordained leadership and tracting, though they served primarily in supporting and nurturing roles. They did not form the separate subculture observed elsewhere,

33. Leeds Branch Manuscript History, 1890-1916, LDS archives.
34. Susa Young Gates, "Relief Society Work in the Missions," *Relief Society Magazine* 5 (July 1918): 365-66.

perhaps due to the more personal character of the church in England which created less distinction between men's and women's efforts and had a more restricted goal. In this mission men and women worked shoulder to shoulder.

It is a credit to the early participants that the Relief Societies succeeded as well as they did, but circumstances were not right. Under conditions of isolation, with their membership always in flux, British women had other preoccupations. In America, they were told, they would enjoy equality, or constructive co-existence, with their Mormon brothers, according to female church leaders in columns of the *Woman's Exponent*. Perhaps they left their records incomplete because they were hurrying to emigrate.

Chapter 6.

Plural Marriage

In 1856," wrote Priscilla Merriman Evans, "plurality of wives was preached to the world." She is wrong about the date. Public acknowledgment was made from Great Salt Lake City during a special August 1852 church conference and published in the British *Millennial Star* that same year. But Evans's testimony may indicate that mission leaders procrastinated announcement from the pulpit, especially in the hinterland.[1] If incorrect about the year, Evans nonetheless vividly remembered the emotional impact among British Mormons:

> It caused quite a commotion in our branch. There was one girl there who came to me with tears in her eyes and said, "Is it true that Brigham Young has ninety wives? Oh, I can't stand that!" I told her that it had not been long since I heard her testify that she knew the Church was true and if it was then, it was true now. She was getting ready to be married and go to Zion. I told her I did not see anything to cry about. So after I encouraged her she dried her tears and when we were ready to emigrate she came with us.

1. Hannah Tapfield King, living in Cambridgeshire, wrote to her brother that "the revelation" was read at meeting the Sunday prior to her 20 December 1852 letter.

In spite of this professed composure, Priscilla and her husband never embraced the doctrine. One wonders if the other woman eventually did.

The other woman's reaction is a common one in the histories: initial aversion followed by conviction followed sometimes but not usually by participation in "celestial marriage" (the order of heaven). Far more frequent is silence. Polygamy is glaringly ignored by seven out of ten of our women who kept journals or penned reminiscences.

Public Denial, 1838-52

Between 1838 and 1852 polygamy was not taught officially to British Saints. During this fifteen-year period, leaders denied the practice publicly both in America and in foreign missions. If British converts of the 1840s knew the truth, they could only have learned it through word of mouth. Polygamy may have been the subject of Mother Dawson's cryptic threat to Joseph Fielding that she would "tell some thing as that we should not like to be told." Even some missionaries—those of local origin—were probably not privy to the truth. During this early period rumors about Joseph Smith's and Brigham Young's wives must have seemed to new converts just another slander from the anti-Mormon propaganda.

Indeed, until 1852 monogamy was preached as the law of the gospel. An "Article of Marriage" prescribing one wife per husband comprised the 101st section of the Doctrine and Covenants until 1876. Furthermore, the Book of Mormon made it clear that a man's hunkering after more than one woman was an abomination and that exclusive faithfulness to wives and families was God's mandate (see Jacob 2:24-27, 30, 35). These teachings thus contradicted not only what was being secretly practiced in Nauvoo but what Mormon converts read (and some believed) about patriarchal practices in the Old Testament.

A study of one polygamous family is instructive of how an early British convert might have come to espouse polygamy.

Ellen Wilding, daughter of a wealthy Lancashire Englishman was one of Heber C. Kimball's earliest converts made while he preached in the old "Cockpit", a rented hall, in Preston. She was the only member of her family to convert. In 1841 she emigrated to Nauvoo, where she became a servant in the household of Edwin D. Woolley, prosperous merchant, friend of Joseph Smith, and later business manager to Brigham Young.[2]

In October 1843 Edwin and Mary Wickersham Woolley (both Pennsylvania Quakers converted in the 1830s) were secretly taught about celestial marriage by Hyrum Smith. No doubt Ellen Wilding was present as well as others. Edwin's younger brother Samuel lay sick upstairs but later claimed to have overheard the proceedings. In a miraculous manner, he wrote, he felt himself in the parlor downstairs, saw Hyrum take out a paper, and heard him read the revelation. "There was a sister present by the name of German who, when he read to a certain point, went to the south-west window, raised the curtain, looked out, then turned around and said, 'Brother Hyrum, don't read any more, I am full up to here' drawing her hand across her throat."

At that time Edwin and Mary Woolley had five children. Their middle child, seven-year-old Rachel, would remember "many more visits" from the brethren at night, after "we children were sent to bed." Unfortunately, she heard only voices, not words. But Samuel Woolley indicated the tenor of what was said. From that day in his sickbed, he was convinced "the revelation was of God, and that no man could or would receive a fulness of Celestial Glory and Eternal Life, except he obeyed that law, and had more than one living wife at the same time."

In her later recollections, Rachel treated with ambivalence her parents' experience with polygamy. To a Mormon public she would say, "Strange as it may seem, mother was the first to receive and accept it [the principle of celestial marriage]." This may well have been Mary's initial reaction, but privately Rachel confessed that "There would be days together that [Mother] would not leave her room. Often I have gone there and found her crying as though her heart would break."

Mary temporarily overcame her feelings, for Edwin took as his

2. Ellen Wilding Woolley's and Woolley family's histories are taken from Leonard J. Arrington, *From Quaker to Latter-day Saint: Bishop Edwin D. Woolley* (Salt Lake City: Deseret Book Co., 1986), 110 and following.

first plural wife a twenty-three-year-old mother of two. Louisa Chapin Rising, whom he had converted while on a mission to Connecticut, was civilly only separated from her first husband. Louisa bore Edwin a son nineteen months after their marriage. But her relationship with the Woolley family and Mormonism proved troubled, and when the Woolleys migrated west three years later she did not go with them. She died in Illinois in 1849.

On 28 December 1843, at or near the time Edwin married Louisa, he also married the British convert Ellen Wilding. Ellen's first child was not born until December 1847, suggesting that connubial relations did not begin immediately. She would bear Edwin five children in all, the last in 1858.

Indications are that communion between the wives was not smooth, and family tradition is that the tensions centered around Louisa. Perhaps first wife Mary's presence made consummation of the plural marriages awkward. Perhaps, too, Ellen needed a period of adjustment from servanthood to wifehood. For whatever reasons, within four months of Edwin's marriage to Louisa, Mary took her new baby and left Nauvoo as well as "Husband and Children and everything that is dear to me, to satisfy others" and returned to her mother's home in eastern Ohio.

Before Mary left, Edwin instructed her to write to him all her feelings, which she did from a lonely hotel room in Wellsville, Ohio, in a pitiable letter dated 24 April 1843:

> I have just gone up stairs to bed where I am locked up in a room by my self with the exception of a little sick baby and while I am watching her I thot I would write a few more lines to thee, I have just been pouring out my soul to my God for consolation in my afflictions, for I have no husband to comfort me, I am deprived of his society whom I delight in, and for why? This I will not answer, let them answer that know better than I but Oh Edwin while thee is enjoying the society of thy children and friends and . . . don't I pray thee forget me for a moment for thee doesn't know all the trials I have passed thru since I left home. This night is recorded in the heavens above and time will come when thee may gaze upon the scenery thyself and realize my own situation and as I am at this time, but there are those I make no doubt that are happy at this time. I ask my God why it is that

one part of his family should suffer so much more than others, the time will come when we must give account of the deeds done in the body, and needs be the offences come but know not by whom they cometh.

This is the woman of whom a descendant told me privately she was ashamed because of Mary's intractability. After all, didn't Mary Woolley have the benefit of direct counsel from Eliza R. Snow—plural wife to Joseph Smith, later wife-in-name-only to Brigham Young, and second general president of the women's Relief Society—to "yield to the lord whom you obey"?[3]

Yet for my part it is difficult to condemn the author of such a letter. Moreover, if the purpose of plural marriage was, as stated in the Book of Mormon, for the Old Testament patriarchs to raise up children unto the Lord, surely this purpose was fulfilled by Mary Woolley and her husband—whose family would ultimately comprise five wives and twenty-six children.

The relevance of this story to our British women is how in several ways Ellen Wilding's introduction to polygamy reflected a pattern. Like others converted in the British mission, she appears to have had no knowledge of the doctrine until arriving in Zion. Once exposed, she came to accept it as direct revelation from God. And any initial aversion or difficulties were surmounted to the degree that family normalcy was eventually achieved.

Most of the histories left the initiation to polygamy unsaid. Even Henrietta Bullock's husband Thomas, later scribe to Brigham Young, scarcely mentioned polygamy in his immigration diary except to say that Brigham referred to "the objections of some men to plurality of wives." Bullock quoted Young as saying "the Elders would marry wives of every tribe" until the Lamanites (American Indians) would become a "white and delightsome people." The dearth of references to polygamy in the diaries is suggestive. The trouble is, suggestive of what? It may be that by the time a woman

3. Sister Snow's advice was penned in Mary Woolley's autograph book, a photocopy of which I was permitted to see in the Woolley collection at archives, Historical Department, Church of Jesus Christ of Latter-day Saints, Salt Lake City, Utah.

sat down to her diary, she found the confirmation of persistent rumors not worth belaboring. Or perhaps polygamy was too dangerous a subject to include in a written record. Another possibility is that a woman's feelings about polygamy were too strong or too ambivalent to contain in mere words. Finally, the women may simply not have been aware of the practice.

Yet, although British women would have known little beyond rumor in the 1840s, by the end of the 1850s most if not all were apprised. Letters from Utah friends and family, a new flurry of newspaper reports and books on Mormons, and private talks with missionaries spread the word to some degree even before the bombshell in the *Millennial Star*. Reuben Hedlock's letter referring to the "spiritual wife system" had been written in 1844, long before the doctrine became explicit knowledge in the British church.

But the letters and private talks must have carried the tenor of Mary Ann Maughan's remonstration to the horrified young Welsh sister: if it was God's church before a woman discovered this unpleasant fact, it was His afterward. If a woman wanted to be counted as one of His daughters, she would have to accept this test of faith. The doctrine may have served to glean the staunch from the less committed. In other words, polygamy may have been one of the dividers between the 50 percent of Mormon converts who gathered to Zion and those who did not.

The New Teachings and the Reaction of British Sisters

When Apostle Orson Pratt (who had once left the church out of aversion to polygamy) tendered the first public *apologia* for celestial marriage in 1852, his proclamation superseded Book of Commandments 101 and the Book of Mormon and created a rationale for the doctrine. Pratt cited Old Testament precedent and gave sociological "evidence" that monogamy was rare and unnatural among world civilizations. Later that day Joseph Smith's 1838 revelation on celestial marriage was read publicly for the first time, "to the great joy of the saints who have looked forward . . . for the time to come when we could publickly declare the . . . greatest principles of our holy religion."[4]

4. *Journal of Discourses*, 26 vols. (Liverpool, Eng.: Latter-day Saints

The immediate reaction in Britain, as noted in the women's histories, was shock followed by apostasy by some of the women's relatives.

Possibly the proclamation led to new doctrinal and organizational tensions among members, although evidence of this is not plentiful. In fact, there is no more mention of the troubles over "spiritual wifery" that had occurred in the 1840s. In later decades the very hint of unrighteous collusion between missionary and sister was nipped by strict mission policy laid down by Amasa Lyman, who:

> instructed the Elders not to escort the young women to and from the meetings. He said he did not wish to have the brethren feel that they were never to allow a sister to take them by the arm, but let it be the aged and infirm who need assistance and not as he generally found it the case, the blooming 17-year-old girl . . .

One of the few women who wrote directly about this tumultuous time was Hannah Tapfield King, the Cambridge landowner's wife. In a letter to her non-member brother dated 30 December 1852, she confessed her feelings following the semi-annual meeting of the Norwich Conference at which polygamy was introduced: "Well now a few words on the events of Sunday last. It was a day never to be forgotten by me! The meeting was held in the splendid Freemason's Hall which was a perfect cram to overflowing. Georgy and I were favored with chairs on the platform. In the afternoon *the revelation* was read which will I expect, set the world in a blaze."

Unfortunately, Hannah did not give even a summary of the speeches. However, if they resembled a discourse by Franklin D. Richards which Hannah wrote about two years earlier, they were Old Testament in flavor. The "pith" of that discourse was that:

> All things would be restored even the sacrifice[.] that in the old laws a child would be destroyed even to sacrifice. That in the old laws a child would be destroyed for being undutiful to his parents, or calling them names—That the adulterer would have his life taken from the earth, and all the laws of Moses would be

Booksellers' Depot, 1854-86), 1:53-66.

restored as he had said they should be till iniquity was put away from the earth. And that there was not a government upon the earth this day where they could be carried out but among the Latter-Day Saints. Oh! Let us be faithful—let us remember that we are a peculiar people . . .

These are bold sentiments. The rest of the letter and later diary entries make it clear that the preaching Hannah heard that day did not set easily with her but caused her intense distress. She continued to her brother:

—Oh!—Brother, I shall never forget my feelings!!! It had an extraordinary effect upon me, for though I had known for a year that such a principle existed in the church, when I heard it read, and some things in it which I did *not* know, I confess to you I became sceptical and my heart questioned with tears of agony, "did *this* come from God?" I could not speak or shed a tear at first. I felt overpowered, *stunned* as it were!

Hannah's daughter Georgiana was engaged to missionary Claudius V. Spenser, son of conference president Daniel Spenser, and would marry him before leaving England later that year. Hannah, Georgiana, Claudius and D[aniel] Spenser left the meeting together in a cab:

Claudius seeing my state of mind got up as he sat opposite to me, and kissed me affectionately and asked me how I felt. That was sufficient. The flood gates of my heart were opened and I wept like a child. He soothed me, and but for the kiss and the kindness, God knows how long the evil one would have held my spirit in bondage. My eyes seemed to rain tears.

Getting out of the cab, Hannah walked up and down the square with Claudius's father, whom she asked "if he *knew* that the revelation was from God."

He, also, was very kind and said everything to comfort and console me, and build up my trembling faith 'till I became calmer—I then went to my lodging close by as I felt too unnerved to go to Mrs. Bray's with him where all our associates were. And there I wept unrestrainedly 'till the agony of my feelings subsided. And after awhile I was ready to go with them all in the evening. Were it not for the righteous men in this church who stand to me as God, I never could stand through these trials.

Hannah's letters and diary entries, profuse as they are, do not tell the whole story. According to the genealogical record, Claudius Spenser—Georgiana's fiance—had previously married. His first wife was Antonette Maria Spenser, to whom he was sealed in the Nauvoo temple. There is no death date for Antonette in the records, which do however note that she and Claudius had "no issue." Had she passed away during the exodus, at Winter Quarters, while crossing the plains, or in Utah before Claudius's mission to England?

If so, then who is the "she" mentioned later in Hannah's journal who welcomed the family to the Spenser home in Salt Lake City (Hannah does not specify which Spenser's home, although at least later it was Claudius's). Was "she" Mrs. Daniel Spenser, Claudius's mother, or Antonette Spenser, his living wife? And if the latter, did Claudius and his father withhold mention of this woman during Claudius' courtship of Georgiana? Surely Hannah and especially Thomas King—that proper, upper-class, non-Mormon Britisher—would not have knowingly countenanced his daughter's marriage to a married man. Yet by the time of the family's emigration it will be evident that Hannah King not only expected, but approved of, plural marriage (see the chapter on the plains crossing).

In Hannah's eyes, the kindness and piety of the Mormon elders enabled her to overcome her natural feelings against polygamy. Even if the doctrine applied to her daughter, she became able to accept it. People without Hannah's trust, and perhaps without her childhood attachment to a loving, sympathetic father, might have been slower to reconcile their feelings. Hannah concluded, "This will indeed prove a 'sieve', a 'mill', a tester to see who is pure and who is righteous, and who is *not* . . . "

Polygamy Here and There

As Brigham Young and other leaders became more open about polygamy, the doctrine became more entrenched by the decade. In a later speech Brigham Young said, "If any of you [priesthood leaders] deny the plurality of wives and continue to do so, I promise that you will be damned."[5] Young's first counselor, Heber C. Kimball, used a psychological tack to persuade members to compliance: "I have noticed that a man who has but one wife and is inclined to that doctrine, soon begins to wither and dry up, while a man who goes into plurality looks fresh, young, and sprightly." As tempted as one is to interpret Kimball's comments as humor, over time a new mentality developed that espoused "enlarged" ideas of masculinity, sexuality and virtue among those considered "the very elect." Yet the British-born sisters seem to have only half-embraced these ideas, for the majority remained monogamous even after emigrating to Utah.

Despite the emphasis in Utah on "the principle" as a prerequisite for heaven, polygamy in the mission fields was uncommon. Fanny Stenhouse said Apostle Orson Pratt took a plural wife in Liverpool "by special dispensation from Brigham Young." Her wording implies that such marriages were exceptional.

Yet if there was little marrying by married missionaries in Britain, there was plenty of courting. When Elder Milford Shipp fell ill, he was cared for by the Hilstead family, and when he returned to Utah at the end of his mission the Hilstead family accompanied him. Eighteen-year-old Mary Elizabeth Hilstead became Shipp's third wife. Virtue Leah Crompton Blackburn became the fifth and last wife of Elias Blackburn, bishop of Provo, when he returned from a Scottish mission and she simultaneously immigrated from Scotland. Virtue bore him nine children.

Ann Faulkner Taylor's husband John Possels Taylor married Ann's sister in 1860, three years after leaving England and soon after the family arrived in Utah. Although it is possible polygamy was not their intent until they arrived in Utah and a church leader suggested the idea to Taylor, they may very well have decided on polygamy while still in England.

That missionaries formed emotional, even romantic attach-

5. Richard S. Van Wagoner, *Mormon Polygamy: A History* (Salt Lake City: Signature Books, 1986), 155.

ments to women is not surprising. Many served long missions—three years was standard, four to five not uncommon—and these lengthy separations from their wives necessitated other social attachments, some of which were bound to be with women. However, the subject of extended sexual abstinence of healthy young husbands is not broached by the women in their histories. After all, they lived in an era whose very name came to mean prudishness about such topics.

As a contrary example, the case of Sarah Elizabeth Smyth Ross affirms that exclusiveness could be maintained between a missionary and his wife during long separations. Sarah married James Darling Ross in 1857. He served two missions while they still lived in England. They emigrated in 1860, and soon after arrival in Utah he was assigned yet a third mission which parted them for seven years. This separation must have affected Sarah and James, but it did not result in his taking plural wives. Why not? Was he kept from access to the temple for such—and so many—prolonged periods that the opportunity did not present itself? Did economic recuperation after each mission discourage taking on additional responsibilities? Did he and Sarah feel that adding polygamy to their already-considerable sacrifices for the gospel's sake would have been too much? Most likely it was a matter of personal preference. It shows that, while Mormon men were pressured to obey the principle of celestial marriage, they could decline without disaffiliation.

How did a missionary pick out a new wife? Most often it was done for him by happenstance. Only occasionally did a man go shopping like the American Priddy Meeks, who with his first wife determined he should marry in polygamy. She picked out "a handcart girl" because the girl had no family—as though, besides being a religious sacrament, plural marriage was a social duty, a charity. Priddy didn't marry his wife's choice but found another woman. Whether or not his wife approved his choice is unstated, but it is likely the new wife was an immigrant and in as much economic need as the handcart girl.[6]

6. Cecil B. Alter, ed., "Journal of Priddy Meeks," *Utah Historical*

There is no instance in the histories of an elder beguiling a young shopgirl into marriage through deception (unless we learn that Claudius Spenser hid the fact of a wife at home). Even Fanny Stenhouse did not accuse the missionaries of using seductive words and looks. These were Victorians, proper and reserved about romance. Understandings were made in seemly ways, the women party to the understandings. Stenhouse questioned men's motives and women's intelligence, and she came to see polygamy as infidelity, a product of superstition, but she did not impute Mormon polygamous men with outright lechery.

Conclusion

If critics needed fodder, Mormon prophets gave it through early dissemblance of the truth about plural marriage. From the 1830s to 1852 they denied both the doctrine and their practice of it, not only to the public but to members of the church seen as too weak for gospel "meat." Many new converts like Ellen Wilding Woolley may well have emigrated to Nauvoo and Utah ignorant of the matter.

But of the two out of our 100 British women's histories to mention this aspect of plural marriage, both hint that they knew about it before it was announced "to the world." Both also show the difficulty women initially had in accepting the revelation. In one case it was the writer herself who wept and argued before regaining her religious composure. Polygamy did not make the immediate sense to their minds that other Mormon teachings had. Yet both histories show these women were not deceived by Mormon elders and that any compulsion to accept the doctrine came from within their own hearts and minds, not from coercion by church minions.

After the official announcement and initial fallout, affairs in the mission returned more or less to normal. Polygamy was not openly practiced in Britain, nor were any more than an exceptional polygamous marriage performed. This is not to say, however, that there was no courting in Britain. For many elders the mission

Quarterly 10:145, cited by Kathryn Daynes in a presentation to the Sunstone Symposium, 8 Aug. 1991.

became something of a marketplace for wives. But it was in Zion that these romances would be consummated, not in England, Scotland, or Wales.

Chapter 7.

Emigration

When in 1838 Mormon missionaries arrived in England and began proselyting from rented meeting halls and borrowed street corners, "they addressed themselves to a mass that was already on the move."[1] This was how a *London Times* reporter of 1857 described a populace agitated by "acute economic difficulties" and "grave social discontent." The populace was on the move religiously, as evidenced by the continuing success of Lorenzo Dow's Primitive Methodism, and on the move literally: between 1800 and 1880 the equivalent of the entire population of Great Britain abandoned the mother country.[2]

Most of these emigrants went to the United States. Others settled in Canada (especially during the Civil War), Australia, and South Africa. Mormon elders followed them and obtained converts from all these places as well.

One out of every four immigrants to the United States in the 1800s was British. Only one out of every 150 of these was Mormon. When considering other immigrant populations, British Mormons were little more than a ten-minute cloudburst in a very wet sum-

---

1. *London Times*, 3 June 1857, cited by Philip A. M. Taylor, "Why Did British Mormons Emigrate?" *Utah Historical Quarterly* 22 (1954): 252.
2. Taylor, 250.

mer. Yet their impact on Utah would be significant, for in the mid-nineteenth century transplanted Britons comprised one quarter of the population of Utah territory.[3]

Historians have debated for a hundred years what motivated the Mormon migration from Britain and Europe. P. A. M. Taylor proposed five different theories but was not satisfied with any one of them. Instead of considering theories of why they emigrated, we will examine the phrases with which emigrants themselves described the adventure of migrating.

Emigration Prose

They "clamored to go."

By some accounts Mormon planners could not keep up with British Saints' keenness to leave. The histories evidence enthusiasm, even though some records are suspect as products of the Utah-centric tradition. But many statements that the woman "had a strong desire to go to Zion" are verified by either the facts of her emigration or the proximity of the historian to her life or both.

My own ancestress, Eliza Ann Clarke Worthington, was said to be "a very religious woman" for whom it was "her soul's desire to come to America and join the Saints." Ann Everington Roberts, mother of church historian B. H. Roberts, was described as "insatiable to go to America where her children would be numbered among the chosen people." This assessment of her drive is borne out by her actions. Unable to accumulate funds to take all her children, she found foster homes for the two older ones and left them in England while she emigrated with the two youngest.

"I want to get home."

Now and then a phrase encapsulates the experience of an entire group of women. Elizabeth Wilkins Steadman's letters to her mother contain such a saying. Her motives might have been to join her older brother who had homesteaded in Utah; to find a

3. I have used population figures from several sources, including Edward Anthony Wrigley, *The Population History of England, 1541-1871* (Cambridge, MA: Harvard University Press, 1981).

husband as she was well into spinsterhood; or because she had caught the emigration contagion (as Taylor calls it) since many of her friends and neighbors had gone to Zion. But during the journey, in a letter to her mother still living in the family house in England, she wrote, "I have no inclination to get married. I want to get home." Being a Mormon, she felt a greater pull from Utah than from her natural home.

"We obeyed the gospel and emigrated."

Emigration was a duty. Gathering to Zion was one of the commitments one assumed in becoming Mormon. One woman wrote, "I was the only one in my family to obey the gospel and gather to Zion."

From the first and second years of the church's founding it had been the intent to establish a gathering place: "The time has come when the voice of the Lord is unto you: Go ye out of Babylon; gather ye out from among the nations, from the four winds, from one end of heaven to the other . . . Let them . . . who are among the Gentiles flee unto Zion."[4] During the first decade the gathering was mostly from New England to Ohio and Missouri. But as soon as Nauvoo was established, English converts began to congregate in Illinois. The first group of forty-one Saints left Liverpool in 1840.[5] Each year a full-page announcement from the First Presidency appeared in the *Millennial Star* encouraging Saints to emigrate, calling for those skilled in needed trades and giving general and specific instruction for preparations for the journey by sea and land.

Sometimes the route to Zion was indirect. One woman who shared the desire to "obey the gospel" was Margaret Blythe, an attractive divorcee of British origin living in San Francisco. She married and then converted John Blythe, a storekeeper. After

4. Revelation dictated by Joseph Smith in November 1831 and later included in Section 133 of the Doctrine and Covenants.
5. Richard L. Jensen, "The British Gathering to Zion," in V. Ben Bloxham et al., eds., *Truth Will Prevail: The Rise of the Church of Jesus Christ of Latter-day Saints in the British Isles, 1837-1987* (Cambridge: Cambridge University Press, 1987), 167.

baptism John neglected to pay tithing in spite of Margaret's warning that he would lose everything if he did not. When fire broke out in the shop it destroyed nine-tenths of John's property. After that, says the history, he not only paid the Lord's tenth but sent $4,000 in gold to assist Brigham Young in defending Utah against Johnston's Army. Within another year he and Margaret had abandoned the store and moved to Utah. Blythe would not be caught disobeying again.

"She felt the spirit of gathering."

A synonym for willingness to emigrate was having the spirit of gathering. Margaret Griffith Morgan joined the Mormon church through her husband, who had seen a newspaper report on Joseph Smith, investigated, and been converted. "In time the spirit of gathering came upon them and they desired to cast their lot among the Latter-day Saints in Zion."

Caroline Lloyd Corbett was the solitary Mormon among her family, but after the deaths of two of her three children, when she sold everything to buy passage across the Atlantic, her mother, brothers, and sisters joined her. They all settled in Pennsylvania for several years, but "soon" she too "felt the spirit of gathering" and left for Utah with her remaining child.

One girl who had the spirit without using the litany was Harriet Tarry, again the only member of her family to be baptized (her mother wanted to join but dared not defy her husband). Harriet did factory work and tailoring until she pre-paid not only her ocean passage but her wagon passage across the plains. In Florence, Nebraska, she was told there were no more wagon spaces and that she would have to go by handcart. This was in 1860. Having probably heard of the difficulties of the 1856 Martin and Willie handcart companies, Harriet refused. Non-Mormon friends offered her a place in their household. Undaunted, she thanked them for their kindness but told them "she was going on to Zion." She hired on as a cook and laundress for a private freight company, earning food and a wagon to sleep in though not to ride in during the thousand miles to Salt Lake Valley.

They were seeking "the blessed place."

Taylor identified "millennial fever" as another motive. A few converts wrote about wanting to go to help establish the city of God, where a pure society would welcome the Savior and where the temporal government was theocratic. They wished to flee the troubles and calamities plaguing or about to fall on "Babylon." Elizabeth Lewis wrote home to her Welsh friends about the "peace, prosperity, and love" which reigned in Zion:

I have not seen a drunken person in this place or anyone quarrelling with another; I have only heard of someone threatening to take another to court, except that he was too ashamed to be the first one in the place to do that. I have yet to hear an oath or swearing on the street; not one murder or theft that I know of in the place, nor have I seen any immorality . . . I fear greatly that sickness, pestilence, poverty, and oppression are causing much suffering to my dear brothers and sisters in the gospel in Wales, which causes me to desire and to pray a great deal to be able to see them by the thousands in this blessed place.

"They decided to emigrate."

For every convert for whom emigration was a foregone decision, another made it a matter of deliberation. Thomas Bullock and his wife "decided to emigrate" after consideration, it necessitating his resignation from a secure position as an excise officer (Henrietta R. Bullock). Margaret Caldwell Bennett's husband travelled to America by way of Canada to look over the country before concluding to send for his family. When he was killed in an accident she "decided to come to Utah" herself. Converts such as these did not act primarily out of group enthusiasm but took their time and made careful preparation before acting.

"They grasped the opportunity."

One might expect economics to have been a partial motive for many families. In 1850 Sarah Hattersley Wells's husband was laid off when "conditions" in their manufacturing town became "bad." With twenty of his company's best men, Samuel was offered a chance to open a branch of the business in America. He and his wife "grasped" the opportunity. Yet their motives were not entirely financial, for before leaving they developed rather satisfactory economic prospects. Left by Samuel with only 30 cents, Sarah still had her craft as milliner and could have used her earnings plus the assistance of an aunt to establish herself in Britain. Instead she spent her aunt's gift on fabric to take to Utah. Samuel could have returned to Britain with his earnings, purchased property, and set up his family in their own home. But Sarah consented to Samuel's working abroad because this meant "the sooner realization of their dream of going to Zion."

John H. Barker, husband of Susan Barker, after becoming established as a jack-of-all-trades in Utah, wrote letters to his sister in England that could well have persuaded another laborer to emigrate. He described Utah as a place where no one was unemployed and even the poor were well off. In England he and Susan had been hired hands at a resort hotel, and very likely one of their hopes for emigrating was upward mobility.

But economics as a primary motive for emigration can be ruled out for many women. Elizabeth Archbold Anderson's husband was a mining engineer who earned a "rather large" income. When they emigrated in 1856, six weeks after their second daughter was born, he left a good job for a poorer one in the Pennsylvania mines. Had their motives been economic, the family would likely have stayed in England as did her brothers who joined the church but left when polygamy was preached.

Jean Rio Griffiths Baker had little financial incentive to leave Britain. Her husband, a civil engineer, had passed away, leaving her with at least two houses, and she had a successful dressmaking business which allowed her to put away savings. Another emigrant, sixteen-year-old Jessie Belle Stirling, took leave not only from her immediate family but from a wealthy aunt who offered her a comfortable living if she would remain in England. Jessie Belle chose to emigrate.

Logic rules out economics as a paramount motive for most women. The family of Elizabeth Wood Bennett, for instance, could have stayed in Capetown indefinitely, for she had a good position earning the family's rent and board as housekeeper for a wealthy man, and her husband earned a salary at brickmaking. Perhaps that is why they delayed emigration to America for ten years. On the other hand, emigration was expensive, and those who would benefit most from moving could not immediately afford it.

"Her family turned against her."

Leaving was easier for women whose ties to family and associates had broken. The break may have been a result of conversion, in which case the woman sought to evade harassment from former loved ones and neighbors. Ursula Chapelle's history explicitly states that she left to escape hostility. Her husband, son, and one daughter disowned both her and her second daughter Naomi upon their baptisms. A sea captain, her husband left on a voyage and never returned, presumably in deliberate abandonment. Finally, "Due to the anger of friends in Malmsbury, Wilshire, they went to London" from where they emigrated to the United States and Utah in 1862.

For years Margaret Davis was punished by her family. Baptized through her grandmother's influence, she was torn from the old woman by her mother at the docks of Liverpool. Later she ran away from home, living with relatives who pawned her off on a well-to-do uncle. The uncle, disliking the girl's religion and possibly her independence, put her in the servants' quarters. When the elders found her again, she was taken in by a local church family until persuaded to marry a Mormon widower, Frederick Thomas, with whom she emigrated (Margaret Rees Davis Thomas).

The most haunting account is that of Mary Nixon Bate Buckly, whose handwritten memoir tells of her three years between baptism and emigration. It is difficult to know how to interpret a tone which is at times hysterical and semi-literate as she describes threats of violence from her husband and others. But whether the psychological abuse was great or small, it prompted her departure. In this sample, notice how her indifference to punctuation gives her narrative an additional eerie quality:

> my Enimies was so powerfull against me it Secmed that it was almost Impossible for me to Endure it being my nearest and dearest Freinds that was Fighting against me, I preached Mormonism to my Husband feeling quite Sure that i could convince him of the truth but the more i tried to Show him the Beauty of

the gospel and the plan of salvation wich the lord had Instituted for the Redemtion of the Human family, the more he raged against it but the lord was very mercefull to me and gave me many Dreames and vissions to comfort me for i was cruely percecuted. My Husband became so cruel that nothing was to bad for him to Say or do it seemed to Fight against me he came Home one day told me in the presence of my children that i had Sent twelve of my Brothers as i called them to watch for him at night and Kill him, and he Said they had pelted him with Bricks and left him for dead, but they where mistaken and he had Settled two or three of them he told the children not to let there mother drag them into Hell where She was taking herself this was Heartrending to me to have my childrens minds prejudiced against me but it grew Harder all the time . . .

Mentally inserting punctuation, one is persuaded by her despair. "After three years of this cruel treatment from my friends my life being threatened continually," she was advised by her branch president to "take some money out of the bank and go to the valley," which she did with her six children, grudgingly followed by her husband.

"She was free to emigrate."

Janet Downing Hardie, who studied obstetrics under a pioneering Scottish physician and authorized using ether and chloroform long before it became universal practice, is said to have decided to come to Utah "after the death of her husband." Hannah Daniel Job and her husband determined to emigrate after his parents died, freeing him from the burden of working the family farm. From these stories it appears that for some women circumstances divested them of responsibilities and death could wean them from their homeland, making emigration a natural course.

Still other women had every reason to stay. Jean Rio Griffiths Baker had lost her husband but enjoyed many friends whom she "collected together" before her departure, "in all human probability never to see them again on earth. I am now . . . about to leave forever my native land, in order to gather with the Church of Christ in the valley of the Great Salt Lake in North America." The only suggestion of personal gain was written in her journal several

{ 140 }

days after sailing: "Little Josiah very weak. Oh how I pray that the sea may return his health."

"She wanted to join her family."

Occasionally women emigrated to reunite with relatives already in Zion. Emily Ann Parsons's family emigrated to Ogden in 1874 to join two brothers and a grandfather "who had come before." Frances Farr Miles was baptized in 1850 but followed her soldier-husband to the British colonies and nursed him and others through several battles before he died in 1863. She and her daughter then went to Utah to join three of her other children. Virtue Leah Crompton (Blackburn) came to Utah in 1862 to be with her five sisters. In England they had been obliged to leave home to find work when their father remarried, but in 1862 he decided to bring them to Utah (the record does not reveal whether he brought his second wife as well). Clara Alice Robinson had little choice but to emigrate at age one with her father, stepmother, and three half-siblings.

Some women married a missionary and emigrated upon his release, such as Ellen Birchall Barton in 1860. Sarah Elizabeth Smith Ross's lawyer-husband served two missions before the family left England. Still other women emigrated with husbands who were in charge of emigration companies. Janet Aicol Gibson's husband William served a nine-year mission during which he presided over several branches. Finally in 1851 he and his family came to Utah when he was placed over a company of poor Saints helped by the church to Zion. Fanny Stenhouse wrote bitterly of the inconveniences of emigrating in 1854 with a company of the poor when her husband was released as president of the Swiss Mission.

Most of these women were personally committed to their religion and were happy to emigrate, but in a few cases loyalty was limited to husband rather than to church. Isabella Lambert had emigrated with her parents in 1844 when she was eight, married James Winner who was killed in the Civil War, and later married Mr. Burgess, a carpenter, who "lost interest" in the Reorganized LDS church and wanted to move to Utah. She opposed him, but in 1874 they went to Utah anyway where she converted and was set apart by church leaders to study midwifery. Edinburgh native Ellen Brooke Ferguson came to Utah from Ohio as an experienced physician. While she visited in Scotland for her health, her husband had corresponded with Mormon leaders and determined to relocate to Utah upon her return. She came with him.

Eliza Chapman Gadd's is a poignant story. After twenty years of marriage, her husband was baptized with several of her older children. Not a member of the church herself, she came to Zion only because her husband wanted to come. She was to qualify for Mormon sainthood unwittingly as a member of the unfortunate Willie handcart company, which was caught in early snows. Death claimed her husband and one son plus a younger son just before rescue wagons reached them. "So through this great sorrow she didn't have the comfort of the gospel as others did who belonged to the Church and lost their loved ones along the way."

Preparations

In spite of enthusiasm for the Gathering, emigration took courage. Prospective emigrants knew from the letters of predecessors that very few families arrived in Utah fully intact. At least one member and often two, three, even four were lost. Consider the perils of a typical 1850 journey half-way around the world: on ship seasickness, smallpox, measles, bad water, bad food, shipwreck, storms, leaks, collisions (especially at port), theft, annoyance from crews, and occasionally hostile captains. At destination, theft again, cholera, and a host of illnesses and misadventures peculiar to a part of the world to which newcomers had not established immunity. Crossing the plains there were wagon accidents, bad water, theft and threats from natives, blisters, sunburn, sunstroke, mountain fever, stampedes, starvation, discomfort, and taxing labor. For women there were also childbirth and "female problems" with medical help often unavailable. For all, the journey meant culture shock, the loss of old associates and surroundings, and braving the unknown.

Once the decision was made to emigrate, families and individuals became like Priscilla Evans: "We were busy making preparations . . ." Because her husband was a missionary, his and Priscilla's fares were paid by the church so that they were able to depart immediately upon the close of his mission. For most members preparations continued for several seasons or even years. One fare—15 pounds—required a year's wages or roughly 50 pounds per family, an amount not easily come by.[6] This was quite an undertaking for people on subsistence incomes, and it took careful, persistent planning. Members went about it in several ways.

The usual option was to remain in one's present situation but intensify wage-earning efforts. Alice Maw Poulter's father and mother "worked and saved" in this manner until her mother became ill and died, after which her father worked alone until he had accumulated passage for himself and three children. Harriet Tarry Hirst worked in a factory by day and at tailoring by night and holiday to earn her passage. Mary Jane Ewer Palmer "worked and saved five years," each day giving her emigration money to her father who handed it over to the church emigration agent.

Another approach was to immediately relocate to Liverpool or another port city to work and await the opportunity to sail. Hannah and Thomas Job did this, moving to Carmarthen upon the death of his remaining parent. Sarah Jane Neat Ashley's family "had such a strong desire to come to America" that "the whole family left their old home and got other work to secure funds for passage." Elizabeth Tripp Gerrard moved to Liverpool where she benefited from the "love and esteem" of the branch. Elizabeth and Charles Wood emigrated to Capetown, South Africa, to find work so as to be able to save toward eventual emigration to Utah. Ellen Bridget Gallagher Cottam's husband relocated to Pennsylvania, sending his mine wages as support so that her midwife earnings could be used toward hers and the children's emigration expenses.

For about half of those who wished to, emigration would have been impossible without assistance. Recognition of their circumstances led to Brigham Young's creation of the Perpetual Emigration Fund (PEF) in 1850. Over the next twenty years 38,000 would be wholly or partly assisted through donations from a few wealthy Saints, tithing from branches, but mostly from contributions and repayments by saints reestablished in Utah. Historians Leonard Arrington and Davis Bitton note that out of 2,312 assisted by the PEF in 1853, 400 emigrated in the "poor companies" (and were

6. Taylor, 267.

wholly assisted by the fund), 1,000 travelled in church companies (and were partially assisted), and 955 came in "independent companies" (and paid their own expenses entirely).[7]

Mary Johnson Talton's family belonged to this "poor" class, even though her father was of respected heritage. Only through the combined assistance of the PEF and two individuals was the family enabled to emigrate. A relative, William Butler, contributed their sea passage, the fund helped them from New York City to Utah, and a prior emigrant to Ogden offset some expenses by hiring Mary's father to protect machinery being shipped from Europe.

The Ashworth family, through disposal of their property and help from the PEF, were able to travel as far as New Orleans, where they stayed and worked five years before being able to continue the journey. Mary Foster Windley's father had been a member "for some time," so the mission president decided to let the family come entirely on PEF funds. Two daughters came first, after marrying their sweethearts just released from missions. The rest of the family followed a year or so later.

Although the bulk of PEF funds came from repayments, a good share accumulated in the form of weekly or monthly deposits made by British Saints. These deposits were recorded in the contributor's name by a local emigration clerk, who then forwarded the money to the Liverpool emigration office.

A few British Saints were in a situation to help more than themselves. Jane and John Benbow, when they emigrated to Nauvoo in 1846, donated the profit from the sale of their large house and farm to pay the fares of associates in the local branch. Ann Jones Rosser, though she never emigrated herself, apparently made regular donations to the PEF. Caroline Rogers Taylor, after receiving an inheritance, emigrated her own family and funded passage for 124 others.

Though well-organized, the church emigration effort did not always go smoothly. Lizzie Weaver Brown's father had a great

7. Leonard J. Arrington and Davis Bitton, *The Mormon Experience* (New York: Alfred A. Knopf, 1979), 131.

disappointment when he and his family arrived in Liverpool prepared to sail. He had been told he could serve as ship's cook in exchange for passage only to learn that the post had gone to another man. "He was rather stunned, at first, to think that the man he had trusted had broken faith with him." But somehow he and his family were able to join a church company to New York where he worked as a stone mason for three and a half years to repay passage and save for the remaining journey.

Mary Nixon Bate and Caroline Lloyd Corbett were among a class of Saints who had sufficient means to emigrate at will. Elizabeth Clark Handley, her husband, and children were able to emigrate through the beneficence of her father who "paid transportation for his whole family" in 1853.

A few women emigrated through unorthodox methods. My ancestress, Eliza Worthington, got to Utah by marrying. Edward Horrocks, a widower, had been a missionary and branch president long enough to justify the PEF's paying much of his family's passage, and Eliza and her daughter Mary were included by virtue of the marriage "shortly before sailing." Jane Stephens and her husband were too poor, so they sent their two oldest children ahead first to establish themselves in Utah. These two then "helped the rest to come" in 1866. Rachel Powell Killian was supposed to join her husband in Philadelphia, but by this time the Civil War had begun and she was advised to take out just enough money to feed herself and children and return the rest to her husband so he could join them on the trail "without tarrying in Pennsylvania."

Emigrants had a pretty good idea of what to pack for the trip due to communiques from church headquarters, advice from experienced missionaries, and letters from friends and relatives already in Utah. Two letters from twenty-seven-year-old Elizabeth Wilkins (Steadman) to her mother back home are informative. From the ship she wrote, "I bought a mattress; they are very cheap . . . You will want some nails, hammer and some string . . ." From Florence, Nebraska, eight weeks later, she added,

> You had need to scratch your mark on all your tin. You need a shallow tin for your puddings. You need baking powder . . . and bring flour if you can and well soak the meat before you cook it.

... Don't carry any more in your hands from New York here than you can help, but bring a water bottle. If you bring a teapot, you can have tea in the cars ... If you have money, you can get bread, butter, treacle [cultured cream], eggs and meat on the way. A tin cannister or two would be handy. Soap and towel to wash with and a cloth in your basket . . . You need some shoes . . . to keep out the water. It is very wet on deck when it is washed . . .

Mormon ship companies were well-organized. Church agents chartered the ships, bought provisions, and appointed captains of hundreds, fifties, and tens. The provisions consisted of meat, crackers, and potatoes, a healthy enough diet but one which must have grown tedious, for Mary Jane Ewer after several weeks of this was given "a snack of real bread and ham" which she remembered as "the tastiest bit of food she had ever eaten." Elizabeth Wilkins, too, warned her mother, "Fancy being without bread for six weeks. The name of the biscuits made many of us feel sick . . ."

Parting with prized possessions must have been difficult for all voyagers, insurmountable for some. Mary Ann Chappel Warner's mother could not part with her prized feather beds, even when another ship rammed theirs in a fog and all excess baggage had to be dumped overboard. She obeyed, discarding all but one "which she said she would go down with."

If a family had the resources to lay aside cash or bring goods that were scarce in Utah, they were that much better off upon arrival. Sarah Hattersley Wells had the foresight, with the help of an aunt, Mrs. William Bland, to buy curtain and dress fabric which she used to make dresses and hats for her daughters in Salt Lake City. She arrived in Utah in 1854; less than two years later during a famine she traded her remaining stash of fabric for "bits of food and flour." After a year she had "disposed of everything but necessities," but her family had not gone hungry.

Mary Bate Buckley described a strange unfolding of aid and betrayal in her preparations to emigrate. Unwilling to endure her husband's threats any longer, she secretly took her four daughters and two sons to the home of a Sister Johnson in another part of London where her branch president had told her she would be safe. "I paid her well for all accommodations," Mary wrote, and after five weeks her family was escorted by the president and his wife to the train station, bound for Liverpool.

But "to our great surprise," at the Euston Square Station tavern they found Mr. Bate, who had been waiting all night, warned by Sister Johnson of the impending departure. "Sister Johnson had betrayed me tempted with five pounds," Mary wrote, although one wonders if the betrayal was also due to second thoughts about assisting an abandonment. For Richard was contrite. In company with Elder James Marsden (a conference leader who would be excommunicated by spring), Richard had spent five weeks scouring England from London to Liverpool to Birmingham looking for his family:

> when they got [to Birmingham] his money gave out so he had to send to London for more, while waiting there for the money to come he said he was in bed two days and could not offer himself any consolation for he said he felt he was like pharaoh when he was persuing the children of Isreal for he had brought it all on himself . . .

Mary's husband was so "subdued" that "we could Handle him," and she got him to promise "on oath" that if she would wait until the following spring to emigrate, he would not only sell the rest of their property and accompany the family but "go with us to the End of the world for he could not give us up . . . "

However, "like pharoah he hardened his Heart again," in Mary's eyes inventing all sorts of troubles and annoyances:

> For about three weeks he Mr Bate took me about to different places of amusement water Excursions and everything he could think of[,] thinking he could win me from the Saints but my Heart was with them and the work of God, his pleasures was nothing to me[,] it was a Sacrifice of time to me but i had to do many things not very agreable to my own feelings to keep him to his promise . . .

One begins to feel competing sympathy with Mary and commiseration with Richard, who was frantically trying to hold onto a wife and family slipping away from him.

Throughout the winter of 1856 the battle between Richard and Mary Bate waged. At one point Richard marched down to the church clerk and demanded the money his wife had paid into the emigration fund. When he could not get it, he merely glared at the clerk but returned home and threatened Mary: "he said he would have the money or my life before he Slept . . . " Mary calmed him by telling him the money had been sent on to Liverpool but that it could be recaptured within a few days. By that time his mood had passed.

The struggle had yet to reach its horrible culmination:

> On the first of January 1857 previous to our Starting in march another little son was born on the tenth he [Richard] came Home fo[u]nd I was all alone the nurse was gone home for a while and he comenced to threaten and act so bad i did not know but he would Kill me and the baby i was almost dead with fear and two weak to Stand or walk So i could not Help myself i put the baby to the Breast and that caused the death of it . . .

Mary, in other words, smothered her baby in panic while fending off her husband's assault. Apparently, Richard left the house in the midst of the confrontation, not realizing what had happened. When he returned and discovered it from the nurse, he went wild. "He was about to Run out of the House said he would go and Drown himself for he could not live." Mary and the nurse talked to him until he was calmer. Strangely, there seems to have been no investigation by local officials into the incident.

The energy gone out of his protests, Richard resisted feebly while Mary sold their remaining houses to a friend ("I sold them to her cheap"). He followed his family to America.

After considering and reconsidering this tragedy for four years, I still do not know what to think of it. There is not enough information to assign blame or even causes. Richard Bate's inconsistencies indicate possible abuse of alcohol, and Mary's abandonment may have been to escape him as much as to get to Zion. Yet he ended up emigrating with her. One wonders if his behavior was inspired solely by a desire "to quarrel with the Saints." If so, how odd that he should agree to live in Utah. I don't believe that anyone could read their story without being saddened and baffled by it.

Farewells

For some emigrants one of the hardest things about "gathering" was leaving family and friends. Jean Rio Griffiths Baker arrived in Liverpool from London on 6 January 1852 with an entourage so large it seems she could not be leaving many behind: it included her five unmarried sons and one daughter, her married son and his wife, the aunt and uncle of her late husband, and another family of six. She had made visits to all her associates in London before leaving. On 8 January, the day before sailing, she went into Cheshire to make one last visit to "an old friend . . . I have now, I suppose, seen the last of all my friends in this country."

Mariah Davies's husband wrote, "Now comes the sorrowful time for us to leave our friends and relations behind us in our native land." But Mariah, too, was fortunate in that her father and mother accompanied her. Imagine the feelings of Jane Graham Laidlaw's aunt and uncle who had raised her from childhood: at age twenty-six she had joined the Mormons, married a Mormon elder, and was taking her children not just to America but to Utah, never to see her step-parents again.

Sarah Hattersley Wells's family supported her emigration plans, yet it must have been with deep feeling that she gave away all her household items to her sister and said goodbye to her aunt. When Susan Dermott Baker saw her mother for the last time, it was to get her permission for marriage. Susan's fiance John walked eighteen miles to say goodbye to his sisters, yet "they would not let me see them."

For Hannah Daniels Job, the parting was so trying, and her fear for her ailing infant daughter so great, that she decided not to go. She returned to her parents' home, refusing to see Thomas or to allow him to speak to his two small daughters.

One family emigrating with the Barkers' company in 1862 met a great disappointment. The ship had already been towed out into the river when the anchor was lowered, and the family, who had taken ill, was sent back to shore by the ship's doctor.

For Mary Oakey the farewells proved too much. From the journal of James S. Brown we learn that Mary had already boarded ship when "a young man who resided at Nottingham, and who had been courting" her, arrived at the docks and begged to talk with her. "The young lady went out with him. The two were never seen again by us. We supposed they eloped."

An Overview of the Emigration

All of our histories, while wanting in detail about the women's younger years, retell the women's emigration experience. It is as if their lives prior to emigration were preparatory, only half-lives. Another reason for emigration detail is that many accounts were written for the Daughters of Utah Pioneers, membership in which requires a woman to prove that her ancestors came to Utah before the railroad was completed in 1869.

Most of our women (46 percent) emigrated in the 1850s. Almost that many (37 percent) came in the 1860s, only a few (9 percent and 8 percent) came in the 1840s and 1870s. The year most mentioned in our histories is 1856. While fifteen of our women emigrated that year, a smaller percentage of the total Mormon emigration did so. Perhaps participation in the 1856 handcart disaster, an episode which took on heroic meaning in Mormon consciousness, inspired more pioneers to write their life histories.

One would guess that, in spite of the success of other handcart ventures, the 1856 fiasco discouraged emigration from that time forward. The 1857 emigration was half that of 1856 and those of 1858-59 even smaller.[8] This was partly due to famine and war in Utah. But among our women the numbers rebounded in the 1860s until they exceeded those of the previous decade.

Boarding

Preparations completed, Elizabeth Wilkins Steadman gives us the best picture of dock life and embarkation.

> We had a pleasant ride down here [to Liverpool]. There are some sharpers here, no mistake. I have not lost anything, nor but one of the rest of us . . . I covered [my belongings and] with my bonnet and all on . . . laid my head on my bed. . . . don't forget [the

8. For discussion of sources for emigration number, see chap. 2, ns 2 and 3.

provisions you will need], and your eyes wide open. We shall be safer, I think, when we get farther from land.

Rachel Powell Killian stated that church agents had difficulty getting a ship for her unusually large 1860 company of 802. They approached the captain of a freighter who declined to take passengers because on his last voyage he had "broken some rules and some sailors had said they would sink him if they saw him again." But eventually he was persuaded. He camouflaged his ship by painting it a different color and plotted an irregular sailing route.

Margaret McNeil Ballard's mother was taken on board early to give birth to a son. Susan Dermott Barker's fiance left his mother's house, said goodbye to his father and brother at the railway station, arrived in Liverpool that day, took their luggage to the ship, and "got on board by night. All was in the greatest confusion and dark, a man fell overboard but was saved." Fanny Stenhouse notes that upon arriving in Liverpool "some of the brethren were appointed to see that the baggage was safely transferred from the railway to the ship." Early the next morning they boarded.

Hannah King was disappointed almost to tears at her family's "gloomy cabin." When she expressed this feeling to Elder Spenser, he only smiled—"as only an American elder can smile." She spent the next twenty-four hours wondering what that smile meant. Perhaps it was a fatherly chuckle over a pampered child about to learn the difference between her "beautiful, delicate bedroom" in Dernford Dale and "this awful hole." Her berth was actually better quarters than most of her peers enjoyed.

Fortunately, missionaries and church agents left records, and both old and recent studies of ship conditions and treatment of immigrants are available. Most Mormon companies were not large enough to charter a vessel exclusively, so passengers included other groups. In these cases the Saints "boarded off their section of the ship" and then divided it into separate quarters for families, single women, bachelors, and missionaries. Each family could then section off its area (using the hammer, nails, string, and sheets Elizabeth Wilkins urged her mother to bring) to create some measure of privacy. Wilbur S. Shepperson notes that the Mormon companies were typically well-organized and well-fitted for the journey compared to other emigrant groups, and that they sang psalms, knitted, and "kept happy and profitably employed at sea."[9] He derives this information partly from Charles Dickens who observed of one Mormon company: "They had not been a couple of hours on board when they established their own police, made their own regulations, and set their own watches at all the hatchways. Before nine o'clock the ship was as orderly and quiet as a man-of-war . . . there was no disorder, hurry, or difficulty."[10] That they were an inoffensive class of immigrants is affirmed by the somewhat snobbish Stenhouse:

> Imagine our disgust when we found that as there were not enough of the Saints to occupy the whole ship, the lower deck was filled with Irish immigrants of a very low order, and that their luggage and ours had been thrown together indiscriminately into the hold. Most of the Mormon emigrants recovered their property when they arrived at New York; but as for our own, personally, we never saw it again . . .

The orderliness of Mormon companies may well have been due to the watchfulness of church agents rather than innate gentility in their charges, for problems did arise between members. Elizabeth Wilkins would warn her mother at the end of the sea journey: "We have some good meetings here but they are not all saints amongst us." Jean Rio Baker described three sisters disfellowshipped "for levity of behavior with some of the officers of the ship, and continued disregard to counsel of the president." She also left a firm condemnation of an elder and a married woman of her company:

> The conduct of [Elder Booth and Sister Thom] has been most shameful ever since we came on board ship, and since they were placed under suspension it has been worse than it was before.

9. Wilbur S. Shepperson, "The Place of the Mormon in the Religious Emigration of Great Britain, 1840-60," *Utah Historical Quarterly* 20 (1951): 207.

10. Charles Dickens, in *The Uncommercial Traveler*, Vol. 6 of *The Works of Charles Dickens* (110 vols., New York, n.d.), 635-38.

Brother Thom is deeply grieved at the conduct of his wife. He is an excellent man and a pattern for every man in the Church. We all hope he will soon be able to forget her entirely. Such a woman deserves no place in the remembrance of a man of God.

After boarding, the emigrants quickly settled into a routine. Jean Rio Baker's diary reveals the itinerary of a shipside day. The bugle sounded at 6 a.m., "when all who think it proper arise." At 7:30 there was morning prayer, followed by breakfast and house-cleaning.

We employ ourselves during the day according to our inclinations. Sometimes a few musical ones get together and have a few tunes. Sometimes [a few] get together and gossip and so the day passes . . . We are most of us getting our sea legs . . . Sometimes a lurch will come of a sudden when we are at our meals, and capsize our teapot, and send us one over the other, but we are getting accustomed to it so we are on our guard.

She noted that each family had its own "department" in front of its berths where members could cook their food however they pleased. Her family, however, customarily took meals on deck. She had praise for President William Gibson, by whom "we are under no restraint whatever . . . I much regret that we cannot have his company to the Valley."

Living procedures varied according to company president, ship size, and ship's captain. On some voyages each family was served out weekly provisions which they cooked themselves. Jean Rio Baker's family "laughed heartily" when they were given their first week's allotment of seventy pounds of oatmeal. They turned sadder when they cooked their last piece of fresh meat three weeks into the eight-and-a-half-week voyage. During Stenhouse's 1854 voyage meal preparation was done in the galley by the ship's cooks, although sometimes the meal was not cooked well, and sometimes it was stolen as it left the galley. During the Isom family's 1860 voyage, with 1,000 passengers, cooking was done by the crew.

The King family aroused some ill feelings from other families by getting invited to use the captain's cabin, "which is the only decent place in the ship." They were told to enjoy the Poop Deck as they wished. "This has already created a jealous feeling but we cannot help that. We shall avail ourselves of the Captain's kindness and they must help themselves as they can," Hannah wrote.

As to the vessels themselves, one historian claims Mormon emigrants came on any ship they could get: packet ships, clippers, freighters. The only packet ship mentioned by type was the *Constitution*, which sailed in 1868 and was "a leaky packet ship," according to Margaret Wright Dunkley.

Sailing ships (presumably clippers) mentioned in the histories, with the year the women sailed, included: the *Harmony* ("a good strong sailing vessel"—1841), *Dan Curlin* (1856), *Golconda* (1852, 1853, 1854), *Horizon* (whose captain wrote, "I'll carry none but Mormons," according Wee Granny Murdoch's historian—1856), *William Tapscott* (which had "stinking water"—1860, 1861), and the *General McClelland* (1864).

Freighters included the *Kennebec* (1878) and an unnamed freight vessel whose captain painted it a different color to avoid retribution from another ship's crew whom he had displeased.

Vessels named but unclassified included: the *Yorkshire* (1843), *Artley* (1849), *Buena Vista* (1850), *George W. Bourne* (1851), *Georgia* (1853), *S.S. Germanicus* (1855), *Enoch Train* (1856), *George Washington* (1857, 1858), *Manchester* (1862), *Bridgewater* (1865), *John J. Boyd* (n.d. but probably 1867), *John Bright* ("an old ship, tossed like driftwood"—1868), *Nevada* (1878), and the *Saint Mark* (n.d.).

The Voyage

During this period an Atlantic voyage took from four to nine weeks, depending on the year of emigration (hence ship technology) but also on the season and route. (During the 1700s an Atlantic voyage had taken eight to fifteen weeks, the average being twelve.[11]) The Ashworth family, with a small Mormon company,

11. Based on information given by Edwin B. Bronner, *William Penn's Holy Experiment: The Founding of Pennsylvania, 1681-1701* (NY: Temple University Press, 1962). Also a Quaker immigrant diary by Gottlieb Mittelberger, *Journey to Pennsylvania*, ed. and trans. Oscar Handlin and John Clive (Cambridge, MA: Belknap Press, 1960), and Albert Cook Myers, *Quaker Arrivals at Philadelphia, 1682-1750* (Baltimore: Genealogical

made the voyage in 1849 "on a tiny ship" in nine weeks. Other histories show that this time was "streamlined" by the 1850s to six weeks and by the 1860s to four to five weeks. An 1879 voyage to New York took only eleven and one-half days, and an 1884 trip ten days.[12] Only twelve of our histories report the specific length of the voyage.[13]

A sea crossing in the mid-1800s could prove to be anything from a lark to tragedy. It was no longer the terrible experience described by Gottlieb Mittelberger, a Quaker emigrant of 1750: a horror of hunger, thirst, cold, damp, fear, lice, dysentery, boils, scurvy, mouth-rot, and more. Indeed, for the Mormon young it seems to have been mostly amusement. Elizabeth Wilkins was not sick a whole day during the entire voyage. Maria Ann Tuckfield, fifteen, struck an acquaintance with a young man who was so helpful to his ailing mother that Maria decided to marry him. Maria Davies and her fiance "enjoyed ourselves very well while traveling on the sea." John described in his journal being towed by steamer to open water where they immediately met a good breeze and "ploughed the Main very fast"; how the cold damp of Liverpool turned warm in a few days and they spent much of their time on deck, where it was "a sight to see the ships sailing on the sea." Their company had a brass band, choir, and string group which played for dances. "We had dancing on the sea," he wrote, and "Bachelors Hall made lots of fun for us on the sea." When the inevitable wedding took place, the bride was hoisted up the mast ("What a brave girl," said the captain) and the groom was carried about deck on a chair.

John Johnson Davies commented on the beauty of the voyage. Davies and Maria, with her parents, set sail 4 February 1854 in the

Publishing Co., 1957).

12. Sarah J. Neat Ashley emigrated with her family to New York in 1879 in eleven and one-half days; Martha Cummings came in 1884 in ten days.

13. Mary Nixon Bate Buckley may have remembered wrongly when she reported a twenty-four-day voyage from Liverpool to Boston, although given the right wind and no delays, a three-and-one-half-week voyage was possible in 1858.

ship *Colcondale* (probably *Golconda*) with 464 in their Welsh company. "There was one thing that gave us joy and satisfaction for we knew that God was with us to protect us on the sea, and we had a good Captain to guide the ship." Davies, as his company's ship sailed up between the Isle of Mann and the coast of Ireland, could see the Scottish hills on the right and quite plainly the Irish houses and farm roads on the left.

Frances Farr Mills had previously traveled with her husband, and it is quite likely that Margery Lisk Spence had joined Captain Spence on local voyages during his long career at sea. Jean Rio Baker, who had apparently sailed before, was in the minority of those whose stomachs withstood the rolling sea, but she compared "the very high wind" to a North Finland gale. She wrote about her clear view of the Irish coast, "mountainous like the Welsh coast," and the schools of porpoises which followed them once they reached warm waters. When "the brethren" hauled one aboard, skinned, and cut it and gave her a piece, she "did not much admire it—it was like very coarse beef and in color, very black."

Jean Baker's diary further tells of one of the exasperating aspects of sea travel in her day: poor winds. Her ship was towed into the river on 15 January. After more than a week a good wind had still not come up, and after two weeks she added, "The wind has not advanced us 20 miles for the past 6 days." Finally the next morning a breeze came up, but 4 and 5 February brought "almost dead calm." It was not until 9 February that they began to make good time—eight miles per hour.

Another inconvenience was the crew. Mary Ann Chapple Warner, when a sailor was seen wearing her father's clothing, helped persuade her father not to accost him over it for "sailors were considered a bad lot and were not past helping one to fall overboard."

Companies which took the southern route through the Bahamas to New Orleans suffered an additional nuisance. By mid-March half of Jean Baker's company was "affected with prickly heat." The captain had a large tub set out in which mothers could bathe their children and themselves every morning, and the men would "don a thin pair of drawers and pour water over each other."

For some women the trip brought more than inconvenience. Mary Jane Ewer was so seasick "she thought she would die." Newly-wed Priscilla Evans, too, was "sick all the way and had a miserable time." Jessie Belle Pack wrote that "Stinking water was the worst drawback." These problems, though not dangerous for most passengers, could bring on dehydration and worsen the condition of a passenger already in weak health.

There was also the possibility of accident and shipwreck. The *John Bright,* which Mary Ann Chapple said was old anyway hence "tossed like driftwood" on the waves, suffered a jagged hole cut in its side when another ship rammed it in the fog. The seventy-five Saints on board prayed and sang songs to bolster their courage while the leak was repaired, and the *Bright* drew into New York harbor only a few days late.

Storms were common, ravaging the spirits of almost everyone on board. The *George Washington,* with my ancestors aboard, was lost at sea for over a week during a stormy 1857 crossing. A storm might last an hour or rage for several days. During squalls the sails were taken in, and the ship would roll and pitch, the water three or four inches deep on deck. For Jean Rio "the sea has never had any terror for me at any time," but when the wind turned against them after having been idle for two weeks, her company spent a "dreadful night" wondering if the ship would overturn. In the midst of this, before dawn "one sister was delivered of a fine healthy boy." During such storms, leaks would develop in many ships, although they were quickly taken care of.

There is not one instance in our records of a major disaster. The real danger was disease, and on almost every voyage this culminated in the death of one or two passengers, usually the very old or very young. The intrepid Jean Rio Baker had hoped a voyage would help her little son, Josiah, who had been "very weak" before they sailed. But one evening before dinnertime, three weeks out to sea, "my little Josiah breathed his last. I did not think his death was so near, though when witnessing his sufferings, I prayed that the Lord would shorten them." Dan Jones's 1856 Welsh company lost five children to chicken pox.[14] Elizabeth Wilkins was happy enough with her voyage until two weeks out of New York harbor when her father passed away. Too stricken to write, she sent word of his death through an associate who was on his way to England. Later, from Omaha, she told her mother:

> I wish now I had sent you a few lines at New York. But I felt very unfit for writing, and I so do now.... He filled in with the dropsy very fast, which you need not be surprised for it was coming on before he left home. He had many nourishments. There was nice gruel made and arrowroot sage broth received. Porter gin and brandy taken round to those who needed it . . . I never saw a pleasanter corpse. I have not much reflection about him. I hope you will not grieve. I hope you will be blessed with health and strength. I would advise you to have a husband if you have the offer from a good man, for it is very awkward traveling without a man (Elizabeth Wilkins Steadman).[15]

Recognizing that the voyage would be harder for her mother than for herself, Elizabeth warned her to bring good shoes, for "it is very wet on deck . . . Sometimes when the ship rocks so you make a mess." Her father had lost his hat the first day at sea by not strapping the elastic band under his chin.

Diseases that pose little threat in our day were dangerous then. Isabella Wade was five when she contracted measles aboard ship. But six-year-old Sarah Isom was vaccinated by the ship's doctor when small-pox broke out among the huge passenger load. She and her family emigrated in 1860. The Civil War dictated a Williamsburg landing which, with the smallpox epidemic, greatly prolonged their journey.

Of thirty-two women whose histories describe the sea voyage, four lost a family member while at sea and another lost two of her

14. Bliss J. Brimley, *The Book of Thomas Job* (Pleasant Grove, UT, 1988). Jones attributed the tragedy partly to the fact that mothers, afraid for their safety, would not take their children on deck for fresh air, not knowing that the real danger lurked below in the crowded living quarters.

15. Note Elizabeth's slight defensiveness. She was no doubt sensitive to what her mother's neighbors would make of her care of her father and his fate under Mormonism.

three children. In at least two of these cases, the family member was already ill at the time of sailing. The other deaths may well have been a result of the voyage, but this is a surprisingly low incidence of death since the religious emigrations of one and two centuries earlier. Jean Rio Baker had not been unreasonable in hoping "to be able to take all my family safely through to the city atop the mountains." Yet the sea voyage proved to be the easier leg of the journey.

Chapter 8.

America and
the Great Plains

In America

For immigrants there were two main gateways to the United States: New Orleans and New York City. Mormon arrivals in the 1840s usually went through New Orleans.

This southern route was described in the delightful diaries of Mariah Davies's bridegroom and Jean Rio Baker. John Davies wrote:

> We had a great deal of amusement on the sea and when we got through the Gulf of Mexico, the Captain said: "Ship about." Then we traveled northwest until we got to that great river, Mississippi. Here a steamer came to meet us and towed us up that mighty river . . . When we came to Quarantine Station, we had to stop for the doctors to examine us. When the doctors came on board, we passed them two by two and they pronounced us all well. We started again and got to New Orleans on the 18th of March, 1854. We made the trip in six weeks from Liverpool to this place (Rachel Maria Davies).

According to Jean Baker, it was 170 miles from the Gulf of Mexico to New Orleans, a city which "No description I have read has ever done . . . justice." The city stretched five miles along one bank of the river, and vessels sat "4 to 5 deep the whole length and as close as they can be stowed." The levee was not level "like the Brunswick wharf" but sloped upward toward the warehouses and was crowded with cotton bales and cargo.

Jean was impressed by the planters' houses "built on the cottage style, with verandas on every side, surrounded with beautiful gardens." Even the "negro huts"—"from 30 to 50 on each plantation"—with their front verandas, white paint and large gardens she found "certainly far superior to the cottages inhabited by the poor in England." Remember that she wrote in 1852, eight years before the Civil War.

From ship Jean marvelled at the massive, human-planted orange groves and wild peach and plum trees as well as wildlife: storks, geese, fox, and raccoon. But she had criticisms as well: "The only thing which detracts from its beauty is the sight of hundreds of negros at work in the sun. Oh, slavery how I hate thee!" And she sardonically noted the Americans' fondness for titles, "Colonel[s], majors, captains, judges and squires being as plentiful as black-berries."

Jean had a letter of introduction from London to a friend's sister in New Orleans who "actually burst into tears at meeting with a country woman." Jean spent two days visiting with this British expatriate, who showed her a female slave market:

> It is a large hall well lighted, with seats all around on which were girls of every shade and color, from 10 to 30 years of age, and to my utter astonishment they were singing as merrily as larks. I expressed my surprise to . . . my companion. "Ah!" she said, "though I as an English-woman, detest the very idea of slavery, yet I do believe that many of the slaves here have ten times the comfort of the laborers in our own country with not half the work. I have been 13 years in this country and although I have never owned a slave, or ever intend to do so, still I do not look upon slavery with the horror that I once did."

Baker was unconvinced by this argument. "The system is a horrible one to English minds. Well might we say . . . 'Oh slavery, disguise thyself as thou wilt, thou are a bitter drought.'"

The Baker family's stay in New Orleans was only a few days while Mariah and John Davies remained two weeks. During this time their company made ready for the 1,250-mile riverboat trip to St. Louis. When finally a small steamboat pulled alongside their vessel and luggage and passengers were transferred, John and his young wife found themselves with more crowded accommodations than the Bakers had enjoyed. He complained for the first time since beginning the voyage, and unlike Jean Baker he and Mariah did not find the six-day trip up the Mississippi "delightful."

But if riverboat accommodations were unimpressive, the river itself was awesome. Jean described it as "about as wide as the Thames at Blackwall." Davies thought it "a wonderful stream" with the great forests of timber along its shores. By now many passengers were too ill to add their observations, but none called it "this foul stream" as did Charles Dickens during his 1842 tour of the eastern United States.[1]

A popular Mormon image of its pioneers is of genteel families on perilous ocean voyages via ships similar to those of the Pilgrims, culminating in Indian- and death-defying treks across the Great Plains. In fact, the most dangerous phase of emigration lay in the riverboat passage up the Mississippi and encampment on the Missouri River. The British had little resistance to cholera, nor did the colliers and factory hands from smoke-festering British cities have the conditioning or stamina to adapt immediately to America's interior.

Dickens noted in 1842 and John Davies in 1855 that the dirty water of the Mississippi River was the only available water to drink, and natives (said Dickens) considered it wholesome. Davies said, "We dip it up to settle it, but it doesn't get much better." Apparently there were no warnings to boil the water. People were told to avoid drinking it only "if they got sick."

Surprisingly, Jean Baker made mention of neither the water nor the sickness which rapidly fell upon the companies. But other travelers did. Sarah Jeremy and her family, steaming up the river in 1849, were among the sixty or more of their 249-member company to be stricken by cholera: "Men and women were lying on the deck, unable to help themselves and no one able to do anything for them. Their tongues and mouths were parched with thirst and

---

1. *American Notes* (Gloucester, MA: Peter Smith, 1968), 198.

they felt as if they were being consumed with fire." In one night three of the Jeremys' small daughters died, and their nine-year-old son would have followed but for his stealing sips of broth out of a kettle of boiling oatmeal. The steamboat stopped long enough for the dead to be buried in rough coffins among the timbers on the riverbank. By the time the Jeremys reached Council Bluffs on the Missouri River the parents themselves could barely stagger down the gangplank.

Leah Dunford lost a daughter on the steamboat journey. Only a few weeks old when the family arrived at New Orleans in 1853, the child died before they reached St. Louis. The boat pulled to shore and she was buried in an unmarked grave.

The Northern Route

During the 1840s and early 1850s only a few Mormon ships avoided the cholera-plagued tropic route. But beginning in 1856 this would change. Disturbed over heavy casualties from disease, wanting to take advantage of the Northeast's expanding railway network, and searching for a way to finance emigration for 20,000 poor British Saints who according to mission leaders "clamored" to come to Zion, Brigham Young and others conceived a new method for gathering in the Saints. In 1855 Young broached this idea to a son-in-law then in England:

> If we can have our emegration come to the eastern citys and the northan rout, it will be much relieve [to] our Brethrern from sickness and deth which I am very ancious to due. There is a raleway from new Yourk City to Iowa City and will cost onley about 8 dollars for the pasedge. Then take hancarts and there little luggedge with a fue good milk cowes and com on till they are met with teams from this place, with provisions &c-[2]

From that time on most Mormon ships docked in New York City, Boston or, during the Civil War, safe ports such as Williamsburg and Quebec.

2. Brigham Young to Edmund Ellsworth, 29 Sept. 1855, archives, Historical Department, Church of Jesus Christ of Latter-day Saints, Salt Lake City, Utah (hereafter LDS archives).

Those among the British Saints who were too poor to emigrate during the first two decades avoided some of the dangers faced by the earlier, more prosperous immigrants. Travel by the new route was not so much dangerous as uncomfortable.

Some routines were similar, such as being detained in the harbor for inspection. Felicia Astle's family was held on ship for several days while the entire body of passengers was vaccinated because illness had broken out while at sea. All ships were met by customs officials who arrived on barges from the Battery[3] along with doctors who might select a passenger here and there who would not be permitted to enter.

Yet New York was not New Orleans. Contrast Jean Rio Baker's pleasant stay in the southern city to Fanny Stenhouse's "miserable quarters" in Castle Garden: "Very cold, and dark, and dreary, were the first days which we spent in the New World." According to Fanny, her husband received charge of their entire company by default, through the "irresponsibility" of the company captain who, she said, disappeared to find former friends. (She did not consider that the official had been separated from friends and family for three years.) While her husband helped others find work and housing, Fanny and the children could only remain

> in that public place, sick and weary, and as destitute of bedding and covering as we had been on board ship. The weather was intensely cold, and, unaccustomed as we were to the severity of an American winter, we suffered not a little. How we lived through that journey I know not, but I am certain that, could I have foreseen what we should have to endure, I would never have left England, whatever my refusal might have cost me.

Fanny's complaints were partly justified. Until 1891 U.S. immigration was directed by the individual states. With the Gold

3. New York City's twenty-two-acre Battery at the southern tip of Manhattan Island was initially a fort. It was then used as an amusement center and later as the immigrant station to which Fanny Stenhouse referred as Castle Garden. It is now called Battery Park, home of Castle Clinton National Monument, a harbor promenade, and the Liberty Island ferry.

Rush and the Irish famine, nearly three million immigrants would pass through New York Harbor in the 1850s.[4] To process these large numbers, the state turned Castle Garden, formerly a concert and amusement hall, into immigration headquarters. While picturesque, the hall was damp and drafty, a good incentive to immigrants to find other quarters fast.

Still, compared to misery by Southern fever, immigrants who took the Northern route were fortunate. "The worst part," wrote Jessie Pack, who was sixteen when she made the inland journey in 1861, were the days and nights en route to St. Joseph in what she called a "cattle car." When the Perpetual Emigration Fund financed a railroad fare, it did not buy first class. Church companies literally rented boxcars which were closed and locked. At night it was necessary to lie down "feet to feet, head to head," in order for all to have room to sleep.

Members of independent companies fared a little better, as suggested by the indomitable Elizabeth Wilkins (Steadman) in her advice to her mother:

> If you bring a teapot, you can have tea in the cars. There are stoves and water closets in them. . . . It is very dusty, and get something to kill or keep the vermin from you. We had them on our heads and bodies too. Their bites are dreadful. They are in the seats. I think some breed them in their flannels by wearing them too long close to their skin.

Elizabeth must have been a self-paying passenger if she rode in a coach with seats, even flea-bitten ones.

The ride by rail to the Missouri River took from six days to three weeks. St. Louis was the destination of most immigrants, although sometimes they went on to St. Joseph and later many went by rail all the way to Council Bluffs, Iowa. Only half (54 percent) went on to Great Salt Lake City the same year they arrived in the states. The other 46 percent settled for a period in Pittsburgh (especially the Welsh, who readily found jobs in the Pennsylvania coal mines), New York City (where some worked as domestics and

---

4. "The History of American Immigration," *New York Times*, 31 Jan. 1897.

others as stone masons or at other skilled jobs in New York state), St. Louis, and the Mormon Missouri River settlements in Iowa and Nebraska.

Before that 1846 immigrants had travelled directly to Nauvoo. One of these, Jane Benbow, arrived just in time to be driven out of Illinois with the rest of the Saints and die from exposure in Winter Quarters, Nebraska.

Immigrants after 1847 who did continue directly to the Great Basin seemed to do so for one of three reasons. They possessed sufficient resources to immediately obtain an "outfit" (wagon, oxen and supplies). They had compelling ties to someone in Utah, relatives already settled in the territory or business associates. Or the husband was assigned by the church to lead a company from Liverpool through to Salt Lake City.

Other families were obliged to settle in the East for one to ten years while they obtained jobs and began the process of financing the rest of the journey. Some delayed the trek west because of poor health or to await the arrival of remaining family members from Britain. Isabella Wade's father initially turned down a job offered by Jim Boyd, "a big railroad man," and went ahead and bought an outfit. But at Grand Island, Nebraska, a few weeks into the trek, he changed his mind and agreed to work as foreman on the Plum Creek section of the railroad. For two years (1866-68) his family lived at the water and feed station, occasionally encountering trouble with Sioux and Pawnee Indians, before they had saved $3,000 to purchase a more comfortable outfit and continue the journey west.

Eliza Ashworth, husband, and family remained in St. Louis long enough for two more children to be born. After four years they still had not been able to go west, largely because of the expense of burying the two infants and a boy hunchbacked in an accident. When in 1854 they finally accumulated the needed equipment Eliza was seven months pregnant again and, in her husband's opinion, in no condition to travel. She insisted, "No I will be all right. Maybe if we wait we will be unable to make the trip for many years. I don't want to wait." At Indian Hollow their wagon company stayed over a day while she gave birth to Benjamin Erastus.

Felicia Astle and her husband were "counselled" to find factory work in Philadelphia. Two years later they went west in the Joseph Horne wagon company. Margaret Ballard's father was advised by retiring British Mission president Franklin D. Richards not to go in the Martin handcart company, "for which we were afterwards very thankful because of the great suffering and privations and the cold weather which these people were subjected to. There were many of the company who froze that year on their journey." Instead, the Ballards stayed at a place called Geneva, "150 miles away from civilization," continuing their journey to Utah three years later.

Another family considered the handcart method of travel and decided against it. Margaret Powell Evans, grandmother of future LDS church president David O. McKay, left England with her husband and several children in 1856, arriving in Iowa City in early July. They helped build handcarts until 28 July, when the last companies moved out and recamped a mile away in Florence to make final preparations. According to her descendants,

> Owing to the lateness of the season, the important question was debated whether the emigrants should attempt to cross the plains that season. Thomas Evans decided he would not take the chance of subjecting his wife and family to undue hardships by attempting the trip by handcart, but would remain in Iowa until he could outfit them so that they could travel with greater comfort.

Accordingly, the family lived and worked in Iowa three years until they had secured a wagon, ox team, and a milk cow.

Lizzie Brown's father, the one disappointed at losing the job as ship's cook, worked in New York City three and one-half years as a stone mason to pay his family's fare. He must have reconsidered his misfortune, for by the time they went west in 1869 the transcontinental railroad had been completed and his family made the trip in relative ease. Said his daughter, "We got here after the worst hardships were over" (Lizzie Brown Weaver).

Poor Mary Nixon Bate's troubles did not abate. Once in America conflict with her husband resumed. Their journey was a circuitous one from Boston by rail to Iowa City where they stayed in a boarding house, then back to St. Louis where they acquired an apartment, stove, and furniture. There a son was born. "It was very expensive eight of us stopping," Mary wrote, even though Mr. Bate had obtained employment. Then disaster struck with his death in 1859: "He died Friday night. Saturday morning I sat down to nurse my baby and the other six all stood around me[.] I looked at them and felt my burden was heavier than I was able to bear. No friends, relations, alone with 7 children, we did not know anything about making a living" (Mary N. B. Buckley).

In the histories one hears occasionally of ministering angels—anonymous earthly benefactors who went about looking for kindnesses that needed doing. An older gentleman of Nauvoo (possibly an Englishman), during the first years of settlement when cholera plagued the young city, went from house to house giving money to those in desperate straits. One of these angels—a stranger although probably a member of the St. Louis branch who heard of her plight—"came in" and gave Mary Bate $20 for her husband's funeral.

There was another sort of angel, too. At Mr. Bate's death Mary had $500 remaining of their life's savings. Wanting to use it wisely, she loaned it out at interest, most likely to a Mormon associate. When the loan came due, she only got $170 back, plus a total of $50 in small payments over the succeeding days and weeks, never seeing the remainder. She now had only $220, so she "went to work at anything I could." For two years Mary and her children worked in St. Louis. It was still her dream to take her family to Utah even though they "couldn't see what I was exposing them to so much trouble for. The prejudices their father had placed were still with them." By 1861 she had acquired a half-sized wagon and a team of full-sized oxen. As the wagon company collected, its captain asked who would be driving her team. Herself, she answered. She couldn't afford a teamster. "What do you Londoners know of driving a team?" he taunted. She said, "My faith is that I can do it" (Mary N. B. Buckley). And she did, by pluck as much as by faith, leading her animals by the reins all the way to the valley.

Mattie Hughes Cannon, who would grow up to be a physician and the first female legislator in the United States, was four when her parents emigrated in 1858. They spent two years in New York "because of her father's poor health." A third child was born there. Caroline Corbett spent several years in Pittsburgh before she acquired five wagons with which to make the trek west in 1862. It was she whose mother threatened to disown her but instead sewed twenty pieces of gold in a skirt she had made for her.

Leah Dunford spent ten years in St. Louis. Her husband worked in a men's clothing store and also served as president of the St. Louis Conference. Her boys, including two future dentists, attended St. Louis schools. The city was "a dirty looking place," according to John Davies, but Dickens gave a more complete picture of St. Louis during this period. The French portion, he wrote in *American Notes*, had narrow, crooked streets and quaint, sometimes lopsided shops and houses. The new parts of town, called the American Improvements, contained sturdy "wharfs, warehouses, and new buildings in all directions" with marble-fronted shops along broad streets. In 1842 four free schools were operating, this number no doubt having increased by the time the Dunfords arrived in 1854.

Rachel Price's was another family which "stopped in St. Louis to obtain work and buy supplies." Perhaps an additional reason for their two-year layover was Rachel's frail condition. Her husband John and the oldest of their five children easily obtained jobs in road construction, but John was used to working underground in Wales. Now he was in the hot Missouri sun day after day. He resisted quitting, but when sunstroke finally overcame him it was so severe that he was unconscious several days and bedridden a year.

The family was then "in dire circumstances." Every child old enough found a job—even eight-year-old Anne. At first she worked as a maid in a boarding house, until a man named Dutch Henry who lodged there saw that "she was working too hard for her age." He took Anne into his home two miles away where each week she was paid a small wage. On Sundays she visited her parents, carrying her wages to help out the family and a small basket of food.

After a year her father recovered enough to think about working again. A friend who was going west offered to get him a job in a coal mine near St. Louis. John was not yet strong enough for heavy labor, but his son Richard accompanied him each day and did the work for him. While Richard was under age, it was common practice in the 1800s for a boy to help his father in the mines.

The King family intended a stopover in St. Louis to give Hannah a rest. She had gone from 168 to 127 pounds during the sea voyage. Accordingly, Thomas leased a house for two months, but within a week they were "ordered to pick up and go off to Keokuk. Accordingly, we set to." Hannah felt loathe to move so soon but, she wrote resignedly, "orders, are peremptory in this church, and there is no dwelling." She took along a bottle of champagne to assuage her reluctance.

One benefit of long stopovers was that eastern branches, many broken up at the 1846 exodus to the Great Basin, were reestablished. Another benefit was unofficial proselyting by Mormon families scattered in towns and cities across the country.

The Collection

In the end all roads led to the Missouri River and, beyond that, the American prairie. In 1841 Mary Ann Weston, the childless young widow, left Herefordshire. She reached the Missouri in a roundabout way, first to Kirtland, Ohio, then to Nauvoo, Illinois, where she met and married Peter Maughan and his five small children and where most of her "fine English china" was broken, and finally to Winter Quarters (near present Omaha, Nebraska) with the body of the Saints in 1846. Henrietta Bullock, too, emigrated in the early 1840s, but late enough to go directly to Nauvoo with her young family. Willard Richards Bullock was born there on 11 February and died of exposure during the exodus.

In the 1850s and 1860s immigrants collected at Iowa City, St. Joseph, Nebraska City, Alexandria, Westport, or Florence (which Fanny Stenhouse called "the starting point of the Frontiers")—all jumping-off places for the Great Plains. Many of them had seen a good deal of America's heartland beforehand, some travelling by way of Canada or the northern canals across the Great Lakes by team to river cities, then by steamboat down the Ohio or Mississippi.

Apparently, cholera had already done its sifting by then, for there are fewer reports of deaths during this leg of the journey. Missouri River trips may not have been as ruthless, but they presented their own difficulties. During this leg of the journey Jean Rio Baker's company lost a fellow passenger who fell overboard and drowned in the eddies and tangles. Two of her newly-purchased oxen were injured through the brutality of boatmen. Yet she was too absorbed with her anticipation and anxieties about the long trek across the prairie to dwell on these misfortunes.

In the 1860s immigrants were able to take the rails not just to Iowa City but all the way to Florence on the Missouri. This mode offered its own unique adventures. Sarah Isom, seven years old at the time, said their mile-long train was driven at "surprising" speed by an evil-tongued engineer who swore he would "drive the Mormons to Hell." He opened the throttle so wide, she remembered, that somehow a baggage car caught on fire and he had to back the train seven miles to a water station. There her parents discovered that nearly all their belongings lay in a "charred mass of wreckage," including their seven-year supply of clothing. When the railroad company reimbursed them, it was in "greenbacks that had depreciated to 50 cents on the dollar."

By the 1870s the collecting was done almost totally by rail, the steamboat journey avoided altogether. As early as 1868 Mary Ann Chapple Warner and her family took a freight car—"crowded to overflowing"—clear to Laramie, covering six weeks of wagon trail (or three-fifths of the plains journey) in a few days. When Martha Cumming Clark travelled to Utah in 1890, her emigration took only two weeks: ten days on the ocean and four days by train to Franklin, Idaho.

But in the early years, the Missouri River was the jumping-off spot even by rail. Here immigrants must have faced the prospective journey with some excitement. Dickens had heard so much about the "paroarer" (as he frequently heard it pronounced) that he had developed "a great desire to see a Prairie" before turning east on his 1842 visit to America. He arose at 4:00 one morning for that purpose, leaving his wife behind as he expected the jaunt to be fatiguing. Jean Rio Baker wrote, "We expect a life of toil fatigue, and many privations on this overland journey to which we are unaccustomed. Still . . . I doubt not . . . I shall enjoy the same protection upon the land that I have had upon the water."

The majority of those who made it this far probably continued. P. A. M. Taylor found little evidence of desertion, though Mormon sources could be "reticent on such a subject." He notes an 1853 *Millennial Star* report of 100 Saints "who stayed in the eastern United States, some to apostatize and some to go on another summer," and an 1856 *Star* estimate that from five to fifty in a company of 500 typically deserted at the prospect of the journey across the plains.[5]

Fanny Stenhouse claimed she would have liked to desert, but, as always at this stage of life, she followed a little behind her husband: "Had I been permitted to choose, I would have preferred to die rather than journey to Zion. . . . ever since my husband had been engaged with the secular papers, we had been getting along very comfortably, pleasant home, many comforts, and little luxuries."

But George Q. Cannon had arrived in New York City to take Thomas Stenhouse's place as Eastern States mission president, and so the Stenhouses were "expected to leave New York within two weeks with the emigrants who were then *en route* from England." Fanny—not her husband—protested that she had a few-days-old baby besides five other children and was in too-delicate health to handle all the preparations herself (her husband being preoccupied with helping the company he would head). She was told to "arise and begin preparations." So she did, though not without resentment: "In the Mormon Church the feelings or sufferings of women are seldom considered. If an order is given to any man to

5. Philip A. M. Taylor, "Why Did British Mormons Emigrate?" *Utah Historical Quarterly* 22 (1954): 268. Taylor cites the *Millennial Star* 15:586 and 18:637. He alludes to an 1844 report of thirty desertions in St. Louis but states there is "poor evidence" for this (268).

take a journey . . . his wife or wives are not to be thought of." She sacrificed their new furniture and belongings "in a reckless manner" and trudged grudgingly after her husband. Fanny was just not cut out to be a Mormon wife.

Priscilla Merriman Evans, on the other hand, was eminently fit for the job. At Iowa City her husband was offered "Ten Dollars a day to work at his trade of iron roller, but money was no inducement to us . . . " By way of justifying this decision, she noted that "Many who stayed apostatized or died of cholera."

At Florence, or whatever gathering place an immigrant was assigned, companies fell in behind their captains. A Mormon wagon train consisted of 60 to 100 wagons peopled by 300 to 500 Saints. There were often several weeks of delays before starting out. Last-minute payments had to be made. Susan Barker's husband wrote on June 28, 1862: "All the money was collected from those going by Church trains." Mary Jane Ewer apparently decided to supplement her share of expenses by doing housework "at Bishop Musser's in exchange for the trip to Salt Lake City." Elizabeth Wilkins Steadman wished she had done so, as she wrote to her mother in England: "I regret that I had not asked if I could [have them] send the money back that I had left when at Florence and come with some independents, and worked my way here. But I had not much spirit for anything." She urged her mother to "come next season": "There was several in the ship I came in that had no money to take them to Florence. There was a gathering for them, and they got here. They were allowed just as much victuals when they got there as the rest, plenty too for a moderate person."

Having paid their share of traveling expenses, some immigrants had to wait while church agents put together an outfit. Several survivors of the Martin and Willie handcart companies wrote that handcarts were still being assembled in late June. Elizabeth Horrocks Jackson, traveling with her husband Aaron, three children, and single sister Mary Horrocks, later recalled:

> The machanics were very busy building handcarts on which to haul our provisions, small children, etc. The Handcarts, or many of them, were built on wooden axles, instead of iron axles, with leather boxes. We had expected to find these vehicles already

prepared for us upon our arrival, here at Iowa City. Thus this work consummed between two and three weeks of the time of which we had planned on being on the road, to Utah.

Elizabeth Jackson's father and stepmother, crossing in 1857, had paid for an ox and two "waggons" to be waiting for them on the Missouri for their family of nine, but "our outfit was not ready as promised" (Elizabeth H. J. Kingsford). Jessie Pack, assigned to an 1861 poor company, spent three weeks with her group in St. Joseph "waiting for ox teams to come from Utah" (Jessie B. S. Pack). Fanny Stenhouse wrote about inconveniences to her family due to "mismanagement on the part of Church Agents."

Jean Rio Baker's company was delayed a week so that their animals could recuperate. "They are in far worse condition than when we left St. Louis thanks to the steamboat men." One of her oxen died, forcing her to spend $36 for a replacement. Yet she did not mind being detained. She found her surroundings four miles outside of Alexandria, Missouri, reminiscent "of days we used to spend in Epping."

Starting Out

Finally a company would pull out. In every decade the first phase of travel, whether across Iowa or from the Missouri overland to the Elkhorn and Loup Rivers, was a training and hardening period. John Davies, whose wife Maria was now nine months pregnant, gives a vivid picture of this scene:

> Now I will tell you about the circus that we had the first few days on the Plains. Our Captain told us to get up early in the morning to get ready to start in good time. After breakfast was over, we got the cattle together and tried to yoke them up. I can assure you that this was quite a task for us and after we got them hitched to the wagon, we started out. Now comes the circus, and it was a good one! The Captain was watching us and telling us what to do. He told us to take the whip and use it, and say whoa Duke, gee Brandy and so on! Now the fun commenced. Then we went after them pretty lively. When the cattle went gee too much we would run to the off side, yelling at them whoa! and bunting them with the stock of the whip. Then they would go haw too much and we were puffing and sweating . . . This was a great

experience and a tough one, but by the time we got half way across the Plains, we could drive an ox team as well as you can any day.

But then John got extra practice, for of the six men assigned to his wagon, "three of them left me at Ft. Kearney, two were sick, and one died on the road." Since his wife had a baby the second night out, that left only John to drive the team.

Bathsheba Smith described the Welsh teamsters:

They did not know anything about driving oxen. It was very amusing to see them yoke their cattle; two would have an animal by the horns, one by the tail, one or two others would do their best to put on the yoke whilst the apparently astonished ox, not at all enlightened by the gutteral sound of the Welch tong seemed perfectly at a loss . . . to know what was wanted of him.[6]

Jean Baker's company started out by traveling fewer than five miles a day, probably not only to give the cattle time to adjust but the people as well. She mentioned their initial clumsiness in the ways of the wild west: "I can just fancy how you would laugh could you see us taking our first lessons in ox driving and our cattle taking every direction except a straight forward one." Yet Jean's family probably learned more readily than most, her children having been trained in horsemanship.

Hannah King, traveling in a new carriage while her son drove one wagon and her husband another, quickly found she liked "this gypsy life." While the pace was slow, she spent her time sewing, writing, and reading Byron and "Woodworth." "I rejoice amid all my trials, and . . . that I am with these people. There is much in them that I like, and the principles I glory in!"

The Trek West

The roughly 200 miles from the Missouri along the north bank of the Platte River to new Fort Kearny did not offer the level ride of a modern freeway. Jean Baker wrote: "Do not expect me to

6. Autobiography of Bathsheba W. Smith, 15, archives, Historical Department, Church of Jesus Christ of Latter-day Saints, Salt Lake City, Utah. Smith is not one of our British women.

describe our road. It is a perfect succession of hills, valleys, bogs, mudholes, log bridges, quagmires, stumps of trees a foot above the surface of the mud . . . Oh, for the good roads of old England. I each day hope we shall have better traveling on the next but as yet it has only been from bad to worse." Since on a good day the wagons could travel twenty miles or more, it took two weeks to reach the fort.

None of our women and few Mormon diarists recorded their observations of Fort Kearny, probably because few if any of them waded the Platte and the three to four marshy miles between the river and the outpost. The Mormon Trail deliberately followed the north bank of the river, avoiding the more crowded Oregon Trail which ran roughly along the south bank and directly to the fort. One or two representatives of a company were sufficient to post east- and west-bound mail and buy last-chance provisions at the shantytown several miles west of the post.

What Mormon immigrants did share with those heading for Oregon and the California gold mines was the Platte itself. They, like the gentiles, considered it "a humbug of a river" with its wide, sandy, shallow bed; its few scraggly cottonwoods that hugged the banks in places; and its many feeder streams whose furrows cut deeper into the Nebraska soil than the main river channel. The water was so silted that grit would settle an inch deep in the bottom of a drinking cup. When the wind blew, the river changed its course like the parting of the Red Sea.[7]

As to the prairie, the histories are likewise restrained. Rachel Maria Davies's husband saw "buffalo by the tens of thousands." Only a handful of visual details was offered by our diarists. Perhaps the landscape quickly became commonplace to people walking every goldurned mile of it.

Beyond Fort Kearny the landscape flattened and the trees became scarcer. Sometimes wood was unavailable, so "as evening drew near and the wagons were drawn into a circle" women and

---

7. For pioneer descriptions of the Platte River, Fort Kearny, and other landmarks along the Oregon and Mormon Trails, see Merrill J. Mattes, *The Great Platte River Road: The Covered Wagon Mainline Via Fort Kearny to Fort Laramie* (Lincoln: Nebraska State Historical Society, 1969).

children would fill their aprons with buffalo chips. Such a fire was smokey but hot.[8]

The most frequent comment about the journey was its tedium. It would become a grand adventure in retrospect, but the actual doing of it was dreary and monotonous. Margaret McNeil Ballard "walked every bit of the way to Salt Lake City barefoot, sometimes carrying my little brother on my back." Fanny Stenhouse admitted that "the incidents which befell" her company were few, but that "every one of us felt weary and worn out." Mary Williams Rees's husband, when she spied a piece of iron on the roadside and stashed it in her apron, asked her why she was weighting herself down with trash. Months later, in their new settlement in Utah, she would carry the metal to a blacksmith who made its nose into a small plow—the first one in Ephraim.

Although Mary Ann Warner and her brothers and sisters "started out with light hearts, our enthusiasm wilted considerable before we arrived at our destination." Sarah Hattersley Wells's family had to share their wagon with her husband's aunt and uncle, hence Sarah, age thirty-one, also walked all the way to Utah. Margaret Griffiths Morgan, blind since the birth of her fifth child, walked many of the miles with her son Owen assigned to attend her. Elizabeth Horrocks Jackson Kingsford said it was monotonous trying to pull handcarts through deep sands and over rocky roads, although tedium was the least of her family's problems.

The young and those well enough equipped to ride much of the way had a happier perspective. Sarah Isom, who made the journey in childhood, found it "perpetual enjoyment" all the way. She gathered rocks and wildflowers, waded in shallow streams, gathered buffalo chips—and rode in a wagon hours each day. Jean Baker's family had extra wagons as well and hauled her piano across the plains. Caroline Corbett came in 1862 with her husband and children in five wagons, an elaborate outfit. And Margaret Powell Evans, whose husband Thomas had

8. Mary Ann Chapple Warner and Sarah Elizabeth Isom Wilson, emigrating in 1868 and 1861, respectively.

elected to hold over in Iowa for three years rather than take his family to the valley by handcart, made the journey "in greater comfort" in 1859.

For any family, traveling and living in close quarters told on the nerves. Hannah King's pleasant relationship with son-in-law Claudius began to wear. She resented an agreement made by Mr. King that at the end of the journey one wagon and team were to go to Claudius—"I don't understand this logic!" She began to feel that the younger man disapproved of her: "Claudius is so very odd and unkind to me." Another annoyance was daughter Bertha who "took poorly" to hardship and who, Hannah concluded, was being punished by the Lord "for a complaining, disobedient spirit to which she has forever given way . . . every step of our voyage and journey."

The manner in which Mormons traveled was unique on the Great Platte River Road. When Joseph Smith led the "Camp of Israel" (a company of 100-plus armed men) from Ohio to Missouri in 1838, he had divided them as he believed the Israelites were organized during their forty years in the wilderness. There were companies of 100 (whether 100 people, wagons, or tents, but usually people), and subdivisions of fifty and ten. In Brigham Young's 1848 division captains of tens took turns standing guard, and on each hour throughout the night there sounded "the cheery call of the guard . . . Twelve o'clock and all is well. Then the next would take up the call until each one of the guards had given the hour."[9]

Other than the occasional administrative snafu (and the unforgettable handcart disasters of 1856), one does not find in the accounts stories of abuse by church minions. Immigrants were sometimes permitted to choose their own company if not company leader, hence John D. Lee's "hard work" raising his fifty: "The people do not like to go with him."[10] Of all the evils, real and purported, of the plains journey, the records testify that the most universal was still plain drudgery.

9. Leonard J. Arrington, *From Quaker to Latter-day Saint: Bishop Edwin D. Woolley* (Salt Lake City: Deseret Book Co., 1976), 192.
10. Ibid., 190, citing the journal of Hosea Stout.

A twentieth-century tourist can drive along I-80 from the Missouri River to Wyoming and almost enjoy the mile upon mile of hill, dale, grass, gully, and sagebrush punctuated by the clackety-clack of tires crossing the seams in cement paving. What did a nineteenth-century woman hear? Wood and iron wheels squeaking? The thudding of hooves on dust and clicking of hooves on stones? We are insulated by tires, steel, windows, even air conditioning, whereas they heard and saw everything, up to half of them walking all the way. They observed magpies, meadowlarks, cottontail, and jackrabbits scared from bushes. They heard the wind, cicadas, frogs, wolves, coyotes, prairie dogs, their own horses, oxen, cattle, and chickens, and no doubt children crying. Out in the sun and wind, they got lean and brown and their feet became calloused. At some camp sites mosquitoes made them miserable. The trek provided a common, unifying experience for old immigrant and new, longtime Mormon and neophyte. It also sturdified the British converts and prepared them for the frontier life they would face in Zion. Perhaps it was no coincidence that 92 percent of the British immigration was accomplished by the completion of the transcontinental railroad. The train eliminated the trek and its function as trainer and toughener.

Some trekkers must have become progressively anxious about where they were headed. Beginning in the bottomlands of the Missouri, travelling through the hilly farmland of eastern Nebraska and the flatter land of western Nebraska, they entered upon the sage plains of central Wyoming where buttes and stone formations appeared more and more frequently. In some diaries the Black Hills are mentioned, but these are so far north that only if you call the Sand Hills and Pine Ridge part of the same range could you say the pioneers saw mountains before they reached western Wyoming. A landmark such as Chimney Rock or Scott's Bluffs could be seen several days away. They traveled at the excruciating pace of seventeen miles per day.

Elizabeth Jackson remembered that it was while crossing the "Black Hills" that the Martin handcart company's "rough experience" began, causing carts to break down and "much delay . . . for the needed repairs." Near here her husband became ill with Mountain Fever and could no longer walk: "Though his appetite was good and he could eat more than his rations he was weak and ambition and strength had gone. All attempts to arouse him to energy or much exertion were futile." Midday of the last crossing of the Platte he fell behind and two men had to retrace the trail hunting for him. "They found him sitting by the roadside . . . he was very weak and they assisted him into Camp" (Elizabeth H. J. Kingsford).

Once leaving the Platte River, the Mormon Trail more frequently shared the route of the Oregon Trail. At Independence Rock one still finds (though most have worn away) the signatures of Utah- and Oregon-bound pioneers, although none of our women mention the stone mountain or carving their names in it. Further on, a hill leading down to Martin's Cove, just past Devil's Gate in central Wyoming, still has the remains of wagon tracks 160 years old. Companies had to cross the river to get to the rocky shelter. A memorial installed by the state of Wyoming mentions the Oregon but not the Mormon Trail.

There are few notations by our women of contact with the Oregon-bound, but Hannah King tells of some "Californians" who came to her company's assistance. One of the Californians killed a buffalo and gave the Kings "a large portion" of it which they fried for dinner.

The land became drier and the air more arid with each mile west. Wyoming's vastness must have been impressive to people from closed-in factory towns. Everywhere they looked were a million acres of open land. For a thousand miles there were no hindrances, few political limits, just as few natural boundaries.

The pioneers had to follow water, not just for themselves for camping each evening but for their animals each noon. Thus water routes dictated the land route. Wherever there was water and grass there were cottontails—small, not pudgy, shy but playful as kittens. In the 1800s, while wolves and coyotes still abounded, rabbits must have been fewer than they can be seen today. Mormons did not participate in the annihilation of the plains bison. A few young bucks from the initial 1846 company rode helter-skelter through a large herd shooting every beast in sight and leaving dozens of carcasses to rot uneaten. They received a tongue-lashing from Brigham Young. Though the buffalo did not survive, the buffalo grass has—finer, greyer, more drought-resistant than bluegrass.

Nearly a million strong, a generation of pioneer campers must have had an ecological impact on the plains beyond the devastation of wildlife. Wood was scarce along the Platte corridor by the 1860s. Much of the buffalo slaughter was accomplished even before the railroad came through in 1869. At least these tourists of 1847-69 were only passing through and stayed within a restricted passageway.

There is some evidence in the histories of resistance by the plains Indians to this invasion, although accounts of actual attacks on wagon companies are extremely rare in Oregon Trail lore. Early Hollywood's stereotype of pioneer wagon trains under siege by Native Americans hurling blood-curdling cries is false, although some women did record encounters with plains tribes. Sarah Isom, six when she crossed the plains, remembered a visit from several braves who demanded payment for the feed her company's animals had eaten. Company leaders obliged with tobacco, tea, and sugar. A member of Mariah Davies's company had a cow killed by Indians. When this incident was reported to the captain of a nearby, unnamed fort, he sent men to confront the offenders. A dispute broke out during which soldiers fired, and in retaliation some soldiers were killed and a fort burned. John wrote, "We thought we would have to fight but they'd had their revenge." For protection the Davies company camped a few nights with a Danish company, but no further incident occurred.

The Spenser-King company interchange in 1853 with an unidentified tribe proved to be diplomatic and Hannah's description of the the Indians admiring. The older Brother Spenser, she wrote, met them "with a military salute or pass, and they responded very gracefully," descending from their horses and squatting "in their not ungraceful Indian fashion." Their leader, Chief Shell, presented Spenser with a letter of recommendation "to all white folks," upon which the Mormon captain offered him whiskey and water. The chief would not drink until the Mormon drank first. Before parting, each family contributed food items for the tribe, who then "drew on one side to allow the train to pass" (Hannah T. King).

Other encounters were less friendly. Eliza Dorsey Ashworth's fifteen-year-old daughter Sarah had long blonde hair which she would sometimes let down. Several visiting Indians admired it and offered a band of horses for her. When the offer was refused, so goes the family story, the braves followed the wagon train for several days, once searching through the Ashworths' wagon. "Up in front with the guards was a slender 'youth' carrying a gun"—a youth with blonde hair hidden under "his" hat. Sister Martha, age six at the time, referred to "many horrifying encounters with the Indians," but apparently no more serious than the threatened abduction (Martha Elizabeth Ashworth Brian).

Hunger was more real than attack by indigenous tribes. One traveler reported that they "came near to starving," not being able to exist on buffalo meat alone. Another developed chronic diarrhea. Equally threatening was the effect of a thousand-mile walk on pioneer feet. Elizabeth Steadman reported severe "gatherings on my feet." Wagon accidents were another concern. Mariah Davies's husband had a wagon wheel run over his foot. A boy in their company was killed when a wagon wheel ran over his head.

Hannah King was amazed that mothers in her company fared so well health-wise. When one sister was confined with a new son and went on with the train the same day, Hannah exclaimed to her journal, "These Mormon women! I think I should have been left in my grave in a similar case. But truly God fits the back to the burden." Mariah Davies suffered a "gathered breast" while nursing her newborn. This was healed by a blessing from John. Elizabeth Steadman sustained an unusual injury—broken ribs caused by a night walker who stumbled over her as she lay asleep in her blanket near the wagon.

A common and more lethal affliction was mountain fever which attacked many company members—most often children. One also wonders how much health hazard was created by the water kept in barrels on the sides of wagons. At the least one girl remembered it as "not very tasty." Bertha and young Tom King nearly died from the fever, and their married sister Georgia contracted a case which would turn fatal at journey's end. Another danger was stampeding by buffalo and livestock. One family gave up their wagon so a coffin could be made for a brother who was trampled in a stampede.

The Handcart Companies

All of these troubles paled compared to the experience of the 1856 handcart companies. Three groups made a successful handcart trek early in the year, including Daniel McArthur's company which included obstetrician Janet Downing Hardie. Most handcart companies crossed the plains in less time and with fewer casualties than the typical wagon company. But two remaining 1856 companies—much larger in number and delayed at every point along the journey—met a harder fate. Fourteen women who participated in these companies headed by captains Martin and Willie left records, and Hannah Job, who traveled with the Hunt wagon company which lagged just behind, wrote that they "suffered nearly as much." When the handcarts began to break down near the Dakotas, food supplies ran low and rationing was imposed, then half-rations. Then winter struck weeks earlier than normal. It seemed God had turned his face away.

Elizabeth Horrocks Jackson Kingsford, stepdaughter of my ancestor and a member of the Willie company, tells in her history of wallowing through snow in late October before and after "the last [icy] crossing of the Platte" River, then of three more days of snowstorms during which her husband's condition continued to sink until he was unable to swallow. One midnight she awoke to discover his body stiff and cold, but she could only sleep beside it until morning since there were no able-bodied men left in the company to help her. That morning he was laid in a shallow grave with thirteen others who had died in their sleep. Elizabeth wrote simply: "I can't describe my sufferings."

During a period of several days when there was nothing for the company to eat or drink, Elizabeth's sister Mary became "deranged in mind." She remained so well after arriving in the Salt Lake Valley. Elizabeth herself "had become despondent" until her husband appeared in a dream to tell her, "Cheer up, Elizabeth, deliverance is at hand." The next afternoon "three men [the vanguard of a rescue effort mobilized by Brigham Young] galloped unexpectedly into camp amid tears, cheers, smiles and laughter of the emigrants."

Eliza Chapman Gadd, a non-Mormon who had come with her husband in the Willie company, lost both husband and a son on the Platte River, then another son on the Sweetwater just before relief wagons arrived. Jane McKinnon Swarts, in the Martin company, pulled her family's cart alone when her husband became too sick to do it. Sitting in the freight wagon one evening holding his head, she watched him die. More husbands died than wives. Participant after participant, both immigrant and rescuer, marvelled that the strong, middle-aged men first went into shock, weakened, and died while their women survived.

With the handcart disaster, pioneer Mormonism lost its innocence. This was trouble caused not by traitors and outsiders but by nature and their own blunders. More than one British convert who had started for Zion in faith, criticizing those who tarried in the east to make better preparations, discovered through the handcart experience that childlike obedience did not protect her from life's consequences.

Patience Rosza wondered in later years if her parents regretted having listened to the elders who assured them the Lord would stay the weather for their sakes. Elizabeth Kingsford would recall two company leaders who "sadly" accepted the instruction of a supervising elder that the handcart people, unprepared for a year's delay in the midwest, should be sent across the mountains before winter.[11] In assimilating the tragedy, Kingsford expressed her abiding faith this way: "I believe The Recording Angel inscribed it in The Archives above. That my sufferings for the Gospel's sake will be sanctified unto me for my good."

Although reduced by about 45 percent from the 1856 emigration, 1857 handcart companies continued to ply the Mormon Trail.

---

11. By this time Kingsford had John Jacques's published account of the disasters before her and was perhaps influenced by it.

In 1860 Hannah Settle Lapish came with a handcart group, traveling with her husband and two infants. Wagon companies of the 1860s continued to include some handcarts until the transcontinental railroad rendered both wagons and handcarts obsolete.

An Adventure

The Mormon emigration was thus marked by cooperation, tedium, hardship, and occasional tragedy. Later the dominant feeling as evidenced in the histories was a marked sense of romance. Sometimes literally, as with sixteen-year-old Alice Horrocks Wood, who was enthralled by a young frontiersman she met at Fort Supply. He made a striking figure in his fringed leather suit and Indian trappings. She liked him so much that a year after her parents settled in Ogden she ran away to marry him. Her family soon forgave them and they became a settled Mormon couple.

Romance and fun. One thinks of Priscilla Merriman Evans's portrayal of her company of 300 Welsh. Her history begins so forlornly, and her voice is so deadpan throughout, that I was slow to recognize the delicious humor peeking between her words. But there it is, in an anecdote about a lady whose ship berth was across the compartment from Priscilla's and who, during a terrible storm, nursed a husband through a woeful bout of seasickness. Worn out, the lady sat upon her trunk which had been lashed with others down the middle of the deck. The violent rocking of the waves tore it loose, and during one huge dip the trunk, with lady atop, slid across the compartment until she and Priscilla were nearly eyeball to eyeball. Then the ship dipped in the other direction, and the lady rode the trunk back to her own berth. She and Priscilla laughed, and the lady promised not to take any more rides like that one.

Later, on the plains, Priscilla listed the members of her tent and wagon who were to guide each other through the wilderness: half did not speak the same language, the other half was comprised of her crippled husband, a man with one leg, a man with one arm, two blind people, and a widow with five children. Compare Priscilla's quick humor to the dim-witted women of writer Theodore Winthrop's immigrant train—blunt-faced foreigners—and one can only conclude that he had missed the point. An entire generation of observers missed the point.

Chapter 9.

Monogamous Lives in Zion

We have followed one hundred British women from childhood to early association with Mormonism to the American West. Most were welcomed in Utah by countrymen (most often a male host) having come before or by the families of elders who had baptized them. Beyond this happy beginning, how did they fare in Zion?

It is a delicate proposition determining if the women, at the end of their lives, looked upon their choice as a predominantly happy one. A woman's original circumstances in Great Britain, her expectations of the new land and whether these arose from promises by missionaries and how realistic such promises were, her initial prospects in Utah territory and whether these improved over time, whether she reached Utah during a famine or an economic boom, and her manner of responding to hardships would all factor into her assessment of her choice. Mary Jane Ewer Palmer, the Lancashire weaver who sacrificed little by leaving England, probably adapted more readily to frontier life than Jean Rio Baker, the London shopowner who for the sake of duty gave up an established business, friends, and devotion to her queen.

Some women believed their lot to be one of sacrifice, this life not being a time of material and personal fulfillment at least for their generation. Other women expected the second coming of

Christ in their lifetimes, an attitude which minimized present hardships. Victorian Mormons—excluding, of course, the frenchified Fanny Stenhouse—would not seek or expect much fulfillment.

Significantly, two-thirds of our British women, along with nineteenth-century Mormon women generally, did not participate at all in the experiment with polygamy. One wonders why they remained monogamous and what their experience was compared to polygamous women and to non-British Mormon women.

Three Were Disillusioned

A perusal of the histories turns up only two monogamous women who expressed regret over their experience in Zion: Jean Rio Baker and my own ancestress, Eliza Worthington Horrocks. In addition, Elizabeth Clark Handley's brief biography depicts the rare family who left Utah in a panic over miseries encountered there. A fourth case wants more evidence than one sentence in the British Mission manuscript history regarding the family's return to England from Nauvoo. After vocalizing their disenchantment the couple was excommunicated.

Eliza Ann Clarke Worthington Horrocks

We start with my third great-grandmother, Eliza Ann Clarke Worthington Horrocks. She was born in 1824 in Macclesfield, Cheshire County, and at age seventeen was baptized by Edward Horrocks, president of the local mission and a Cheshire native. About 1849, at age twenty-five, she began to live with a nonmember, James Samuel Worthington, who by some accounts was a professional tailor.[1] Eliza and James's only child, Mary Worthington, was born 7 February 1850. James would not accept the Mormon gospel, and family tradition is that because of religious differences "they parted."[2]

1. Birth registration for Mary Worthington (witnessed by the landlady), Eliza Ann Clarke, mother, father unidentified. There is no marriage certificate on record for Worthington and Clarke. Vital Records, Somerset House, London.
   2. Worthington family papers in my possession, including a short biography of Eliza Clark Worthington Horrocks, an autobiography of

Daughter Mary claimed that Eliza's parents also turned against her. This is surprising since her father, Joseph Clark(e) of High Street, Macclesfield, was baptized when Eliza was an infant. However, a year after Mary was born, Joseph Clark(e) was "cut off" from the church for unnamed reasons, and even though this was a common occurrence (Eliza's staunch second husband was also cut off a year before his appointment as branch president), her father was never rebaptized. This apparently left Eliza on her own.

Eliza married Edward Horrocks on 28 April 1856, a year before they emigrated. The marriage certificate identifies Edward as a "silk manufacturer" and Eliza as a "spinster." Edwards's daughter wrote that after Mother Horrocks's death her father hired Eliza to work in the home and take care of his children, and that Eliza proved "a wonderful companion" so he married her. When the Horrockses emigrated, it was with six of his children and Eliza's daughter Mary (Elizabeth H. J. Kingsford).

All records agree that their emigration was flawed. It began with a stormy crossing on the *S.S. George Washington*. They were seven weeks before reaching Boston. When they arrived at the starting-out point for the plains, the outfit they had ordered and paid for was not ready, causing another delay. They must have felt apprehension, since a year earlier Horrocks's two older daughters had been trapped in the Rockies with the Martin handcart company. One daughter had lost her husband and the other had become temporarily deranged as a result of exposure, starvation, and exhaustion. Yet for Eliza and her party the plains phase of emigration was spotted only by normal hardships: quicksand, stampede, mountain fever, and for Mary too much walking which proved "hard on a seven-year-old girl."

In Utah the Horrockses settled first in Ogden, thirty-five miles north of Salt Lake City, where they started a mercantile establishment "known throughout the area" as Horrocks Brothers.

Mary Worthington Coon, histories of these two women by Eliza's granddaughter and great-granddaughter, copies of Eliza's patriarchal blessing and Mary's birth certificate, and research notes made by my grandmother from British census records, LDS Records of Members, and Macclesfield city records.

Their first winter was meager, the family subsisting on bran bread, bran mush, and squash. Mary liked to tell how her mother once decided to vary this diet with an apple dumpling pudding. The trouble was she did not have any apples, so she used sweet onions instead. Mary remembered this steamed pudding as "very good."

When three years later the little town of Huntsville was established in beautiful Pineview Valley in the mountains east of Ogden, Edward moved his family there and began a freighting operation between Huntsville and Ogden. They could not have been wealthy, as no settlers to that area were entirely comfortable. From age twelve, daughter Mary hired out as a domestic, doing housework, milking cows, making butter and cheese. She once worked all summer for a pair of shoes, two dresses, and yarn for stockings.

In 1865, eight years after arriving in Utah, Edward was hurled into a ravine by a snowslide which knocked his freight wagon off the road and killed him. He was fifty-nine and left Eliza with two small sons and a daughter besides Mary. His own children were by this time married or self-sufficient.

Not much is said in the family records about Eliza's later life, a reverse of the tendency to be brief about the British years while detailed about emigration and life in Zion. She married again, to Thomas Sleater "for time"[3] in the Logan temple, but this third marriage ended in divorce, possibly a casualty of trying to mix step-families. Eliza eventually moved to Mary's home in Pleasant Green (now Magna) where she died.

It is the footnote to Eliza's story that is of most interest. A strong tradition has passed from daughter to daughter that Eliza asked to be sealed for eternity to "her first husband" rather than to Edward Horrocks because Horrocks was mean to her and she

---

3. Both in pioneer and modern times, marriages of worthy Mormon couples may be performed in a temple "for time" rather than "for time and all eternity." This is necessary when a woman has been sealed to a previous husband, for Mormons believe that in heaven men will be allowed any number of spouses (although on earth, at least for the present, only one living wife at a time), while women will be permitted only one husband. Thus Eliza could have married Thomas Sleater for eternity only if her eternal sealing to Horrocks had been set aside.

regretted marrying him. Eliza may well have been unhappy with a husband eighteen years her senior, and it is true that Mary, who was said to "remember her father well," never adopted the Horrocks name.

This tradition is so strong that my grandmother badgered LDS authorities for over twenty years to have Eliza's temple marriage to Horrocks revoked and another vicariously performed to Worthington. Because of this family experience, my family has a high tolerance for out-of-church weddings.

Thus of all the British women's histories, my own ancestor's turns out to be the exception to the rule that at first blush seems to prove the stereotype: she could well be the naive proselyte who listened too credulously to Mormon elders and lived to regret it. Yet Eliza did not spend her Utah years in bondage. Though simple, hers was not a life of want and abandonment. She was never a plural wife, although she might have become one had Horrocks lived long enough. She did not repudiate other tenets of her faith.

As for Eliza's descendants, daughter Mary married a Mormon and raised sixteen children. Six generations of descendants have proven more-or-less faithful to Mormonism. As a great-great-great-granddaughter, I have to agree with my ancestress that it would have been the better thing to stick by her first husband. Yet where would I be, and my brothers, sisters, and cousins, had she not?

Jean Rio Griffiths Baker

A history sumptuous in emigration detail while tantalizingly terse about her life in Zion is that of Jean Rio Griffiths Baker Pearce. Open, vividly observant, always interested, Jean described her departure from friends and associates in the London hat business, her family's voyage across the Atlantic and up the Mississippi, and the wagon trek across the plains.

Jean had obtained the name Rio (pronounced rye-oh) possibly from her mother's French birth and Griffiths from her Scottish father. Her first husband, civil engineer Henry Baker, died in London. She converted to Mormonism in 1848 where she was a member of the Whitechapel Branch, and three years later emigrated with her six children, losing a small son at sea.

Upon arriving in Salt Lake City Jean wrote, "I can hardly analyze my feelings, but I think my prevailing ones were joy and gratitude for the protecting care [who] had over me and mine, during our long perilous journey." One of her early observations was "the singular fact (at least to us English folks)" of clean air "enabling us to see objects at a very great distance ever since the Missouri River."

Within a week Jean purchased a small Salt Lake Valley house and one-acre garden that pleased her highly with its Indian corn, potatoes, cabbage, carrots, parsnips, beets, and tomatoes watered by a small stream. She bought a three-year-old heifer. The house had only four rooms, she noted, but "we can manage for the winter."

Her life might have turned out differently had she remained in Salt Lake City. But Jean had larger agrarian ambitions. That winter she turned the house over to an aunt and uncle so she and her sons could "go farm" on twenty acres she had purchased in Ogden. It was a ruinous step for a London shopkeeper.

The diary tells this only in retrospect. It lapses for nearly two decades before entries resume in a far different tone from her happy scribblings upon first reaching the valley. On 29 September 1869, Jean wrote: "I have been 18 years this day an inhabitant of Utah Territory and I may say 18 years of hard toil and almost continual disappointment. My 20 acre farm turned out to be a mere salaratus patch . . . I am now in Ogden city living in a small log house and working at my trade, as a dressmaker." Looking back to the famine of 1856 and the Utah War and move south of 1858, she said, "we passed them both, and a bitter experience it was." She had buried her next-youngest boy in 1860. Her son William had been married since 1858, and Edward and John had left for California within two years of arriving in Ogden: "they could not stand poverty any longer so ran away from it." As a last blow, after fifteen years as a widow, she had married again only to see her new husband live but six months. Jean continued,

> I have tried to do my best in the various circumstances in which I have been placed. I came here in obedience to what I believed to be a revelation of the Most High God, trusting in the assurance

of the missionaries, whom I believed to have the spirit of truth. I left my home, sacrificed my property, broke up every dear association, and what was and is yet dearer than all, left my beloved native land, and for what? *A bubble that has burst in my grasp.*

These words were not written in the immediate throes of grief. Her second husband Edward Pearce had been gone five years, so one can assume that such words reflected her dominant feelings. "It has been a severe lesson," she continued, "but I can say, it has led me to lean more on my Heavenly Father, and less on men's words."

Eight weeks after writing this, Jean succumbed to Edward's and John's implorings and joined them in California. There she saw her boys for the first time in ten years and met John's non-Mormon wife whom she called "my new daughter," commenting, "I like her much and she seems a thorough, whole-souled young woman." The following spring Jean wrote, "it has been a very pleasant winter . . . It is like being in a new world." A few other relatives soon followed her from Utah, all settling on rented farm land on a place called Sherman Island.

California agreed with Jean. At age seventy she would write (as the last entry in her "Utah" diary) that she had good health and was "spending my time among my children, sometimes at one house and sometimes at another." Although in California too the family suffered "many disappointments, many trials," Jean now had "every temporal comfort my heart can desire . . . "

Except for a twenty-one-month visit to Utah in 1876 to see family, Jean remained in California. During this visit she found her "remaining children and friends . . . As the members of one household of Faith, irrespective of creed . . . " Her son William, after eleven years of married life in Ogden, had moved to Richfield in central Utah and taken his young Scandinavian housemaid as a plural wife. This girl's fiance had died, so she married William for time only, being sealed for eternity to the dead fiance. But after bearing William twelve children, the earlier sealing was revoked and a new one performed with William. Jean's only daughter

married in the church, later divorced the man, married an Episco-
palian, and "left" the church.

Experience broadened Jean's comprehension of the world and
made her less sectarian. She learned to distinguish the Zion of the
heart from real estate. Yet according to a descendant, even her
family does not know if she died in the faith. Her California
journals have been lost. Her funeral was a non-Mormon ceremony,
although this may have been her sons' choice.

A statement which appears in quotation marks at the end of
Jean's diary leaves the strong possibility that she stayed loyal to
Mormonism. It is dated 1880, after twelve happy years in California. "I have but one wish unfulfilled and that is that I may live to
see every one of my children and grandchildren faithful members
of the kingdom of God." It seems that however muddied the trail
became, Baker held to the path she chose at conversion in
Whitechapel.

Elizabeth Clark Handley

The histories of Jean Rio Baker and others reveal an initial
"honeymoon period" during an immigrant's first weeks in Utah
territory. We will see more of this tendency in the next section. But
a biography which intimates nothing of the kind is Elizabeth Clark
Handley's, which belies a checkered existence in Utah from the
beginning. Elizabeth was born in Chesterton, Cambridgeshire, in
1824. In 1844 or 1846 she married George Handley. Their first two
children died in infancy. About 1852 most of Elizabeth's family
converted to Mormonism, and in 1853 her father, B. Thomas Clark,
paid the emigration fares for the "whole family."

These converts may have been overly-expectant, or perhaps
they just ran into an unusually heavy share of bad luck. Certainly
the timing of their arrival was inopportune. It was the middle of
the famine of 1856. The family record states that "privations and
sufferings caused [them] to leave Utah Territory and in 1857 they
went to Council Bluffs" (Nebraska). There they lived and worked
five years, after which time they returned to Utah where they now
"found things more favorable." Their story is a seldom-seen aspect
of the settlement of Utah and sheds some realism on the romanti-
cized stories of blissful happy-every-afters and the sensationalist

claims that hordes of Saints crowded the Mormon Trail on their way out of Zion.

The genealogical record reveals some of the obstacles which caused the Handleys to become discouraged with Zion. George and Elizabeth emigrated with a two-year-old daughter. A son was born on the Wyoming plains but died the same day. In Salt Lake City the next spring they had stillborn twins. Sons born in 1855 and 1857 lived, but 1856 and 1857 were years of famine, drought, and grasshopper plagues.

Iowa treated them little better than had Utah. During their exile in "the States," four more of the Handley children died, three in a single five-day period just before Christmas 1861. Perhaps the Handleys decided that God had cursed them for retreating from Zion, for in 1862 they returned to Great Salt Lake City.

If they were cursed, they brought it with them. A son born that winter died five weeks later. At this time Elizabeth and George must have feared they would leave no posterity at all, with only three of thirteen children surviving and these so young that their futures were uncertain. The couple could not have predicted that one son and a daughter, born in 1864 and 1867, would live to comfort Elizabeth's old age.

Just before completing the book I came across a microfilm record on George Handley previously overlooked. It turns out that as Elizabeth's childbearing years came to a close George took a second wife—an English girl, possibly a servant in their home, Sarah Ann Briggs. In marrying again, George, forty, robbed the cradle, for Sarah Ann was not yet fifteen. Here is one family among our histories which contributed to Utah's relatively low marrying age.

Sarah Ann would bear George four children before his early death in 1874. (She was more fortunate than Elizabeth in that only one of her children died young, a daughter at age nine, five years after her father's death.) It does not speak well for the institution of polygamy that at age twenty-three Sarah Ann Briggs was a widow with four dependents.

If only there were more information on what became of these two women. The record shows no remarriage by Elizabeth Clark

Handley, although she must have had opportunity. Sarah Ann remarried, this time to a man her own age: Arvis Scott Chapman.[4] Early marriage and widowhood may have disabused Sarah Ann of her teenage impressionability in matters of religion. Only two of her children were baptized and these late, one at age twelve, the other at age fifty-four. Sarah was buried in Salt Lake City's Mt. Olivet Cemetery, a burial ground not commonly used by Mormon families, suggesting that Arvis was a gentile.[5]

All three of this section's stories suggest mixed feelings at leaving Great Britain, confirming in individual cases though not in cumulative totals the stereotype of the bitterly-disappointed Mormon dupe. The stories are tragic. Mormonism was no refuge from the solitary aspect of sainthood. The group did not supplant the individual, however much it may have wanted to. What the stereotype did not recognize was the dupe's ability to learn from self-perceived mistakes.

Four Were Glad

Neither Eliza Worthington Horrocks nor Jean Rio Baker left a clue as to why she eluded polygamy. The case of Elizabeth Wilkins Steadman is important because in a letter she made direct reference to her marriage decision, an exciting find among our histories.

Elizabeth Wilkins Steadman

Elizabeth was born in 1835 in Buckebury Berks near Newport, England, the youngest daughter of a blacksmith. She was twenty when her entire family converted to Mormonism. They emigrated in stages, beginning with two brothers. Charles settled in South Cottonwood, Salt Lake Valley, where he married and produced five children. Christopher, while still in the east, was persuaded or waylaid into joining the Union Army. His family heard nothing from him for three years, whereupon they received a letter which

---

4. The records show her remarrying twice, but "Doctor Chatwin," born in 1851, must be Chapman, also born in 1851.

5. Information on Sarah Ann Briggs Handley Chapman taken from family group sheets on computerized Ancestral File, LDS Family History Library. Details about her marriage to Chapman could not be found.

revealed, "I have been on the battlefield, and it is terrible to behold." As a band musician he had not fired a shot or received a scratch.

The decision was made that the next to sail would be Elizabeth and her aging father, who sadly passed away two weeks out of New York harbor in 1862. Elizabeth's letters to her mother (published in *Our Pioneer Heritage*) begin with her excited observations just before sailing and continue with her plaints about cows and babies several years after arriving in Utah. They reveal her to be mature and independent for twenty-seven, of a practical bent, observant, interested in her traveling companions, and prone to put a matter-of-fact, even optimistic, construction on most events. Her first letter from Zion reads:

> SLC, Sept. 1862
>
> Dear Mother, I was glad to have a letter from you, but almost afraid to look at it. I was sorry to hear Sophia is dead. It must be very dull for James and you too . . . I wish you could come next season. . . . I was very hearty at Florence, I got so that I could hardly get about. When I came along the plains I got thin enough. I had the diarrhea a month before I got here and a very bad appetite. I had five or six gatherings on my feet which made it worse. I have not the least desire to come back. If you could get a little cinnamon to bring you might get a little milk for that purpose [as a cure for diarrhea].

Elizabeth added that her brother Charles had a comfortable home and she liked his wife. This letter was written within days of arriving in Utah, yet Elizabeth was already making decisions about the future, for she concluded, "I can stay here as long as I like but I suppose that won't be much longer. I have my choice to have a single man or a man with one wife and I don't know what to do, nor anybody can't tell me, for both are very good men . . . "

Her mother must have waited eagerly for Elizabeth's next letter, which was dated the next February:

> I seldom go to sleep but I am dreaming about all of you and that I am back there but I am glad I am here . . . I should have more pleasure in writing to you if I had something cheering to tell you. That I would have some chance of sending for you but I don't at

present. . . . I am glad Charles had not got to pay it [her Perpetual Emigration Fund debt]. My man pays that. I was married on my last birthday to a single man, four years older than myself. We live comfortable together so far . . .

Characteristically, Elizabeth stuck mostly to practical details about her situation. Her husband George Steadman, a Sussex convert, was sharecropping a South Cottonwood farm near Charles's place. The newlyweds already had acquired two cows and hoped to get another that summer, and had traded one cow and a pig for oxen and a good new wagon. Elizabeth wrote of George, "He is a good fellow to work and to make things handy and comfortable indoors and out."

Elizabeth tried to tease her mother into emigrating right away: "I expect to have a little boy the latter part of February and I want you for a nurse . . . I hope you will have strength and health and be able to keep up your spirits and live to come here."

This letter and one written a year later show that soon enough the newlyweds were receiving a balance of luck and trouble. They had to move from South Cottonwood when the pregnant Elizabeth came near to dying due to diarrhea, a liver complaint, and a "canker." "George had to be about so much nights he said he could not work days." By moving they had to forgo harvest on the first property and they arrived too late in the season to prepare a crop on the new place, which meant living "hand to mouth all the long, cold winter." In addition, their brand new wagon was conscripted by the church to be "sent back to the States to fetch the Saints. We bought another, an old one." Finally, Elizabeth was bedridden nine weeks before childbirth. Her letters show that the first glow of arriving in Zion had been replaced by workaday cares. She commented, "If people come here for nic nacs and comfort they have to wait until they can make them and they that don't pay tithing here, can hardly live." She probably meant that people got by only through God's help, although she may have also meant that only through assistance from the church—which non-tithe-payers did not enjoy—could a family survive.

Actually, George and Elizabeth were doing relatively well. They had a house, a good garden, peach and plum trees and currant bushes, and a new baby daughter—"a poor little thing but very healthy and hungry . . . not a day's sickness since she was born." And they had no debts. The new wagon surely paid off her Perpetual Emigration Fund loan, and they had acquired the new house by trade using wheat and the South Cottonwood property.

Unfortunately, the letters end here. The rest of her story must be pieced from computerized genealogical data found at LDS church headquarters. These show that Elizabeth's childbearing years were short compared to many nineteenth-century women, perhaps because she had married relatively late. Seven children were born between 1864 and 1876. It took George six years to obtain a son to help him on the farm. They were fortunate in not being torn from their second farm and sent to colonize an outlying valley but spent their entire married life in the Millcreek and Taylorsville areas of central Salt Lake Valley. In 1877 Elizabeth and the three children who qualified were rebaptized, probably in a gesture of recommitment to the church. Except for George Jr., who remained a bachelor until his death, all their children married and lived to old age, although not as old as their parents. Elizabeth died in 1918 at age 83, George a year later at 88.

In retrospect, Elizabeth had no reason to complain about her life in Zion. A spinster on arrival, she married within a few months to a man who treated her well and proved a compatible companion. They endured the predictable afflictions of a nineteenth-century family: the ups and downs of scraping a farm living, the sometimes-annoying demands of the local and central church, illnesses and diseases that were sometimes life-threatening but did not take the ultimate toll of either adults or children.

Elizabeth Ann Claridge McCune

A family which was not allowed the luxury of remaining on their early homestead was that of Charlotte Joy Claridge. Charlotte was born in Houghton, Huntingood, England, in 1819, the daughter of James Joy and Sarah Skinner. She married Samuel, nine years her junior, in 1849 and was baptized into the Mormon church in June 1851. It did not take them long to prepare to emigrate. The very next year she and Samuel carried their two infants, Samuel and Elizabeth, to Utah. It is daughter Elizabeth Ann Claridge McCune who is the main subject of this story.

Elizabeth's parents had another son just after arriving in Utah and a daughter was born in 1857 who would later marry one of Brigham Young's more prominent sons. The family set down roots in Nephi, several days' wagon ride south of Salt Lake City, where many of the family would be buried over the next seventy years.

The Claridges made several ties to Brigham Young's family. Besides the daughter who married Brigham S. Young, the oldest daughter Elizabeth would become lifelong friends with Susa Young Gates, called "The Thirteenth Apostle" for her energetic involvement in church and Utah politics. Susa was a prolific writer, founder of the *Young Women's Journal* and long-time editor of the *Relief Society Magazine*. She occasionally succeeded in getting her wealthy but very private friend Elizabeth to write articles for publication.

One such article tells of Elizabeth as a fifteen-year-old helping the little town of Nephi prepare for a visit from the First Presidency. Local bands practiced for weeks, girls prepared flowers to be strewn along the visitors' path, and females made new hats to copy "the stylish city folks" who would accompany the Brethren. With this story Elizabeth meant to show the love and loyalty Nephi families offered the church authorities.

About the time Elizabeth's parents might have settled into somewhat comfortable middle age, Samuel Claridge was called to help establish the ill-fated Muddy River mission in southeastern Nevada. Elizabeth later wrote that she sobbed at her father's leaving but would have felt disgraced had he not accepted the call. In time her mother joined him. Elizabeth herself stayed behind to marry a young Nephi man, and she later had some exciting adventures of her own when, with her first baby, she traveled alone to visit her parents now ensconced on the Arizona frontier.

What Elizabeth did not say in the story is that her father was also called to take a second wife, Rebecca Hughes. No information beyond the marriage date—3 July 1865—has been found about this woman. But the marriage probably took place just before Claridge joined forty-five families on the Muddy River as part of an effort to establish a cotton colony. Within a year only twenty-five families remained there, and by 1870 all remaining settlers voted to withdraw when given a choice by Brigham Young. It is not known if Samuel Claridge was one of the faithful twenty-five.[6]

From Nevada the Claridges relocated to Thatcher, Arizona, and first wife Charlotte died there at age sixty-five. She lived long enough to recapture the prosperity she had lost in leaving Nephi and to know that her children prospered as well.

Elizabeth was twenty when she married twenty-three-year-old Alfred William McCune. Alfred was born in Calcutta, India, of an English doctor and wife who were converted and emigrated to Utah sometime before 1857.

Alfred and Elizabeth had nine children: six boys and three girls, all born in Utah between 1873 and 1891. Otherwise they were not a typical frontier couple. Against the trend established by church leaders who tried to develop an agricultural rather than mining economy in Utah, Alfred became a mining engineer and partner in ventures from Utah to South Africa which yielded fortune after fortune.

Elizabeth came from a too dedicated religious stock to enjoy fully the cosmopolitan possibilities as wife of a mining magnate. When Alfred moved her into a lavish mansion above the temple in Salt Lake City she was embarrassed. During one of his many extended travels, she moved herself out of the ostentatious villa into a modest house across from Liberty Park on Ninth South. Later she willed the mansion to the church.

From a letter Susa Gates wrote to Alfred but never sent, it appears his preference for business over religion was a point of strain between himself and Elizabeth. Yet it was probably through Alfred's financial prominence, as much as Elizabeth's friendship with activist Susa and a sister's marriage to an apostle, that Elizabeth enjoyed many opportunities to help women and serve her church. Over the years she acted as a trustee for the Utah Agricultural College in Logan, appointee to the National Council of

6. Lawrence B. Lee, "Homesteading in Zion," *Utah Historical Quarterly* 28 (1960): 29-38.

Women, member of the general presidency of the Young Ladies Mutual Improvement Association, and member of the Relief Society General Board. She died in 1924 and was buried as she would have wished in Nephi. Extravagant wealth had not turned her from the faith of her parents. Alfred outlived her by three years and died at Cannes, France, but he too was buried in his boyhood home.

Mary Nixon Bate

Few Utah families proved as materially fortunate as the McCunes. Mary Nixon Bate was the London housewife and property owner whose power struggle with her husband over her religion culminated in the accidental smothering of their newborn. Mary was thirty-five, Richard Bate forty, and their other children thirteen, ten, eight, six, two, and four months when she joined the church. After three years of emotional abuse, Mary took what money she needed from the bank and stole away to Liverpool with the children, where Richard caught up with them.

That Mary was pregnant again shows marital relations continued despite their problems. The family went by train to Iowa City, then spent two years in St. Louis where Richard died in 1859, only forty-five years old. Mary was now widowed with seven children, having spent most of her money just getting to St. Louis.

Mary's early years in Utah were as difficult as her emigration. Just after she arrived in Salt Lake City a man borrowed 100 pounds of flour plus a half bushel of white beans, never paying it back. This repeated a similar experience in St. Louis. Yet, while there were parties in church circles willing to relieve a widow of her surplus, others were honest. A man to whom she had loaned $13 in Iowa City looked her up in Salt Lake City to repay her in provisions. She also still had $50 and a team of oxen which together paid for a house with sixty acres.

Within a year of arriving in Utah, Mary married William Brewer, about whom nothing is known except that she and all her children were soon sealed to him. What became of Brewer, and why her name is given in the history as Mary Nixon Bate Buckley, can only be surmised. No record could be found of Buckley.

Apparently Mary stayed in the Salt Lake City house only five years, for by 1866 she was in Provo forty miles south, finally settling in nearby Springville two years later. There her history ends, hopefully because her life had become comfortably mundane. Several of her descendants remain in Springville to this day.

In spite of troubles, Mary never regretted her decision to gather to Zion. In 1881 she left her testimony in the form of an account of her conversion and immigration, a handwritten document which was sealed with others in the cornerstone of the St. George temple until 1931. Before submitting the document, she devoted three months in St. George to working in the temple. "I never spend [sic] such a happy time in my life," she wrote at age sixty-two. "I bear my testimony to the work of God that has been revealed in these latter days for the redemption of the Human Family."

Did Mary ever reconsider the consequences of her early decisions? Apparently not. One line in her history mentions "the darkness of my Traditions," but this refers to her not fully appreciating the dreams and visions she enjoyed during the warfare with her husband, "whisperings to my soul wich gave me joy and peace." The family group sheet on Richard, Mary, and their seven children has this notation: "Do not seal to husband"—a final insult to Richard Bate who had already lost everything else to a faith he did not embrace. He may be one of the handful of real victims of Mormonism.

Hannah Tapfield King

Hannah Tapfield King was converted to Mormonism through readying dreams, prayer, and tears. Her journals indicate that she remained loyal to her death. Yet her story not only resembles but very well could be the prototype for Maria Ward's image of the comfortable matron beguiled by initially charming, solicitous Mormon elders and as a result losing her happy British home, British honor, and earthly prosperity.

Hannah almost emigrated to Zion without her spouse. At virtually the last minute her husband decided to sell their property and follow Hannah and the children. This meant splitting up his ancestral home forever. Hannah herself had mixed feelings about this:

I felt a weight upon me I could not shake off, for I knew it was only the almighty love he had for his family that made him make this great sacrifice. Well it is a great sacrifice for me also. I have loved my home as much as he can have done . . . Now it will be broken up and disbursed . . . to the four winds. It is also a great, a very great sacrifice to my children. Yet, bless them, they are ready to make it.

But the sacrifice must have been harder for Thomas, a yeoman who loved rural English life and not Mormonism. Hannah admitted, "At present he is looked upon as a man victimized by his wife—an object of universal pity and commiseration. But God, not they will be my judge! . . . Poor dear man! How distressed he was all the afternoon."

Here is a slight twist on the story of the gullible matron—Hannah was able to bring her adoring husband and cherubs along. She was made painfully aware that her "father and mother are wretched too about it." During a last walk in the family garden she agonized: "Oh, nothing but the conviction that I am doing the will of God could urge me forward to make the stand I have done. And many trials are yet in store for me!"

The Kings' trials were swift in coming. Before crossing the plains their oldest daughter, Georgiana, "the twin spirit of [Hannah's] soul," married the missionary who had converted the family, Claudius Spenser. It is clear that by the time of the trek Hannah had espoused polygamy in doctrine if not practice, for when another daughter, Louie, vowed "she would be the first wife or not be married," Hannah wrote: "It seems to be incorporated into [Louie's] system—the idea of being *great* according to *her* notions of greatness. Perhaps she will learn better in time."

As noted in the previous chapter, travel by wagon train had frayed the devotion between mother and son-in-law Claudius. Then, less than a week after arriving in Salt Lake Valley, Georgiana died from mountain fever. It left Hannah "almost paralyzed with surprise, sorrow, and sadness. [She] was taken very ill 5 weeks."

In a bizarre manifestation of the excesses of polygamy, only a few days after Georgie's death Claudius began urging Hannah to give him younger daughter Louie to wife. He persisted even while

Hannah lay ill, causing her to see in a new light his behavior during the wagon trip. She now believed that he had been "always after [Louie] either by a 'dumb expression' or otherwise . . . As I now feel, I shall never give her to him." Yet his implorings finally wore her down and "At last I said, 'Cease . . . I give you a release . . .'" On 9 October 1853, less than three weeks after losing Georgie, Claudius took both Louie and another immigrant, Susannah Neslen, as plural wives.

One can only speculate on Thomas's opinion of his daughters' marriages. At least "Mr. King" (as Hannah referred to him) and Hannah made an effort to enjoy Mormon society. They donated $50 to the Perpetual Emigration Fund. It would be the last donation they would make for a long time. Next year, when a builder tried to collect what they owed for construction of their Salt Lake City house, the Kings were unable to pay him.

For the first time in their lives there were days with no breakfast to eat. They were even poorer than most Salt Lakers during the famine of 1856, for at April general conference that year, when Brigham Young asked the congregation for $100 in donations for the poor, Hannah found she had not a cent to give. "Felt rather sad at my poverty, for I would have loved to have given something as all the rest were doing."

Louie and Bertha helped their parents by supplying flour, sugar and eggs, and Hannah asked President Young to find work in the church offices for sixteen-year-old Tom Owen King. Young obliged, and soon Tom was running errands for the Express Company, a freighting outfit organized by church leaders and merchants. In addition Hannah operated a school in her home, although her health ended this enterprise after two years. Hannah's journal tells nothing of efforts by Mr. King to contribute to the family's living.

In the midst of these difficulties, Hannah went to President Young again and donated to the church a piece of land in England—a legacy from her father—while reserving some as an inheritance for her children. The prophet responded by sending the Kings sixty pounds of flour, a more valuable commodity in Utah that spring than English land or cash.

In addition to money, Hannah found herself lacking friends in Zion. She had decided even while crossing the plains not to confide in her husband: "I dare not tell Mr. King many things that trouble me ... It might injure the things of God, and do me no good." When a young man who had become her confidante on the plains boarded at the King home, tongues set to wagging. "I feel I have a secret enemy somewhere," Hannah wrote. And apparently Old World class differences still told in Utah territory, for after tea with several other Mormon matrons, Hannah confided: "Did not like the feeling of these women ... they feel I am different and are rather in awe of me ... we belong to different orbits." After one Sunday meeting, she wrote: "Went to the Ward Room, enjoyed it pretty well. But the women seem spiritless, only three brethren present ... I do not feel unhappy but there is a void. I feel alone."

While kind most of the time, Mr. King tended to be "cross and fault finding" about some matters, occasionally causing Hannah to reassess whether she wished to remain yoked to an unbeliever. She wanted to be true "until death do us part," yet she worried that she might thereby forego "a fullness of salvation," consigning herself to the role of a "ministering spirit" in heaven by not seeing to it that she was "sealed" in the Endowment House to a worthy male. However, when one sister urged her to get herself sealed "to Joseph" (the prophet Joseph Smith), Hannah told her that in this case she preferred to walk by sight, not by faith.

Neither were Hannah's children always a comfort. Bertha, who had caused such friction in England that the Kings once considered sending her to boarding school, would slip away evenings in Salt Lake with friends without permission. At age nineteen, to her mother's grief, she married a Brother Candland. Less than a year later she divorced him, again against her parents' counsel. Once again living at home, Bertha was described by her mother with these lines: "I cannot get her to assimilate with me, and this morning she showed such a spirit as I never saw exhibited in her before." Finally Bertha left to live with an older female friend. Independence must have mollified her rebelliousness, for a year later she was helping to support her parents.

Louie, married in polygamy to Claudius Spenser, soon delighted Hannah with a grandchild, and Hannah resumed a courteous relationship with Claudius but never again the trust and adulation as when he and his father were officials of the British Mission. No record is found of Louie's children living to maturity. Bertha remarried but likewise left no offspring of record. Only the youngest child, Thomas, would live to old age and insure the Kings a posterity through his eight children. Eventually Hannah made a few friends "firm as the hills, and true as steel." She may have been referring to her associates in the Polysophical Society, a debate/arts/social club formed in 1854 by and for the intellectually-starved. Hannah frequently gave readings at society meetings. But even this comfort was to be denied her. She was greatly disappointed when the club became "a stink in the nostrils" of Apostle Jedediah Grant, fiery promoter of the Mormon Reformation of 1856-57. When Heber C. Kimball jumped on Grant's bandwagon and forced the society to disband, Hannah was deeply hurt.

The Reformation itself was another cross for Hannah. From youth she had resisted Calvinist religion, and she suffered acutely from the hell-fire-and-damnation tenor of Reformation sermons. Far into the 1870s she would recall, "Never shall I forget the darkness, desolation, and horror of those times!" Her journal describes her ward bishop and two teachers catechizing the members:

> How well I remember them coming to our house. There was no one at home but Tom Owen and me. They asked if I desired to be questioned in a separate room. I said no, and smiling at Tom I asked him if he did. Poor boy, he was but 16, he looked as guileless as a child and said no. They then proceeded with me. It began, Have you committed murder, ditto, ditto—adultery? ditto-ditto—robbed?—Spoken slander of your neighbor?—Broken down your neighbor's fences?—Brought your children up in principles of righteousness, etc. [The Catechism] was over a foot in length!! Blessed were those who could answer in innocence.

She claimed that many members were frightened into confessing sins they had not committed. Hannah could never bring herself to criticize President Young, whom she credited for ending the Ref ormation. "At last one Sunday Brigham rose up in the stand peaceful and benign. Told the people to stop their confessions . . . " She would not outright state that the whole episode was misguided. "Only I know it was a fearful ordeal, and fear is a slavish passion and is not begotten by the spirit of God!"

A final misfortune curiously did not wring the usual tears and poetic effluence from Hannah: the death of her mother. Regarding this event she wrote with peculiar detachment: "She [Mary, Hannah's only sister] says she died broken hearted! Poor thing! Well, I expect the time will come when she will bow all things, and then all will be right." Hannah seems to have long before reconciled herself to the alienation from family that her religion had created.

On her fiftieth birthday Hannah sat at her writing desk to compare her life in Utah to her former life at Dernford Dale:

> Formerly I had servants to keep my house clean and in order as I directed. I had children, and their governess who grew to be my friend, whose love to me was wonderful! "Passing the love of women." I ruled in love, and we had a home of peace and order, and above all *love*. I maintained a dignity of manner and character that comforted me and returned blessings on my head, and I felt great and good.

Now she wrote ("I am not complaining, only stating facts"):

> Now I am literally a servant in my own house, with not a human being under me. I am everything but my own mistress. I am poor even to often wanting the necessaries of life. [Once] I could comfort myself by comforting others . . . All this is past, and now those I would [do] good to receive my kindness with, at best apathy, and alas! often with repulse. Truly has the gospel brought *not* peace, but a sword in my family, and has cut almost every heart string I had under the old regime!

Her troubles were offset by her great love for Mormon leaders Brigham Young and Heber C. Kimball. Upon first meeting the prophet she wrote, "He looked and spoke like a man! He is the very man I saw in my dream in England." And Kimball made it a point to befriend her at balls and socials so that she always felt cheered by his attentions.

Hannah lived to be seventy-nine, contributing poems and

prose writings to the *Women's Exponent* until shortly before her death. Thomas King, Sr., never converted to Mormonism but died in Salt Lake City at the age of seventy-five.

How does one assess Hannah King's experience with Zion? There is the temptation to simply accept her own appraisal—an unshakable personal vision which translates as dogged Mormon orthodoxy. Two years after arriving in the territory she wrote, "I bear my testimony here in writing that I am rejoicing as ever in the work of the Lord. I feel . . . that He has been my Father . . . and never has the thought crossed my mind that I wish I had not given up my home and come here, or a regret that I have entered into covenant with Him . . . " Twenty years later these were still her sentiments. Confiding only to her diary, with no one to impress or deceive, these were presumably her honest and predominant thoughts. Perhaps maturity buffered her from disillusionment over conditions and attitudes found in Zion. After all, her life in England had not been idyllic, either, with losses through death, estrangement, and depression. "We must have the evil and the good in about the same ratio," she philosophized.

Yet there is an equal temptation to condemn her. It was she who dragged Thomas to Utah, obviously a bad move for them materially. She also bears major responsibility for her daughters' embroilment in polygamy and her son's forfeiture of his birthright at Dernford Dale. And Zion drew only a little closer to her Christian ideals than had the society of her English homeland. So one must look further in the attempt to understand Hannah King not only by her own measure nor by criticism but by the standards of distance and objectivity.

One of her diary entries reports a lecture given by a Dr. France in Salt Lake's Social Hall. His subject was midwifery and diseases of women. Hannah wrote: "He spoke good. Says he means to teach the men a few things one day. That *the world* said it was good for the men to have license in these things, but he said 'commend me to the man who can command his passions with only one wife, or no wife at all.' This was what Paul taught." To the doctor's words Hannah added her own opinion: "Verily, such is the man for me!"

Then she appended: "I long for the time when the Celestial

Law will be established. It will be a good day." Did she refer to polygamy, which was then commonly referred to as the Celestial Law? Or to virtue and mutual consideration in any marriage situation? Or to self-denial, even abstinence? For this third choice was soon implemented in her own marriage. A year later she would write, "Mr. King has been kind, and I sleep alone, which adds to my good feelings, for this has long been my desire." Did Hannah harbor a biblical or Victorian ideal of manhood which her husband did not fulfill?

If so, one cannot help feeling a bit sorry for Thomas King. In England he forfeited his livelihood, inheritance, and the regard of his peers by following his Mormon wife. In Mormondom he was an object of condescension because he did not go through the official motions of "him who should stand in his lot and place, and be a father and husband in Israel!" Though he sacrificed as much for the Kingdom of God as Hannah, at his death he was not even honored with an obituary in the Mormon newspaper. Here the tenets of Hannah King's pioneer religion seem unjust, even shallow, and one wonders what private ordeal Thomas endured because of them. Hannah did recognize the love which had motivated King to leave wealth and influence for obscurity and frustration. "That is something," she admitted.

What further clues are to be found regarding Hannah, her choices, and the outcomes of those choices? On board the *Golconda* Hannah had written to her brother, "I will not complain, for we are in a school that will do us all good." Later she noted in her journal about the emigration experience, "If I was proud, as my mother said, here came the humbling." And a notation in her diary after four years in Zion indicates that she felt the "school" of Mormonism had indeed further matured her: "Am I as happy as I used to be four years ago? Yes, withal I am quite as happy. My views are far more extended. I seem to take a mightier range, in fact, 'old things have passed away ... All things have become new.' The vacuum is filled which never was before in my happiest times."

For Hannah the development of the immortal soul took precedence over material considerations. And she was not alone; many

Victorians viewed life as a school that would teach virtue in the kiln of experience. So in Hannah's diary there are many entries like the following: "O! help me to improve, to gain ascendancy over myself, over my selfishness . . . Preserve me from the powers of darkness, from the weakness of my own imperfect nature."

She herself probably did not fully recognize some of the refinements to her character brought about by her Utah experience. Zion indeed leveled and made her more democratic. Remember the governess who received such effuse praise as a bosom friend in Hannah's later diaries? Actually, Hannah had earlier kept the girl firmly in her place out of concern for maintaining a position as lady of the household. Servant Ann, who had joined the church and emigrated with the family—doing chores while the King daughters giggled in the wagon—became more appreciated after Georgie's death when Ann tended Hannah "like a daughter." And Hannah's Utah diaries contain fewer of the complacent early entries in which she contemplates her untiring wisdom in managing her household.

The less-privileged life of Mormondom also taught Hannah to be more self-sufficient. "Why is it that I do not journalize as I was want [sic] to do?" she had written a year after settling in Salt Lake City. "One thing is I haven't time. . . . everything so different that I have not yet found my level, but I am rejoicing still in the work of the Lord."

It appears that, for all Hannah's aristocratic, self-absorbed delicacy, she produced strength and persistence in seeking her idea of God above self-interest. If this is not sainthood, it surely is an impressive attempt at sainthood. Perhaps it is impossible for twentieth-century readers, we being even more privileged than she, to comprehend this non-materialistic point of view or accept her (and Thomas's) sacrifices as meaningful.

Two Are Unknown

Tracing two women has been especially difficult. Alicia Allsley Grist was the young matron who wrote to the *Millennial Star* urging women to broaden their sphere of influence. Bright and articulate beyond the average, Alicia's fate in Zion is of interest.

Alicia Allsley Grist

Alicia appears in the Utah genealogical records as Elicia Allely Grist, born 1827 in Birmingham. Apparently Zionism tried her and husband John Knapp Grist from the start. They lost three of their five daughters before or while emigrating. A sixth was born in Salt Lake City in June 1866 but died that September.

John himself died the next year, only forty years old, the cause of his demise unknown. Elicia continued in the faith, having her youngest daughter baptized at eight years of age just as she had the older children. She remarried twice to gentlemen her own age, first a Mr. Surke, next Oliver Garthwaite, but nothing else about these marriages was found. Elicia herself died in McCammon, Idaho, at the premature age of fifty-eight.

One wonders if she went pleased or disappointed. We look further into the records to find meaning in her commitment to Mormonism. Since John and Elicia Grist had no sons who lived, the family name died with him. But Alice, Elicia's oldest daughter, married at age eighteen and bore fourteen children. Evangeline, the second daughter, married at twenty, had seven children, was widowed, married again, and lived to be seventy-two. Elicia Knapp Grist, the youngest, married at twenty and lived to be 89, although she apparently left no descendants. If numbers count—and in Mormon values they do—Elicia and John left a significant posterity numbered among the Lord's people. For now this is all we know of Alicia Grist.

Elizabeth Lewis

Another woman about whom there is little information is Elizabeth Lewis, the immigrant who wrote such shining reports from Manti to her friends and relations back in Wales. Some facts about her life can be gleaned from her two letters. She left father, mother, sisters, and brothers in Wales. She was married but preceded her husband to Utah, surmounting many obstacles to do so. She considered Gathering a duty and worried that her friends back in Wales would postpone baptism irrevocably and forfeit salvation.

She bore testimony to the Mormon gospel in eloquent, musical phrases, describing its "great sweetness to me" and the power, wisdom and love of God in the plan of salvation. She was certain Mormonism was "the religion of Jesus Christ."

In her letters she expressed satisfaction with the pious, democratic tenor of life in Zion where the leaders were chosen "from among ourselves" and the "only thing fashionable" was religious demeanor. She perceived this devout society as granting its members rights, enjoyments, peace, freedom and beauty.

After her initial delight at the absence of swearing or ungodliness, did the hard work of survival dim her enthusiasm? We do not know. At least twenty Elizabeth Lewises appear in the LDS church's genealogical records for the early 1800s. Our Elizabeth might have been born in 1824 in Merioneth to Robert Lewis and an unknown mother, and married Edward Giles Roberts eight years her junior (which may fit the unsubmissive tone of the letters). This Elizabeth Lewis died in Malad, Idaho, but she had two daughters born in Wales after 1850, the date of the Manti letters.

Or she might have been born in 1821 in Bedwelty, Wales, the youngest of seven children of Llewellyn Lewis and Mary Harry. This Elizabeth would have been a twenty-nine-year-old spinster in 1850, but there is no evidence she ever emigrated. Hopefully future research will identify Elizabeth Lewis, the Utah correspondent, and throw light on her destiny in Utah.

Conclusion

Perhaps British women were by and large a sour lot. As best they tried to fit in, their dissatisfaction seemed to persist. It was not Mormonism so much as Utah and the recurring insensitive husband that they found so difficuilt to embrace. Some gave up and returned to Britain. Some were too proud or poor or demoralized to admit defeat. Others adopted their new surroundings with resignation.

It is clear, however, that, among the odd libidinous maidens were mature, young-to-middle-aged women who, far from being coerced, brought their reluctant husbands across ocean and plains. Once here, what these women lost in cottage and garden, in happy families around a warm and plentiful hearth, they found in inner-growth and spiritual peace.

Chapter 10.

The Polygamous Minority

One of the surprises of women's history lies in the reality of Mormon polygamy. In contrast to the stereotypes, monogamy surpassed polygamy among rank-and-file marriages by a margin of at least two to one. Among polygamist marriages, a variety of family styles and circumstances was exhibited.

As with traditional marriage, there were happy and unhappy polygamous marriages, those in which the husband dominated and others with a decisive wife, some with shared power and decision-making, marriages marked by formal or informal separation, those interrupted by death and divorce, those which produced large families and some which were childless, couples in affluent circumstances as opposed to families which endured various degrees of poverty, and mixed-religion and mixed-race marriages.

Once an early convert assimilated the reality of polygamy, she no doubt looked about and reviewed these other, less sensational aspects of marriage relationships in her culture. When outsiders noted only the surface pattern of a male-dominated church hierarchy and inferred repressed and powerless females, the women felt discounted, resentful, and introspective.

The purpose of this chapter is to look closer at six polygamous women. Each of the six meets two criteria: (1) her history was told in enough detail to give a more-than-cursory look into her experience, and (2) she, if only in some superficial way, resembles one of the major stereotypes of Mormon women: naive shopgirl, gullible matron, or lowly fishwife.

The Naive Shopgirl

In the anti-Mormon literature the shopgirl was unmarried and of lower-class origin. According to the standard plot, she was converted by a Mormon elder, emigrated to Utah, and became another of the prisoners of Zion. Four of five ensuing histories follow this stereotype skeletally.

Susan Dermott Barker

We know a great deal about Susan Dermott Barker through lifelong journals and letters left by her husband. Susan was born in 1843 in Southampton, England. Upon her father's death, when she was eleven, she left school to help support her mother and three younger sisters. At eighteen she and John H. Barker, a nineteen-year-old waiter, were both working at Radley's Hotel in Southampton. He baptized her in 1861.

As a boy John and his sisters had been placed in foster homes upon his law clerk-father's imprisonment for debts. When his father left prison, his parents separated. Later John lived in London with his mother, who now supported herself as a seamstress and had joined the Mormon church in 1848. John had been baptized in 1859. Before meeting Susan, he was engaged to two separate girls, at least one of them a Mormon but both of whom died.

In April 1862 Susan and John received notification to emigrate on the ship *Manchester*. They borrowed money from John's brother for supplies and obtained a letter of permission to marry from Susan's mother. They were wed in the tent of company captain John D. T. McAllister just before starting across the Great Plains.

Nine years, four moves, and five to six children later, John and Susan were living in relative prosperity in Cache Valley, northern Utah. Through a brother who cowboyed in Texas, John learned the whereabouts of his younger sister Jenny, of whom the family had lost track in the breakup many years before. John began a campaign of annual letters in which he tried to entice Jenny to Utah, and through these letters he indirectly revealed much about his wife Susan's situation in the Mormon Zion. One of the earliest letters shows basic contentment at this time of their lives:

> I have worked at every kind of work a man can do in this country, harvesting, farming, building, driving team, school teaching, mines, but at present we live in our own house on our own land and I drive my own horse team and make my living by a little farming, a little school teaching (in winter) and working some little for others at the Silver Mines . . . It is a life that I like very well as there is no one to call master, it is all my own (letter dated Nov. 1871).

Eight years after this Susan and John's situation underwent a drastic change, although his subsequent letter (dated May 1879) to Jenny did not reveal it: "Susan is well and as nimble as a young sixteen and sometimes feels as young and as full of mischief—today is her birthday and I have taken her to Logan and bought her a new dress and a wringing machine." John mentioned attending April general conference in Salt Lake City but declined to tell Jenny that he had gone alone and, during his stay, taken "a young Danish girl" and "another Danish woman" as his second and third wives. There is no clue whatever in his journal or letters as to what motivated these marriages, but his taking two wives at once suggests a decision based either on principle or a directive from a church superior. Such directives often came to a man or couple who were thought to prosper.

About this time John acquired a town house in Logan besides "the farm house" in nearby Newton. The summer after his plural marriages, he wrote Jenny that "Susan has been living at the farm house and taking care of the cows, but we are now all at home in town . . ." (Aug. 1880). Unable that winter to find a job offering cash wages, he hired on with the Denver & Rio Grande Railroad, and later the Utah Northern, for five months. It proved a disappointing venture, costing so much in travel and living expenses that he decided not to repeat it. It was disillusioning in other ways as well, for the next year he kept his sons on the farm, insisting they avoid the railroad and mining camps "where they would be exposed to every evil." He himself spent that summer working as a shipping clerk in Logan Canyon during the weeks, returning home only on Sundays.

Four and one-half years after entering plural marriage, in November 1883, John wrote that Susan was "getting very heavy and fleshy and not able to do as much work." This is the first mention of Susan's health problems, and because of the timing one could construe her putting on weight and John's commenting on it as intimation of stress in the marriage. On the other hand, one could also view health and economic strain as predictable conditions for a middle-aged couple.

Certainly, the pressures of earning a living (no doubt attentuated by the additional families) took a toll, for as John's children from three families increased he wrote Jenny: "Perhaps you have heard of the eternal push and rush of the Yankee—we have a little too much of it here, we seem to live and work in a hurry & rush" (Sept. 1885). In a new country, he continued, with so much to be done, the residents wanted it all done at once or in one season. His own sons were "growing up with just such a spirit . . . It would be much better could we go a little slower . . . "

In 1886 John wrote Jenny that he wanted to visit her in Germany (where she was then living) but could not as "it takes some labor and thought and care to provide for my families." Work outside the farm was hard to get, and he was "not safe from the persecution now going on against the Latter-day Saints." In addition, Susan's health was "not very good." A year later John confided to his sister that Susan had stayed for two months in Salt Lake City "to consult the doctors about her sickness . . . Her health and life depends on care in eating and drinking and good nursing." Susan was still able to "be around but with more or less pain."

On 30 May 1888, at age forty-five and twenty-six years after arriving in Zion, Susan died. In telling Jenny, John confirmed the hints he had dropped that he was a polygamist: "I . . . have failed to inform you of my circumstances, for fear that in your want of understanding of the principle you might condemn me. In 1879 I took Christene M. Benson to wife who now has Myrinda 8 years old who often says, 'Father, why don't Aunt Jenny remember me as well as Jennie and Birdie,' and also Irvin 3 years old" (June 1888).

They had "all looked for [Susan] to live for some time yet" as her disease had not seemed to progress severely, "but she was taken . . . Oh, how lonely for the rest of us . . . there is NO SUSAN AT HOME NOW." He was sealed to his two previous fiancees (who had died in England), John continued, and now Susan was "with them and I have a place and home to go to when God shall please to call me hence."

John had obviously not discarded his first wife on the dung heap because he had tired of her. His letters suggest some of the strain and disappointment of polygamy, including the heavier financial burden and Susan's ill health which was perhaps aggravated by the sudden and continuing blow of having to share her husband. Otherwise the difficulties seem no more than those endured by many couples on the western frontier. Only one was unusual: John expected at any time to be arrested by federal authorities for cohabitation. He wrote Jenny that he foresaw a prison term but would not deny his plural wives and thereby "disgrace the children."

Susan's death was followed by a rift in the family. The plural wives had been living in Ogden during Susan's last illness, and John now moved Christene to Cache Valley. She would eventually bear him eight children. Johannah proved "false to her religion," in John's words, and refused to leave Ogden. In 1889, within a year of Susan's death, she sued for divorce, leading one to wonder if Susan had been the glue that held this plural family together, even if only as a diversion of jealousies. According to John, Johannah remarried "a worthless man" who "in one month . . . beat her and she has left him—and she is now alone in the world with my two Boys." Thus John once more found himself "with one wife and free from persecution . . . I feel lonely at times and have the Blues, natural to dyspeptics" (June 1888).

Susan Barker's story does not end there, for it is partly tied to that of her sister-in-law Jenny, whom she never met and who outlived her by forty-six years. John continued to write to Jenny about family life and economic conditions in Utah. The fall of 1889 brought a real estate boom and growing trade to the territory. The next spring Jenny, at age forty, wearied of her work as a governess to British families who had taken her to Ireland, the Austrian Tyrol, Italy, and Germany, and she agreed to come to Utah. John paid her passage. Jenny stayed a short time in Logan, then became a traveling companion to the wife of a Salt Lake City mining magnate and continued her adventurous life by traveling to Alaska and many western sites. Jenny liked Utah well enough that she married her employers' gardener, Stephen Stanford, in two ceremonies since he was LDS and she was Anglican. He lived seven years.

Jenny lived until 1934. The family history does not precisely state that she left Salt Lake City after her husband's death, but since John took a mission to Britain in 1909, the year Stanford died, it is possible one of his purposes was to escort Jenny home and that she passed the rest of her life in England.

If we were to combine the stories of Susan Dermott Barker and Jenny Barker Stanford, we might come close to the stereotype. Yet neither was a prisoner or abused, though disillusioned perhaps. Add to this Johannah's choice to leave her husband and Jenny's choice to remain Anglican after acquiring a Mormon husband, and we see considerable freedom to live and marry as one chose in the Mormon capital. Jenny was known by her Mormon relatives as "a gentle, refined lady, kind and generous, dearly loved," not as an outsider. The irony, I suppose, is that Christene and Johannah, though family, may have been treated for a time as outsiders.

Mary Elizabeth Hilstead Shipp

Another of the "shopgirl" class of British converts was Mary Elizabeth Hilstead Shipp, born in 1852 in Hull, York County, off the beaten track of Mormon conversion centers. She was a teenager when Milford B. Shipp, on one of his fourteen missions, became ill and was nursed by her parents, members of the local branch. About 1870 the family gathered to Zion, and Lizzie was eighteen when she married Shipp.

The family she married into was to become one of Utah's most accomplished, and as a plural wife Mary served both as agent and participant in this achievement. Polygamy seems to have been the catalyst for tremendous personal growth among at least some Shipp family members. Their story gives new meaning to the principle of enlargement. Unfortunately, Lizzie left no record of

{ 220 }

her life. So the story must be told mostly through the record of one of Milford's other wives, *The Early Autobiography and Diary of Ellis Reynolds Shipp, M.D.*

Ellis as a child was brought to Utah from the Midwest by her grandfather. She worked for a time in the home of Brigham Young, who took a father's interest in her. In time she was courted by Milford Shipp, considered a poor suitor by Young partly because Shipp's two previous marriages had ended in divorce. But Ellis married Milford anyway and made the marriage last.

Milford was ambitious throughout his life, volunteering for missions, seeking out polygamous life, and eventually law school. One Mormon myth about polygamy is that it was always undertaken with the first wife's permission. This was not the case for Ellis. Milford simply came home one day with the dramatic announcement that he was bringing "a sister and companion" into the house. Regarding this and others of her husband's behaviors, Ellis wrote, "It was many years before I believed that my husband could err—if he did, I always blamed it on myself. I should have known that every mortal is but human, and in this earthly probation we cannot expect perfection." Later Milford brought home another wife, and Ellis said, "I do not allow myself to become low spirited." Then he brought a fourth wife into the family, Lizzie Hilstead.

In the summer of 1873 Ellis was pregnant with their fifth child when she heard general Relief Society president Eliza R. Snow broach a plan to send sisters back East to study medicine so they could teach territorial midwives better obstetric methods. Someone asked Ellis why she did not go: "I thought it would be what I would love and delight in, if this knowledge could be obtained here. But the thought of leaving home and loved ones overwhelmed me and swept from me even the possibility of making the attempt." Maggie, the second wife, went instead. But Maggie stayed in the East only a few weeks before returning homesick.

Leaving her sons in the care of Milford and a childless wife, Ellis decided to go to Philadelphia to medical school. It was 1876; Ellis was twenty-nine years old, Mary Hilstead twenty-two.

At about half past three o-clock on Monday morning the old

whistle gave the signal of our arrival in the far famed city of Philadelphia. A crowd, a rush, extending of welcoming hands, friendly greetings, loving embraces (for others) . . . I was left *alone*, where a policeman had told me to remain until he could show me to the waiting room. Oh what strange sensations—to be alone in a strange City at such an hour.

Ellis slept on a bench in the station until dawn, then took the car to 1324-22nd Street where another Mormon woman, Romania Pratt, was staying. Romania took her over to the college and helped her register, pay fees and begin classes. "For a time I felt almost bewildered," Ellis wrote, "but soon my interest was awakened and I began to feel my desires for knowledge increase as I began to see and realize how little I knew." At times during the next few weeks Ellis almost decided to go home. When she did not receive letters on time she could not sleep. She was an early riser anyway, causing her roommate enough disturbance that Pratt finally asked her to find other quarters. Ellis fought a tendency to become depressed:

> A lady remarked to me today, "You always appear so sad, as though you were grieving over something." I wonder if it is really true . . . I endeavor to be cheerful or at least not to be melancholy. I know I have much to be thankful for, much that should make my heart rejoice, but it requires a constant struggle, a continued watchguard to keep myself from feeling lonely and despondent. My darling sweet little children, how Mama longs to see you. Oh, how my heart aches—oh, Milford, if I could just have one word from you, one look at your dear face.

Back home Milford had taken up legal studies, aiming to complete them by the time Ellis returned, an intimation of competition or pacing each other in this family becoming remarkable. Once Milford wrote to her somewhat sharply, and Ellis confided to her diary: "If I did not know him so well and understand his great desires for my success I should feel hurt, at times. His words, though bitter and sharp, have a good tonic effect and urge me ever onward." But there was so much to learn. Ellis was eager, and her excitement and triumph came to dominate her school journal. Back home, Lizzie Hilstead Shipp must have almost as eagerly read

{ 222 }

Ellis's letters, judging from her later devotion to Ellis's work. The entire family helped Ellis. From Mary, the childless wife, Ellis received letters telling what the baby was learning. From Maggie she at least once received a $20 bill. On another occasion, when Milford was too poor to send Ellis anything, Lizzie sent $50 she had earned from braiding and selling hats. Without these sister-wives, Ellis could not have finished medical school.

Ellis is credited with founding modern medicine in Utah. Returning home, she would train hundreds of midwives who in turn would take new ethics of cleanliness, sound anatomy, and safe delivery methods to settlements from Idaho to Mexico. Her midwives were far ahead of frontier doctors.

There are many interesting entries in Ellis's journal written before and after Philadelphia which reveal her grief when Milford took other wives. Ellis thought he did not love her or she did not satisfy him. He took another wife after Ellis returned home.

Yet in this case polygamy seemed to relax the demands of Victorian wifehood to allow Ellis a full-time career. She was not constrained by the old dilemma of how to manage the home front while in the workplace. She did not need to worry about a tendency to faithlessness by her husband since he had other women under a system which legitimized multi-partner sex for men, held them responsible for its consequences, and protected the women involved from many abuses short of grief.

What about Lizzie Hilstead, the poor English girl who happened into Milford's and Ellis's life? After Ellis's return Lizzie studied under her, read the medical books Ellis brought back, and eventually moved to Fillmore in central Utah where she taught classes, practiced obstetrics, and bore four daughters. Perhaps because of Ellis, Lizzie seems not to have suffered so agonizingly the pangs of her model elder wife who ended a book of poems with this statement: "Great minds are they who suffered not in vain. If wondrous True, we have suffered not in vain. I do not feel my spirit Great. But Oh, I have suffered—and pray it has never been in vain."

Hannah Greenwood Fielding

Another convert whose story conformed superficially to the

shopgirl-proselyte stereotype was Hannah Greenwood Fielding. The youngest child of a working-class Lancashire couple, Hannah was of the population that Theodore Winthrop ridiculed in *John Brent*. Lancashire women were said to have tongues like rattlesnakes and minds that could not comprehend anything not literal and prosaic, minds susceptible to the manipulations of wily Mormon elders.

Hannah joined the Mormon church on 15 March 1838, one of a thousand to be baptized in the Preston area the first year of the British Mission. One of those early missionaries was Joseph Fielding, a forty-one-year-old English bachelor who had emigrated to Canada, joined the church there, migrated to Nauvoo, then returned to England to introduce the gospel to former friends and relatives. Joseph's journal is one of the finest sources of information about the British Mission and its womenfolk.

On 11 April 1838 Joseph made a notation in his diary about a meeting which went "till near midnight" only to resume the next morning. Its proceedings were "for the greater Part spent in blessing. Many Tears were shed; a great Blessing was pronounced upon Sister Ann Dawson . . . And a good and great Blessing was confirred upon Sister Hannah Greenwood." Two months later Joseph married Hannah Greenwood. "Her age is near 30," he wrote, when actually she was nineteen. Either the family typist misread the original diary or Hannah misled Joseph, perhaps so that he would think himself only twelve years her senior rather than twenty-two, the reverse of the Mormon Elder deceiving the Proselyte. Joseph wrote in his journal, "I have not sought for Money in this nor do I get much of [it]," referring no doubt to the lack of a dowry. What he got was criticism from local members who worried about the burden a missionary's wife would place on branch and member finances.

This resentment probably increased when Hannah became ill and had to quit her factory job. It was in December 1838 that Joseph described things in the mission as "very dark," when their landlady Sister Dawson was contemplating moving to a smaller house "to get rid of us," and his missionary companion Willard Richards and wife were suffering from an extended "affliction" of some kind. But a year after their marriage Hannah and Joseph were still living with the Richardses in an apartment belonging to Mrs. Dawson, with predictable tensions.

Later in 1839 the Fieldings moved to Manchester, and in 1840 Joseph's work took them to Liverpool. By 1841 they were back in Preston where Hannah's first child was born. Joseph was Hannah's only attendant until "at the time of delivery" a woman from the branch arrived "as if by chance," followed by two other branch sisters. Joseph's diary entry gave thanks: "Freely our Bread has been given us . . ."

In 1842 or 1843 the Fieldings emigrated to Nauvoo, Illinois, in time to visit the temple before it burned in 1846. Three days after their temple sealing, Joseph was also sealed to Mrs. Mary Ann Peake Greenhalch, a forty-four-year-old Lancashire widow. She participated in the exodus from Nauvoo with Hannah and Joseph and bore three children between 1846 and 1848. All we know of Mary Ann Peake is that she continued in the faith until at least 1854 when she was rebaptized in Salt Lake City, and that she outlived Hannah by eight years even though Hannah was sixteen years younger. But this was after both she and Hannah spent many years as widows due to Joseph's early death.

Hannah may have been of poor socio-economic status and become enamored of a Mormon elder, but it appears that it was she rather than he who did the captivating. She felt free to speak her mind, and her husband was as frustrated to prevent it as any Victorian husband. In Preston, readers will remember, she had sharp words for the church for overloading her husband's schedule. Richards threatened her with disciplinary action. Though the details are sketchy, it seems that she permitted her husband to take a plural wife, neither of whom was disillusioned enough by this event to leave Utah after being "freed" by their husband's death.

Fanny Warn Stenhouse

Another English lass who fell in love with a Mormon elder was Fanny Stenhouse. This time the bachelor was the handsome, intellectual Scottish missionary, Thomas Brown Holmes Stenhouse, and Fanny would spend twenty years in the Mormon faith. Then, after apostatizing with her husband, she would take up the pen "to plead the cause of the Women of Utah" in two books, *Polygamy in Utah* and *Tell It All: The Tyranny of Mormonism, or An Englishwoman in Utah*.[1]

Born in 1828 or 1829 at St. Heliers on Jersey Island in the English Channel, Fanny was "one of the younger members of a large family" of Baptist parents and an invalid father. "When I thought of the future," she said, "I readily saw that if I desired a position in life I should have to make it for myself." At a plucky fourteen she went to France as governess to a British Army family. Soon she was teaching English and needlework in a French girls' school and taking instruction in Roman Catholicism. Perhaps to insert a romantic element in her story, she told of becoming engaged to "the wealthy Constant D———," brother to her gentleman master. But after several years, her desire for "an honorable social position" waned along with the appeal of Continental culture and religion. Fanny returned to England.

During Fanny's long absence, her parents had converted to Mormonism and moved to the mainland. Her older sister remained at St. Heliers, however, and Fanny visited her long enough to hear anti-Mormon stories from her and the brother-in-law, both by then disaffected members. This was the first Fanny had heard of the faith, and it was not a very encouraging introduction. She was told "the turbulent experience" of the St. Heliers LDS branch, where "improper conduct" by some elders had, according to Fanny's sister, "disgusted the people with their doctrines." Fanny had to agree that Mormonism must be "a vile delusion."

Yet Fanny felt the new church must have some merit if her parents had joined. Reunited with her parents and younger sisters in Southampton, she took it upon herself to attend a Mormon lecture with them. She was surprised to find Mormon teachings "in accordance with Scripture." In addition, she found her family changed. Her sisters were no longer silly, light-minded girls but now delighted in more serious things such as reading scripture

1. I have used the Travelers' Classics edition strangely attributed to T. B. H. Stenhouse of *Tell It All*, a reprint made in 1971 in New York by Praeger Publishers.

and serving the missionaries. There was new love and harmony at home which she attributed to the influence of the Mormon gospel.

Her resistance to the faith was not completely overcome until a young elder, of whom she had heard great praises from her parents and associates, spoke at a meeting. Over thirty years later Fanny would write almost nostalgically about this experience and the early days of the British Mission:

> Mormonism in England then, had no resemblance to the Mormonism of Utah to-day. The Mormons were then simply an earnest religious people, in many respects like the Methodists, especially in their missionary zeal and fervour of spirit. The Mormon Church abroad was purely a religious institution, and Mormonism was preached by the Elders as the gospel of Christianity restored. The Church had no political shaping nor the remotest antagonism to the civil power. The name of Joseph Smith was seldom spoken, and still more seldom was heard the name of Brigham Young . . .

Polygamy, blood atonement, the Adam-God theory, "together with the polytheism and priestly theocracy of after-years" were at that time "things undreamed of." The young elder talked about "the saving love of Christ, the glory and fullness of the everlasting Gospel, the gifts and graces of the Spirit . . . fortifying every statement with powerful and numerous texts of Scripture." Years later, in spite of revulsion at what she had come to perceive as the tyranny of Mormon patriarchy, she would remember these early days in English Mormonism as "among the most pleasant reminiscences of my life."

Fanny was baptized within three weeks of meeting Elder Stenhouse. Her baptism experience is described in the conversion chapter. Several months later she became engaged to Thomas and they were married on 6 February 1850. Not four months after the wedding Thomas was appointed to accompany Apostle Lorenzo Snow to open the Italian mission, and Fanny's grievances with Mormonism began.

Pregnant, unemployed, dependent on Thomas's family and local members for rent and food, she felt abandoned. By her account it was several months before she could obtain any sewing commissions, during which period she claimed to have gone two weeks at a time with only dry bread and water to eat. Her comment on this period of her life may be more an indictment of Thomas than of Mormonism: "Men who look for miracles, and count upon special providences for daily bread, are not generally very prudent or far-seeing in their domestic arrangements." In preparing for his new assignment her missionary-husband had had no thought for himself "and certainly he made no preparation for me."

Thomas found Italy hard ground for the Mormon gospel, and just days before Fanny's daughter was born he was reassigned to work with the Waldensians in Switzerland. He spent the winter learning French. Before this new mission began, Snow returned to England and discovered Fanny's situation. He chastized the local branch and summoned Stenhouse home. Donations were gathered, and when Stenhouse returned to Switzerland Fanny and little Clara went with him.

The years in Switzerland were said to be years of frugality, while in actuality Fanny had a Swiss handmaid the entire time who followed the Stenhouses to Utah. Arriving in Great Salt Lake City for the first time, Fanny found not the golden, godly society, but log houses and poverty, although she exclaimed joy upon first glimpsing the valley.

From her early marriage Fanny had heard talk that the apostles in Zion had plural wives. In England, when she questioned Thomas, "He did not deny it, but he would not talk about it, and did everything he could to banish the thought from my mind." Finally in 1852 he told her that the doctrine was to soon be publicly acknowledged, and when two elders early the next year delivered the issue of the *Millennial Star* which published the revelation on celestial marriage, Fanny was so upset she had to leave the table.

Fanny herself preached polygamy to female converts in Switzerland. From this point on Fanny's book is absorbed with polygamy. Though she claimed early rejection of it, such decisiveness was slow a-borning in this young wife so eager to live up to her husband's expectations. Long into her career as a Mormon, when a female friend admitted, "How I hate Polygamy! God forgive me; but I cannot help it . . . and yet I believe that it is true," Fanny's response was, "Poor child! I understood her too well, for her position was exactly mine."

Fanny said that Thomas promised early in their marriage never to take a plural wife. But once in Utah, his increasing influence and affluence as a newspaper publisher and his daily interaction with church leaders made this more and more untenable. Increasingly after 1852, polygamy was a qualification for advancement both spiritual and economic. Fanny's accounts of conversations with associates, selective as these accounts are, show that there was social pressure not only from church leaders but from friends and other polygamist wives. Yet Thomas "held out" for five years, perhaps because of his wife.

Fanny really did not have a chance. Thomas was ambitious, and she ambitious for him. When he began furtively courting a girl, Fanny looked on silently. When one day he asked her to meet with Eliza R. Snow, Fanny obeyed even though she guessed the purpose of the summons.

Sister Snow was the Prophetess of Mormondom. Although not the first plural wife of Joseph Smith, she was the most widely known of his widows and was assured a measure of autonomy and prestige in Utah by her marriage to Brigham Young as well as by her successful revival of the female Relief Society, which had been dormant since Nauvoo.

Fanny recounts in detail her conversation with Snow. By now Fanny had already consented to Thomas's taking a second wife but was not happy about it. She argued that her husband was not yet in a financial position, that he did not really want another wife, and that her own feelings made it an unwilling and thus ineffectual sacrifice. Sister Snow countered with arguments which could be interpreted as either good pioneer sense or calculated plays on guilt: "Where would the kingdom of God be if we had all talked in this way? Let your husband take more wives, and let them help him, and you will feel blessed in keeping the commands of God." And, "Your husband is a very good man, and desires to live his religion, and it is a great grief to him to know that you feel as you do." Finally, "If you had a loaf of bread to make, and you made it, and it was pronounced good, do you think it would be of the slightest consequence what feelings agitated your mind while you were making it, so long as it was well made?"

Personally wooed by Zion's elite, it was no wonder Fanny and Thomas succumbed. Indeed, Fanny was given far more time and attention during her struggle than most sisters. That she took the ministrations earnestly and tried to adopt the orthodox attitude is apparent in her account of daily self-attempts "to subdue my rebellious heart." She believed that her husband's lot was "irrevocably cast with the Mormons—I knew that when I married him."

Thomas's second wife, wooed both in Fanny's home under her eyes and at socials and the theater while Fanny sat home with the children, was the young and pretty Belinda Marden Pratt. Belinda's mother, Belinda Marden Hilton Pratt Box, had divorced her first and third husbands and was widowed by Apostle Parley P. Pratt.

By her own admission Fanny was barely civil to Belinda who lived with her the first year. Fanny says Thomas courted a third woman during the birth of Belinda's first baby. Belinda and Thomas divorced,[2] and the third marriage never took place.

To Fanny's retrospective delight, Thomas associated increasingly with non-Mormons and became embroiled in the Godbeite schism by 1869. Although Fanny's own daughter Clara was now a plural wife to Brigham Young's eldest son, Fanny wrote, "I took my stand with the heretics; and . . . my own was the first woman's name enrolled in their cause."

Thomas went to New York City to write his *Rocky Mountain Saints*, a somewhat objective work, and on her own subsequent visit to the East Fanny fell to writing a less reasonable book about her Mormon experience. She later lectured in major eastern cities about Mormon polygamy and theocracy. The Stenhouse children apparently abandoned Mormonism as well, for Clara Federata

2. International Genealogical Index 2.16—British Isles and Ancestral File 4.02, computer files of the Church of Jesus Christ of Latter-day Saints based on submitted family records, not verified by official birth and life records.

Stenhouse Young is the only one of the four mentioned in LDS genealogical records.

Fanny's autobiography is not as easy to evaluate as some. It would be facile to say that she came into the church murmuring and left it still complaining. Yet she sprinkled her book with deprecations, vague allusion, and loaded statements which tell only half the story. The paradoxical thing is that Fanny seems to have been sincere. She avoided outright lying, yet she appears to have seen, especially in her later life, only that which colored Mormondom as diabolical. She ended her autobiography with these words:

> Full of love for them—my sisters, my friends, the companions of my life hitherto, whose religion was once my own, whose hopes and joys I have shared, whose sorrows and trials have been also mine—with hopeful prayer I lay down my pen and present my labours to the world. And if my humble efforts shall have conduced, even in the smallest degree, to keep one sister from entering into this sinful "Order"; if they shall have aroused the women of Utah to investigate the foundations of their faith, to calmly and impartially consider the iniquities of the system of Polygamy to renounce the man-made slavery of the "Celestial Order" . . . I shall feel that my endeavours have been abundantly rewarded, and that my labours have not been bestowed in vain.

How could a woman's view change so radically? Perhaps by a process resembling a mid-life crisis: too many stresses which culminated in the uncovering of some early-laid fault lines. The breakline is distinct: polygamy was more than she could bear. By her own forthright admission, she lacked the emotional composure to make sacrifices with much grace. When asked to undergo the ultimate test, she broke. It was a mistake for her to have ever acquiesced to "celestial marriage." Through coercion she became a victim and spent the rest of her life getting revenge.

Throughout a re-reading of Fanny's book, one wonders why she did not divorce Thomas. Instead she insisted on beholding him in a stubbornly positive light, overlooking his frequent if non-violent cruelties to her and their children:

> During all his efforts to obey counsel and build up a "kingdom,"

my husband, I know, never ceased to love me. For the misery which he then, in—as I firmly believe—his conscientious endeavours to live his religion, inflicted upon me, I have long ago freely and fully forgiven him. I think that during all that time he never ceased to entertain the fondest affection for me; and, if he was foolishly confiding in those who he believed were divinely authorized and speaking by inspiration, can I blame him when I remember that I myself was actuated by the same faith?

Thomas gets off Scot-free. Fanny's worst blind spot regarded her own husband, from whom she called the idea of divorce "repugnant."

It is my opinion that Fanny's judgment snapped—that Thomas's willingness to enter polygamy was an unendurable reality to her mind. One wonders what would have happened to her marriage, much less her sanity, had Brigham Young not been available as an emotional stand-in for Thomas, with whom she never lost her temper.

Ironically, the woman who thought pioneer Mormonism deprived women of identity has been denied her eternal identity by modern Mormonism. In 1973 Thomas's standing in the church was reinstated while Fanny's inexplicably was not. All but her birth information was either never entered or was expunged from the Mormon record. Poor Fanny! Mormonism is less forgiving of female heresy than of wife abuse. Her consolation will have to be that her books sang a strong melody in the swan song of polygamy.

The Gullible Matron

The second stereotype is of the British wife struck twitless by a charismatic elder. She deserts her happy, middle-class hearth and cherry-faced cherubs only to be brought to ruin under polygamy. This type is rarely represented even on a superficial level among our histories. Most of the married women of the sample did not enter polygamy.

Hannah Daniel Job

One of the few who did was Hannah Daniel Job. Born in 1828 near Carmarthen, Wales, Hannah is the eighteen-year-old whose thirty-five-year-old fiance was studying for the Baptist ministry when Hannah became pregnant, dashing his plans.

Thomas has an interesting history more detailed than Hannah's. As a boy he was bright, eager to read and write, though his first chance to do so did not occur until he was sent to the parish school to learn the alphabet at age twelve. Later he attended a free Welsh school for two months where he learned to read but poorly. Then at age sixteen he "was put in school again over the winter to learn arithmetic . . . This was all the school my parents intended that I should have."

As a youth Thomas and a friend trained snakes. Later he became interested in alchemy, both of which disturbed his Methodist mother. She thought he was "playing with the devil when he played with snakes." His father considered her theory nonsense but insisted that Thomas be doing something "useful." So the boy was put to work as a mason's attendant and farm laborer. His wages went to his father, but whenever he could get extra work he would save the earnings to buy paper and pens with which to copy those few books he could borrow. These, in keeping with Welsh folk education of the day, turned out to be mostly about mathematical games, alchemy, astrology, and conjuring.

What Thomas really wanted was to go to college in the city, which eventually he was able to do through an offer from a generous acquaintance. This education, too, was cut short when he returned home on a visit to find his parents ailing and about to lose their farm with no sons left to work it. Pressured to remain with them, he stayed ten years, his dreams of further education destroyed.

It was while working his parents' small farm that Thomas met Hannah Daniel, whom Thomas's mother considered slightly evil because she was Church of England and danced. Later Thomas, Hannah, her mother, and her sister all became Mormons through the influence of Thomas's uncle. Between 1848 and 1853 Hannah bore three children, all girls.

After the death of his parents, Thomas felt free to emigrate, moving his family to Carmarthen for this purpose. But now it was Hannah who held him back. She, her sister, and her father wavered because of stories told about Utah Mormons, and she refused to subject her weak infant daughter to the voyage. This caused a rift with Thomas who had already paid their fares. Hannah took the children and returned to her parents' home in Abergwilly.

The family history states that before emigrating Thomas made one last visit to Abergwilly. Hannah would not even see him, but when two-year-old Elizabeth ran out to greet him, he picked her up and took her away to Carmarthen and to Utah. Hannah could do nothing under the laws of that time, he being the child's father.

Hannah was not the only wife left by an emigrating husband. One recalls Jane Strachan Heggie who refused to be baptized. Andrew Heggie left her with funds to emigrate should she change her mind, instructing her that he would wait five years before remarrying. Faithful to his word, he waited.[3]

Thomas Job, in contrast, met a Welsh girl on board the *Golconda*, Elizabeth Davis, who was also without family. She had worked in a woollen mill since age nine and had joined the church by herself. Her boarding was delayed because for some reason she was not listed on the emigration clerk's register. Thomas became interested in her, and they were married in August 1855, possibly even before arriving in Utah. The family history extenuates this by noting that it was not until two days after the wedding that he received a letter telling him baby Anne had died and Hannah and her mother were back in the church. He immediately wrote to Hannah offering to pay her fare to Utah but did not tell her about Elizabeth. It was only when he met Hannah's wagon train in Salt Lake City that she learned about the new wife.

Hannah now refused to live with Thomas in spite of his pleading that he needed her as he kept "two maids in the house always." She had to find a place for herself and daughters, but because no one would take a servant with children Thomas kept the girls. The strange story is told that Hannah found employment

3. Jane Heggie was born about 1815 in Scotland and married Andrew Walter Heggie, ten years her junior, a dye worker, and shoemaker, in 1848. They had one daughter. Andrew was baptized in 1852 and spent eight years trying to convert Jane before emigrating in 1860. He did not marry again until 1865.

as a housekeeper to a South Cottonwood widower, Albert Miles. Hannah "spoke only Welsh, he only English, and when he asked her to marry him, she brought him a glass of water." Miles took Hannah to see Brigham Young, who married them—in English. The point of the visit was not immediately clear to Hannah.

She was never very happy with Miles, who drank heavily, but family tradition is that she blamed herself for her situation. Her second marriage, she said, "was no more than I deserve," and she named her first son Thomas. Eventually she and Miles lived apart, and she spent her last years philosophically alone except for extended stays by daughters and grandchildren and a rare letter to her first husband.

Thomas's second marriage was reportedly a happy one which resulted in eight children, but he had his troubles as well. The daughter he had abducted ran away at age thirteen to live with her mother before marrying young. Thomas became uncomfortably persistent in his mathematical and astrological theories, writing letters to church leaders, apparently being alternately ignored and admonished for presuming to tell authorities what to do. When he began teaching that the Nauvoo church was the true one, he was dismissed from Mormonism. He served for many years as regional mission president for the Reorganized LDS church (led by Joseph Smith's son, who had remained in Nauvoo), a masochistic undertaking in Mormon country where Reorganites occasionally suffered mob violence.

In Hannah's case the stereotype of the gullible matron may apply, though she did offer resistance. Still, through illiteracy and trickery she was duped by two husbands, both Mormons, with perhaps unwitting complicity by the Mormon leader who married her to Miles. The wrongs are not clearly one-sided, for who knows what was said between Hannah and Thomas at that last parting at Abergwilly. And family tradition is that one reason for Albert's roughness was Hannah's refusal to love him. Yet Hannah had obvious reason to be disillusioned with Zion.

But she was not. Hannah's remarks in later years imply that she felt that if she had emigrated as counseled she would have kept her family intact. As time passed, rather than feeling imprisoned,

Hannah became more orthodoxic Mormon in her outlook, regretting her early defiance of polygamy and seeing the situation of a plural wife as preferable to separation from her children and an unhappy second marriage. When her son-in-law contemplated taking a second wife and her distraught daughter ran home for comfort, Hannah advised her to return to him "if she loved him and he was good to her, even if she had to share him."

One wonders if Hannah, like Fanny Stenhouse, was too forgiving of her first husband. She certainly seems to have been too hard on herself. To the modern reader she was shabbily treated. Yet in the context of the times, her perspective was perhaps unavoidable. Men ruled the roost. So when she weighed her travails against the virtues of home and family, she blamed herself for the way things turned out. A jaded view would be that in Utah this age-old story simply had a peculiar twist.

Ann Steel Murdoch

A woman who to all appearances overcame any ambivalence she might have felt towards plural marriage was Ann Steel Murdoch. This Scotswoman and her husband of four years were converted by her brother in 1850. They followed the brother to Utah two years later. On the steamboat voyage upriver to St. Louis, several of their children died. John blamed this on voyage leader John S. Higbee, who he felt did not provide enough food for survival. A proud man, John found himself begging for food but being turned down. One of those who refused later changed his mind and offered nourishment, but by then the Murdoch baby had died.

John had been brought to Utah to herd Brigham Young's sheep. When Young's livestock manager introduced John to the prophet, Young said "he had rented his sheep to brother Lorenzo Young for five years and didn't need anyone now," so John was without a job. Young told him to rest, eat, and the way would be opened for him to get work. John did a month-long stint as a laborer on an outlying farm before Young hired him to dig potatoes, which gave John "much joy though the work was hard, as he was working for a Prophet and the greatest man on earth."

Ann and John lived in Salt Lake City for seven years before

moving to Heber City near relatives, where they prospered . . . so much so that when the time came, John and Ann both "were impressed with the importance and necessity of observing this principle [polygamy] as well as any other of the gospel."[4] It is unlikely the Murdochs felt much external pressure, since their stake president and much of his high council were stubbornly monogamous in spite of threats of dismissal over the years by various church presidents.

The second wife turned out to be Isabella Crawford, a beautiful, dark-eyed twenty-six-year-old who had been thrown out by her English parents upon joining the LDS church. With four other mill girls, she emigrated to Massachusetts where she worked for five years before walking to Utah. There "Bella" continued in mill work. During a visit to an old mill friend who had married and was living in Heber, Isabella met John and Ann Murdoch. She married them in 1862.

Ann bore fifteen children (seven of whom died young); Bella bore seven. John was able to build "a large and comfortable home" for his large family, and it is said "both wives and all the children lived together [in different areas but] under one roof for many years in peace and harmony." One child was said to have been nursed by both mothers. Others joked that they sometimes did not know who was their real mother. Bella was known for her easy personality, listening to the children's troubles, and telling them stories. On John's and Ann's fiftieth wedding anniversary, formal camera portraits were taken of John with each wife.

The family had its difficulties. Late in life all of John's considerable herd of sheep was stolen by a hired caretaker and never recovered. John was imprisoned along with many other Mormon men for cohabitation. One wonders if Ann was initially as complacent under the husband-sharing system as the second wife who had not endured the dugout years. Yet Ann, her husband, and Bella became "a noble trio." In old age, after the deaths of Ann and John, Bella left the following testimony with her children:

4. Some of the narrative may be colored by the grandson who wrote the family history.

What am I that God has been so good to me and brought me, a lone girl, to this favored land and given me all the blessings and privileges of the gospel; where I am surrounded with prophets of God and the holy priesthood and friends on every hand? And I have had the privilege of associating with men and women of God and had a patriarch of God to be the father of my children. So I say, "What am I?" And now this world has no charm for me. I am waiting to go, and your father and mother are coming every night to me and I am waiting to go with them.

It is no surprise that some women suffered under polygamy. What is surprising—at least to me—is that other couples, so far from Fanny Stenhouse's experience and evidently out of pure devotion to their religion, triumphed over their natural instincts to create generally loving relationships among all parties. One has to be touched and even somewhat awestruck at this achievement.

An Informal Statistical Summary

Ninety-three of our histories were specific enough to answer some questions about Zion's treatment of immigrant women. Eighty histories that give definitive information show that fifty-one women were monogamous and twenty-nine polygamous, or 64 percent versus 36 percent.[5] Kathryn Daynes's study of Manti, Utah, found that second wives in polygamous households tended to be recent immigrants.[6] She also found that plural wives tended to have no family in Utah and to be disadvantaged economically usually through the absence or death of one or both parents. She proposes that young women whose parents were both living or who had other means of support married into polygamy less frequently.

Besides being predominantly immigrants, orphans, and indigents, plural wives tended to have been daughters of polygamous

---

5. This is apparently higher than the incidence of plural marriage among Utah women generally. Vicky Burgess-Olson concluded that 5 percent of Mormons were polygamists. But Ben Bennion compared two localities in nineteenth-century Utah and found that the percentage varied dramatically between areas, raising questions about the overall incidence.

6. Paper presented at Sunstone Symposium, 8 Aug. 1991.

parents. Sixty-six percent of polygamous daughters married in polygamy, whereas only 14 percent of monogamous daughters did so. This means that many of the daughters of our British women probably became plural wives. Finally, plural wives tended to be young, which conforms to the stereotype of the young exploited shopgirl. In 1860 the average marrying age for women in Utah was sixteen and one-half in spite of the numbers of widows, divorcees, and older women who had opportunity to remarry because of polygamy. The marrying age for U.S. women at that time was twenty and one-half, although one suspects it was younger for immigrant women. A surge of plural marriages among teenaged Utah girls during and after the Mormon Reformation of 1856 was largely responsible for this low marrying age, but in other decades as well the average age of Utah brides was dramatically younger than for women of any other region of the country. Only toward the end of the century, after 1890, did it rise.

If economic need was one factor in polygamous marriage, women in adequate economic circumstances should show a lower-than-average rate of plural marriage. Of our 100 histories, only thirty-three contained definitive marital and economic data. Of eleven who had satisfactory means of support, three married into polygamy anyway, one married monogamously, and the others did not remarry after divorce or a husband's death. Of twenty-two who could be considered in economic need at the time of marriage, nine married polygamously and thirteen married monogamously.

Another class of pioneer women should be considered—the unmarried. Among our histories, no woman remained unmarried, not even John Barker's spinster-sister Jenny. A governess in England for most of her life, within a year after arriving in Utah she had married an English gardener and widower, even though he was Mormon and she was not.

The question of our women's motives for entering plural marriage or choosing monogamy remains unanswered. Only Elizabeth Steadman wrote directly about her choice, and she did not give her reasons. Her letter reveals that she had her pick between single and polygamous suitors and she chose the single man. Was it because she preferred monogamy or George Steadman? We may be justified in supposing monogamy, for little romance seems to have been involved in this short courtship. Whatever her reasons, Elizabeth took a calculated chance on a man she hardly knew and saw it turn out well.

It is significant that two matrons who I initially thought were monogamous turned out polygamous: Charlotte Claredge and Elizabeth Handley. One wonders how many others, when further evidence comes in, will prove to have experienced polygamy, and how much this would skew the two-thirds/one-third finding. It was apparently not as easy to avoid plural marriage as I had first thought.

Of Charlotte Claredge's daughters, one became a plural wife and one did not. Elizabeth Claredge McCune did not because her husband was a "backslider." We assume that Jean Rio Baker's second husband, the one who lived only six months after their marriage, was a widower and not a polygamist. And Elizabeth Lewis's fate is unknown.

For so many first wives the choice was not theirs but their husbands'. Ellis Shipp would have liked to have kept Milford to herself. Yet for the Heber City Murdochs, it seems to have been a joint decision by all three parties. The Handleys on the other hand may have entered polygamy out of desperation to leave a posterity. Jane Ewer Palmer, Ellen Wilding Woolley, and others who came to Zion as spinsters apparently fell into the program because it was their only offer. Interestingly, nowhere in the histories does a woman eschew plural marriage because she did not like the idea.[7]

It should be noted that Vicky Burgess-Olson studied records of over 120 plural wives and drew the following conclusions. First wives, she thought, entered polygamy for the sake of "the princi-

7. In 1983, while teaching an American history class, I read a term paper from a student the subject of which was his ancestress from Heber City. It told how, when her husband was called to take a plural wife, she, the first wife, just said no. The husband accepted her decision. They were subsequently called to colonize a site in Utah's Dixie at which time they relocated. Regrettedly, I no longer recall the student or the ancestress's name.

ple" or under persuasion from the church hierarchy. Middle wives were motivated by economics in addition to theology. Youngest wives, exhibiting what Burgess-Olson labeled the "Amelia syndrome," had economics and status as their primary motives.[8]

What of our women's experiences as mothers? Of forty-two women about whom the histories give family information, only six were so fortunate as to have all their children live to maturity. Most families, mongamous and polygamous alike, lost infants and, less frequently, adolescents. Unlike Burgess-Olson, I found that polygamous women bore no fewer children than monogamous wives but almost precisely the same number: 7.74 births per woman compared to 7.75, of sixty-seven women total. The number of children of monogamous women to survive to maturity was 70.6 percent compared to 64.4 percent of polygamous women, but infant deaths in the Shipp family alone skew the figure against polygamous families.

Half of our women had only one husband during their lifetimes. But this does not mean that half lived in traditional, monogamous marriage to old age. Only fourteen (of seventy-four) enjoyed this privilege. Ten were widowed prematurely and six died in middle age. The rest were plural wives. Thirteen married twice and three married three times.

Ten out of seventy-two women elected divorce or estrangement from a husband, seven of them from a plural marriage and three from monogamy. This incidence of divorce is probably understated, for each time I found further information on a family another divorce or separation was discovered.

Does the higher number of polygamous divorces indicate dissatisfaction with polygamy? Only in some cases. Some women left one polygamist only to marry another. Maggie Shipp was one. She married B. H. Roberts after divorcing Milford. What the divorce rate suggests is that women unhappy with plural marriage were not chained to the system as the stereotype claimed. Some

8. Vicky Burgess-Olson, "Family Structure and Dynamics in Early Utah Mormon Families: 1847-1885," Ph.D. diss., Northwestern University, 1975.

husbands provided for ex-wives. And given the availability of marital prospects in Utah territory, a divorcee could be fairly confident of remarrying.

Regarding life expectancy, polygamous women outlived monogamous women. Of fifty-eight giving information, forty-one monogamous women lived to an average age of sixty-nine, while seventeen polygamous women lived to an average of seventy-four. This most likely means nothing, yet it is worth considering that polygamous life meant the sharing of domestic chores which in frontier poverty could be exhaustive. This may have been partly what Dr. Ellen Brook Ferguson meant when she argued that polygamy brought the redemption and salvation of women, although one suspects her meaning was also political and sexual.

By their own assessment, how did Zion treat British women immigrants? Only twenty-eight of the histories reveal directly or indirectly opinions about their experiences. Seventeen (fourteen monogamous women, three polygamous) indicated that the experience was a positive one. Four (two and two) expressed dissatisfaction. Six (four and two) characterized their lives as predominantly hard but expressed either resignation or acceptance. Three (three and zero) said Zion was a mixed bag of good and bad.

I have attempted to rate each woman's external circumstances as either poor, fair, good, or excellent. The allocations are subjective. Nevertheless, out of sixty-eight giving information on this subject, twenty-seven or 40 percent can be characterized as poor throughout most of their lives in Zion. Of these, eleven were polygamous. Seventeen (25 percent) were fair (only three of these were polygamous), twenty-one (31 percent) good (nine polygamous), and three enjoyed excellent economic advantages (two polygamous). These comparisons suggest that a plural wife's circumstances tended to be either good or poor, not mediocre as was the lot of many a monogamous woman.

If we asked whose lives were made difficult for at least one sustained period of several years to a decade because they followed Mormonism, thirty women would respond affirmatively. Seven women sacrificed considerable money and property in emigrating. Six women obviously suffered because of poor economic and farming conditions in Utah or because they lacked the skills to master the frontier. The church made life hard on many women through cumbersome church callings which took their husbands away from home.

We have already discussed the problems of plural marriage peculiar to Mormon affiliation. But other church doctrines also created hardship. For instance, an order to pioneer a new community brought new dangers and prolonged hardship. Charlotte Claredge experienced this; Felicia Astle relocated three different times by calling and exigency.

Another two women suffered greatly through persecutions directed at Mormon converts. Mary Ann Maughan lost her bridegroom of several months to consumption after he was tarred and feathered by an anti-Mormon mob. During divorce from an abusive husband, Margaret M. Blythe lost custody of her children because of her religion; she spent many years in Utah "yearning" for them. Happily, in her later years she was able to visit them in the east, and a son eventually settled in Utah while others vacationed there.

Finally, at least one woman may have died from the massive toil of establishing a kingdom in the desert. Rachel Jones Price lived only into her forties, never seeing beyond the family's most difficult years in Sanpete County when her husband strip-mined coal by Brigham Young's direction. Only after her death did he acquire a store and postal franchise and live an easier life with his second wife, a widow.

But if some women suffered because of Mormonism, others just as clearly benefitted in one way or another. Sarah Hattersley Wells's husband could find no work in England; he had no trouble finding work in Utah. Susan Dermott Barker's husband bragged that "the poorest in Utah are better off than the poor in England." Though he sometimes had to scramble for cash for his three families, he was never disappointed with the opportunities available in the Mormon kingdom.

People who had no chance of owning land or becoming full citizens of Great Britain found multiple opportunities for homesteading in the Great Basin. Mary Jane Ewer Palmer, for all the ruggedness of her life in Skull Valley, improved herself in status and property by leaving England. Even though William Budge's missions slowed his economic progress, moving to an outlying settlement proved a smart choice and the family prospered. Sarah Jeremy called her little home in west Salt Lake City "The Willow Basket." It was pretty, and she owned rather than rented it as did most Welshwomen their row houses in Carmarthen. And while those who took up farming in arrid Utah thereby took up their cross, most were glad for the opportunity.

Some women could not have done worse than in Britain. Veronica Giles had such "a hard life" in Scotland that frontier poverty could only have been a step up. Martha Cumming Clark would most likely have spent her life in menial labor had she not emigrated to Franklin, Idaho, and met and married an indulgent widower. Elizabeth Wilkins Steadman and Jennie Barker Stanford hailed from better circumstances, but they may well have remained spinsters had they not gone to Utah.

One happy benefit of emigrating was reuniting with friends and family from the old country. In Salt Lake City Anna Evans Jenkins was offered a furnished house by her son David, but she opted instead for Samaria, southern Idaho, where many of her Welsh friends had settled. Says the history, "The weariness of her journey disappeared instantly when familiar voices called, 'Anna, croesaw i America. Yr ydum yn gobeithio y byddwch yn gysyrus yma.'"[9] She would recount this welcome many times to her children and grandchildren. When later she moved to Malad Valley so her sons could obtain land, the parting was eased by Samaria's proximity and the success her sons would make in farming, livestock, general merchandising, and grist milling.

Many female immigrants experienced intellectual, educational and career opportunities not possible for them in the old world and scantily available in eastern America. Until Congress took away the female franchise as a condition for statehood, Utah women were full citizens with the rights to vote and hold office.

9. Loose translation: "Welcome to America. We hope you will be happy here."

One British immigrant, Dr. Martha Hughes Cannon, ran against her husband and was elected to the state legislature. Scores of female immigrants became trained midwives through obstetrics courses taught by Dr. Ellis Shipp, and others were "called" to study medicine at eastern colleges. Polygamy freed some wives from home duties so that they could practice their professions.

Among our women, most kept the faith. Of fifty-three who wrote enough to draw conclusions about their choices, it is safe to say that forty-seven were followers of Mormonism to their deaths. Only six left the church, were excommunicated, or expressed serious doubt about the value of Mormon doctrines or of Mormonism as a way of life. Dr. Ellen Brooke Ferguson, after spending twenty years defending Mormonism and polygamy at international women's conferences and before Congress, retired into Theosophy in 1897, was eventually excommunicated, and died in New York City. Sarah Evans Jeremy was excommunicated for unknown reasons. She may have aligned with the RLDS church whose local leader Thomas Job attracted a large Welsh following. My ancestress, Eliza W. Horrocks, ultimately rejected counsel to abandon non-believing spouses but retained other Mormon beliefs. Fanny Warn Stenhouse, of course, threw out the bathwater if not the baby.

Two women were non-members who remained essentially friendly toward Mormonism. Jane Barker Stanford never joined, though she married Mormon Stephen Stanford. Eliza Chapman Gadd emigrated only because her husband wanted it and appears never to have been baptized although she assumed the burdens of Mormonism including accepting a church call to go east to study midwifery. She eventually delivered 2,000 babies.

Conclusion

A fitting end to this lengthy chapter is the abbreviated but purposefully-chosen history of Mary Jane Ewer Palmer, the home weaver who chose to emigrate rather than hand over her five-year savings to bury her younger siblings. The poverty of her childhood was so relentless that emigration even now seems to have been her only hope of a future. What became of Mary Jane Ewer in Zion?

She left for Utah alone in 1866. In Salt Lake City she obtained some kind of work and sang for a year in the Tabernacle Choir. Perhaps that is where she met James Palmer. In August 1867, less than a year after arriving, she became at age twenty-one his third wife. James, who was not wealthy but had marketable skills as a contractor and stonecutter, joined the church in England six years before Mary Jane was born. His first wife married him in 1842, his second in 1851. How burdensome his family responsibilities were cannot be ascertained due to absent genealogical records on the other women.

James apparently meant to support Mary Jane by homesteading. Perhaps by church counsel, he set her in Tooele, a pretty settlement on the west slope of the Oquirrh mountain range a long day's ride west of Salt Lake City. Their farm in Tooele was not an immediate success. The first year brought low yields for unexplained reasons, and the second year most everything was eaten by grasshoppers.

James then moved Mary Jane further into the west desert to Skull Valley, described by a daughter as bleak, desolate and lonely. It had its amenities, nestled against the west slope of a minor range which caught the clouds and created rainfall to feed a few small streams and springs—but it was forty miles from the nearest settlement. Here all but one of Mary Jane's thirteen children were born (only eleven of whom are listed in the LDS genealogical records). One of the hardest conditions was fear of Indians. Several pages of the history are taken up with tales of unnerving but non-violent encounters with Goshutes.

James worked in the city to earn cash for improvements and could have spent at best no more than half of each month with his third family. So five-foot, 120-pound Mary Jane did most of the homesteading, working by hand, heating water which she hauled from the creek a block off on an outdoor fire, making her own soap from lye. In the early years, when she and her small children ran low on food, they picked watercress, pigweed greens and sego roots. Her babies came at regular two-year intervals, and four days after each birth she was up baking bread. It was a rough pioneering way, but it must have provided the hope of a good life. At least she was her own boss and the land was hers (if legally James's). She planted an orchard which in a few years began to bear.

Other than work, there were few diversions in Skull Valley. Settlers walked or rode eight miles to church, a cabin which Mary Jane arrived early to clean each week. Mail was delivered once a month. James's visits must have been a bright spot once or twice a month. He taught Mary Jane to read and write and began a tradition of accompanying hers and the children's singing by playing his clarinet.

Mary Jane's main solace must have been her children. One guesses at her sensibility of this, as she gave each of them Ewer as a middle name. At ten Henry, the oldest, helped her till, sow and harvest one hundred bushels of wheat and vegetables of which they were proud. For a time they made charcoal to be sold by James to the forges in Salt Lake City. One wonders what James did with the cash. Surely it went to advancing the farm, for later Mary Jane described those twenty-three years in Skull Valley as "years of poverty, trial and finally years of plenty." She told her daughter Fannie she did not mind the constant hard work so long as she was able to keep her family healthy. "She had trained herself to take her pleasure at her work, no matter what situation arose."

Mary Jane lost her second child at only a month old. A more profound tragedy was the death of Henry at eighteen by appendicitis. After this, wrote Fanny of her mother, "she was no longer happy on the farm." In 1890 Mary Jane moved to Grantsville to be nearer her married and working daughters and closer to medical care for her younger children. Apparently she bore two more there. The last would have come in about 1892 when Mary Jane was forty-six. How she supported herself in Grantsville is not told, perhaps from the sale of the farm.

In 1894 James, now seventy-four, married a fourth time. The records do not show the woman's age, whether she bore him children, and if this further diluted his time and influence with Mary Jane's still-young family. Nine years later James died, leaving Mary Jane with at least three teenagers still at home, the youngest thirteen. She lived a widow in Grantsville thirty more years.

{ 247 }

On the surface, Mary Jane's treatment by Zion seems dismal, her existence there a half-life. With exquisite understatement, she herself summarized it in these words: "Marriage is not a bed of roses. The trials of life begin with marriage. When things get hard, stand by your mate and don't weaken . . . " She added, "I have no regrets except that I might have lived a more perfect life." Her attitude reminds one of the Quaker poet's philosophy: "Clearly if there is beauty to be found/ I must seek it within me."[10] Perhaps the crowded drudgery of her English childhood prepared her for an adult life of stark isolation. On the other hand, perhaps her adult life was not stark at all but rich in children, a good if sporadic marriage, her own ground to till and plant and build on, neighbors and community on Sundays. One thing is clear: Mary Jane subordinated many expectations for this life to her hopes for the next. Like many Mormon pioneer women, she chose to see her external world through the inner eye of eternity.

Mary Jane's most lasting accomplishment was her children, including Fannie Palmer Gleave, the daughter whose keen attunement of the material and spiritual and even keener style of expression provided Mary Jane a memorable epitaph. It might serve as epitaph for an entire generation of Mormon women: "It was said of her that few women of civilized countries gave more and asked less of life . . . Thousands like her have been missed by historians."[11] Mary Jane Ewer Palmer reminds us that to a great extent Zion prospered on the backs of its women whose voices have yet to be heard.

10. Excerpt from Bayard Taylor's poem, "Home Pastorals," from Henry Seidel Canby, *The Brandywine* (New York: Farrar and Rinehart, 1941), 252.

11. Fannie Ewer Palmer was Mary Jane's eleventh child and fourth daughter, born on June 17, 1888, at Skull Valley. Fannie waited until age twenty-six to marry John Ernest Gleave, and she resided for years at 971 Diestel Road in Salt Lake City. She rather than children of the first wives came into possession of her father's journals.

Conclusion

After all is read and considered, were the stereotypes true, the Victorian image of "suffering Mormon womanhood" valid? Were they dupes in the beginning, docile victims in the end?

With some exceptions, the quality of women's lives in Zion seems not to have deteriorated from what they had experienced in Great Britain but rather improved in important ways. In Utah they had new opportunities to own land, enter careers, and raise children under the precepts of Mormonism. Church could be an annoyance and hindrance to economic stability, but just as often church society was a buffer against privation. Most saw tithing and mission calls as prepayments on heaven's blessings—"fire insurance," if you will. They viewed obstacles through the eyes of faith rather than materialism.

A woman's first weeks in Mormondom were frequently a honeymoon. Then reality set in. This was not Nirvana nor did most expect it to be. There was no escaping the real world of working, paying bills, fighting insects, surviving natural disasters, starting and settling family squabbles, coexisting with neighbors, and enduring selective government policies. Zion had its unscrupulous men: those who took more than they gave, borrowed and did not repay, landowners and agents who sold useless farmland. But women's disappointments usually centered on dead-beat husbands rather than on church leaders. There were no harsh words for Brigham Young, Heber C. Kimball, bishops, or stake presidents, except from Fanny Stenhouse. Not that victims can be counted on always to recognize the sources of their abuse, but, aside from the patriarchal realities of the time, women seemed to have as great a shot at happiness in a caring Mormon setting as in an indifferent Old World environment.

For two of every three British immigrants, their lives were what today's middle-class would call hard physical circumstances, yet usually not as stark as in the factories and sweatshops of

Manchester and London. Infant mortality was high. Six out of seven women experienced the death of a child. Only one in five enjoyed a traditional, one-spouse-'til-death marriage. One in five ended a marriage by divorce or separation.

For those of fortunate estate in Britain, Zion often proved an upender and leveler. If a sister arrived with cash in her purse, within a short time she was likely to find herself no richer than her neighbors either through her generosity, illness, sharpsters, or a church directive. One imagines Brigham Young eyeing families for signs of prosperity and calling on them to make a sacrifice. The oblation might take the form of adopting another wife, filling a proselyting mission, or colonizing an outlying corner of the Great Basin.

A couple had the option of saying no, and some did, but not many. Gentiles looked at Young's power, his comparatively grand homes and properties, and called him a hypocrite. With at least twenty-seven wives and fifty-six children, he did not skimp in the family arena. He employed twice as many as he wed or adopted. True, he never left the territory to proselyte, did not relive the hardships of colonizing yet another satellite community, and at his death his funds were inextricably mixed with church funds. But he came to see the church as his family and himself an indulgent father. With that view came both the benefits and pitfalls of paternalism. There was a level of security and love, but he expected obedience and respect in return. Many immigrants believed they needed the kind of direction and support the system provided. Others chafed under its regimentation.

The greatest social and economic leveler was not Brigham Young but the frontier. This was especially true in the early decades, although subsistence farming would always be precarious. Even today visitors from the Midwest, where farmsteads are immaculately white- and red-washed, wonder why Utah farms look so down-in-the-mouth. The answer is that Minnesota farmers do not have to irrigate.

Utah farmers deal alternately with drought and flooding along with grasshoppers and rocky soil. When they might have been painting their barns they had to build reservoirs, grade and line canals, repair reservoirs, dredge ditches, shore up reservoirs, take water turns, and rebuild reservoirs. Later, when open channels gave way to enclosed, pressurized watering systems, the workload shrunk to morning, noon, and middle-of-the-night pipe rearranging.

Immigrants like Jean Rio Baker, who dreamed of becoming a Jeffersonian gentlewoman farmer, came to a place better suited to sheep ranching and mining. The more prosperous families engaged in the latter, or merchandising, rather than agriculture. The Great Basin was not a bread basket.

Thus, most everyone in Utah had problems. If an immigrant came expecting to be "at ease in Zion," she was soon disabused of her hopes. Many understood this and were not surprised at the drudgery required to grow roses in the desert. Like Elizabeth Lewis, they wanted to build the City of God where no one blasphemed, profaned the Lord's day, or found fault with the prophets of God. Material success was less important than spiritual citizenship.

But what of the spiritual kingdom? How did the women fare in this respect? If speeches from the Tabernacle are an indication, the priesthood brethren derived spiritual identity from "wearing the pants" in the church and flexing leaderly muscles against women. For all their protests of estrangement from Victorian society, they shared the era's most basic attitudes, particularly in their strict definition of sex roles. He was considered a poor priesthood holder who could not control his wives or who allowed a woman to make family or church decisions. One expression of this ethic was the quashing of the Polysophical Society.

Was there a dark side to Mormon patriarchy and polygamy? Of course. As one non-British pioneer woman put it, "The ordinance is from the Lord; but it would damn thousands."[1] In a system that ratified female subservience, women were bound to suffer. For starters, the thoughtlessness in relationships with pre-

---

1. "History of Sarah Studevant Leavitt (Copied From Her History by Juanita Leavitt Pulsipher, June, 1919)," mimeograph booklet in my possession, 23.

sent wives and inconsideration in selecting new ones seemed driven by the idea that polygamy was a male right rather than a sacred dispensation. Husbands' callous disregard for wives shows that men who shunned the very idea of dishonorable treatment of a fellow did not necessarily extend these scruples to women and children.

Very early, a theology developed to rationalize plural marriage. In 1852 Orson Spencer was already saying that monogamy was "unnatural," implying that either reproductive facts or masculine libido or both justified more than one sex partner for men. There developed a preoccupation with the doctrine of celestial marriage. It became a primary, indeed paramount, principle of Mormonism. It also evolved into an overweening measure of a man's fitness on either side of the veil.

Perhaps not everyone bought into this attitude; then again, maybe monogamists did not have the means or clout to take a place among the dominant members of society. Among our women, the percentage is two to one for monogamy. Although polygamy was the norm for Utah's elite, it was not the lifestyle of choice among common Mormons even during its heydey. On the occasion of the Manifesto, Susa Young Gates, Brigham Young's daughter, chided the sisters for their complacency toward the Principle. One guesses most of her readers did not beat their bosoms in self-reproach.

For every woman who expressed disillusionment with the Mormon system, two others saw things more favorably, often without losing a sense of realism. Rebecca Elizabeth Howell Mace phrased this when she heard that a friend, Dr. Harris, had joined the church: "I told him I was pleased to hear it, but I told him he would find many stumbling blocks to overcome, but the actions of men does not change the truth of the Gospel." She meant by men's actions the actions of individuals. But her choice of words leads to the point that overbearing men were known to exercise their authority unreasonably.

It should be recognized that Victorian attitudes toward masculinity and feminity were embraced by Mormon women as well as men. There is the ironic fact that under the Mormon system of male dominance and plural wives, females assumed unusual freedoms. The mechanism of this phenomenon should be further explored, as well as why Mormon society has not continued in the vanguard of feminism but has actually fallen behind in recent generations. The catalyst could have been necessity; that, through sharing one man, women were left to make their own economic way and in so doing learned independence. Perhaps polygamy was not the catalyst at all, and a group of extraordinary women and men were simply social innovators. Keener examination of the Shipp family could provide some clues to this question.

If polygamy took on other purposes than religious and procreative, it proved to be a viable form of marriage for hundreds of Mormon families. Kimball Young, interviewing in the 1920s surviving wives and children from these early polygamous families, concluded that 50 percent of the families had been successful. Other studies of Mormon polygamy are rife with positive judgments by survivors of the great experiment.

There were, if not apparent then at least available, escape routes from polygamy and its desert society. Some women left Zion altogether, moving to California, returning east, or back to Britain. Others stayed but left the church or retreated from it emotionally or married a non-Mormon.

Marriage was fairly fluid in pioneer Mormondom, getting into and out of it relatively easy. Even the monogamist majority did not enjoy the one-partner standard fitting the popular perception of the Victorian days. My grandmother used to say that divorce was not an option for women of the "old" days. The histories do not bear this out. I suppose the attitude of my grandmother's generation evolved later. Fanny Stenhouse, perhaps showing her French Catholic influence but making a valid observation, complained that divorces were granted too casually in Utah. Very possibly the increased demand for wives stimulated by plural marriage made it feasible for early Mormon women to leave unhappy situations.

Divorce was not the norm, but spouses who did not get along lived apart or obtained a dissolution of marriage from Brigham Young. The prophet did not condone this—indeed, forbade at least one of his own daughters to separate (although she quickly obtained her divorce after Young died)—but apparently considered it worse to lock a woman into a relationship she did not want. Fourteen percent of our histories report divorce or separation.

We see evidence that some of our women became more independent as they grew older, daring to express views not in strict accord with church doctrine. But for every such woman there was another who is described as gathering her grandchildren around her to tell exciting and faith-promoting incidents from her spiritual trek for the gospel's sake.

It is tempting to conclude that a woman's attitude toward Zion depended on her experience with it. But this theory does not hold true. Many who endured the hardest conditions were the most stalwart in their loyalty. What they lost materially, they felt they had sacrificed for their own and their descendants' ultimate betterment.

Despite the tendency of the Mormon frontier toward leveling, the rich becoming poorer and the poor improving their situations, there appears to be surprising diversity in the women's lives in other areas. There were career women like Maggie Shipp and homebodies like Bella Murdoch. Some became interested in social causes, others in arts and letters. In short, there is a story in the records for every reader.

One can find, among my one hundred women's histories, confirmation somewhere for nearly any stereotype. But in every woman's history is also a resounding repudiation of the composite stereotype. No one woman even comes close to resembling the rude, mean, thieving, superstitious, perverted, abused, abandoned, verminal subhuman of the Eastern and European presses. It was probably inevitable that these women would inspire curiosity and contempt from their conventional contemporaries—just as Utah's modern fundamentalists baffle today's Mormons. We don't understand them. We have difficulty imagining a woman choosing to remain in such an arrangement. Mormonism has in many ways turned from its past, until the polygamous, isolationist, millennialist ethic of the pioneers now seems a peculiar code of a peculiar people living in a peculiar time.

If the stereotypes are not valid, how should these women be

defined? Perhaps by comparing them to today's Mormon women. If there are affinities, devotion to Mormonism would be the most obvious. Another is the ideal of dedication to children and husband over material, career, and personal development.

Miscellany of circumstance is a third similarity. After several generations as predominantly white, middle-class, and American, Mormonism has again become a meeting ground for people of many origins, expectations, situations, and viewpoints. Today's worldwide church is no more homogeneous than was pioneer Utah. The pilgrimess's progress from preparation to initiation to sturdy devoteeship is once again the primary and sometimes only shared experience between Mormon women.

As to differences, it could be ventured that twentieth-century, college-educated sisters are not as trusting as the Victorians were but are more sophisticated toward, even skeptical of, institutional authority. Yet some observers would claim just the contrary, that modern Mormons are overly socialized, placidly conforming to church, husband, and other authority.

One could also speculate that Mormon women of the 1990s, while generally supportive of priesthood authority, are more sensitive to women's issues and less accepting of female subordination. Yet it would be hard to find less subservient females than those early contributors to the *Woman's Exponent*, the Polysophical Society, and the Relief Society in pioneer Utah.

Another point of departure between generations is in physical circumstance. It may be impossible for us to comprehend the isolation, direct dependence on nature, and need for self-sufficiency of the pioneer experience. Recently the writer spent two years in central Utah in a pioneer adobe cottage without heat, hot water, or bathroom. While exhilarating, this adventure was also sometimes frightening. We might wake up to rain leaking all around our bed and know that morning would bring another 18-hour day of hard labor. There were times when we wondered, trying to survive as outsiders in a deprived economy, whether we would literally lose all but the clothes on our backs.

But there was at all times a buffer between us and starvation. Little more than an hour away was the city with plentiful supplies and our leased-out suburban house. Still, we wanted in the worst way to succeed. It took many months for us to buckle under our failure to grow enough food at 6,000 feet altitude in dry, rocky soil, the exasperation of trying to get ahead without a tractor or a water share. Thus we began to understand, in small degree, the ruthlessness of those pioneers' lives. They had no buffers but their own hands and God.

So if it is untenable to compare ourselves to them, and if they were not the lowly creatures of the literature, who were they? Statistics and generalizations do not adequately define them. Perhaps the best measure is the intangible one. Twentieth-century readers may be too steeped in materialism to put much stock in romantic notions such as, "It's not in whether you win or lose but how you fight that counts." Our great-great-grandmothers put stock in character development. What did Zion produce in the way of feminine saintliness?

Jean Rio Baker gave up home, business, friends, family and country for the privilege of years of frustration. Yet, instead of wasting herself in bitterness, she turned philosophic, grew closer to her Creator, and tried to enjoy the trip. Elizabeth McCune could have lived in any home on any continent she wished, associating with only the privileged in great luxury. She chose instead a relatively modest cottage among common neighbors with service through church committees.

The Shipp family had its contentions and disaffections, but they managed to turn these problems to good. The contribution of this curious but remarkable family has only begun to be estimated. The Murdoch trio—Ann, John, and Bella—lived in one house in general love and harmony for several decades. The Murdoch children grew up with little idea of the forbearance exercised daily by the adults in their lives.

Could any good thing come out of Skull Valley? Yet Mary Jane Ewer Palmer wove a selfless, productive life out of the sparsest of materials. She created happiness from her work and her farm and from matters of the heart and spirit. She worried only that her children had medical care and that she had not given enough of herself.

Susan and John Barker maintained humor and affection for each other not only through the tribulations of homesteading, illness, supporting nine children, and doing duty to church and community, but through two additional wives and the wives' children. They did not despair, did not divorce, did not give up the fight.

Elizabeth P. Davis became thrifty so that she could afford to be generous. Says her historian, she would patch and mend to save a dollar to give to the needy of the church. During the immigrant season, it was usual for her to provide one hundred meals a week to newcomers. On one occasion a friend arrived in the valley "almost fainting" from having lived on roots for three weeks with a baby nursing blood from her breast. Elizabeth gave the girl bread and tea and "the best she had in the house . . . joyfully." Moreover, Elizabeth enjoyed her martyrdom: she loved to attend dancing parties at Social Hall in Salt Lake City, meeting with Welsh people from the Thirteenth, Fifteenth, and Sixteenth wards to share her merry smile and enjoy old Welsh tunes. She also loved a good joke, such as the one about the old Welshman who summed up his reasons for divorcing his wife with this: "And look you, she cleans the bottom shelf first."

One must even admire Fanny Stenhouse. She longed for the uncommon pampering of an upper-class English matron, with a husband who came home to one hearth and one set of toddlers. Instead, as the outfall of Thomas's religious zeal, she had to support her family through thick complications and keep her marriage together through thin incentives. Orthodox Mormonism may judge her harshly. She violated a code which considers doctrinal heresy worse than personal treachery if only the latter is selective and directed toward the unimportant. From the perspective of a hundred-plus years her sins seem mild. And tarnished though her exposé may be—the product of an anguish and, yes, self-interest she herself may not have plumbed—Fanny emerged a decisive woman.

Perhaps my assessment is polyannish. But these are the views the women took of themselves, and they thought they looked from the perspective of eternity. Who is to say they were wrong? A great advantage to studying history is the opportunity to see how things came out in the wash. The distance of years makes it possible to follow these women's selections, occasional revisions, then pursuance of their dreams despite heartaches and discouragements. We can identify some of the long-term consequences of their choices, not all of them comforting, as in the proliferation to this day of polygamous cults throughout the American West. But here the waters get muddy. It will take closer, more skillful study than the present one to determine whether polygamy established a pattern of emotional exploitation of women and unviable burdens of guilt and resentment on orthodox daughters such as Fannie Palmer Gleave.

Although some of the women's choices are difficult to countenance, on the whole their lives do not shine across the years as doltish or fishwifish. Even many who entered plural marriage do not appear to have greatly lamented it or to have suffered much beyond what a monogamous wife did. In fact, polygamous family life seems to have had perquisites not enjoyed by the monogamous.

It is a pleasant thing to discover that these women were after all much like ourselves, with choices to make, dichotomies to endure, consequences from which to learn. They made mistakes, as did their leaders, and one would not wish to deny this and shut out the fascination and lessons of the women's stories. But if the women were not angels, neither were they fools. They are likable. They're worthy of emulation. Their lives had meaning. They demonstrated that virtue has unlikely habitats, could even sprout in a place scorned by the Other Victorians as the least promising for the nurture of goodness: that spiritual chamber of horrors, that Eden betrayed, that whited sepulchre, Mormondom.

Bibliography

Aland, Ellen Sarah Harding. Biography in Edith P. Haddock et al., comps., *History of the Bear Lake Pioneers* (Bear Lake County, ID: Daughters of Utah Pioneers [hereafter DUP], 1968), 1-2 (hereafter *Bear Lake*).

Allred, Clara Alice Robinson. Grant Borg, "Interview with Mrs. CARA — Spring City, Utah, Sanpete County." Federal Writer's Project (hereafter FWP), 2/9/1939, carbon of typescript (hereafter ts), 5 pp., Utah State Historical Society, Salt Lake City (hereafter USHS).
   Family group sheet under name of Reuben Warren Allred, LDS Church Family History Library, Salt Lake City (hereafter FHL).

Allred, Isabella Wade. Elvera Manful, "Pioneer Personal History: Mrs. IWA." FWP history revised 3/9/1937, carbon of ts, 6 pp., USHS. Written from an autobiography.

Archbold, Elizabeth. Biography in Kate B. Carter, comp., *Our Pioneer Heritage* (Salt Lake City: DUP, 1961), 4:57 (hereafter *Our Pioneer Heritage*).

Ashley, Sarah Jane Neat. AlDean Ashley Roberts, "George Ashley and SJNA," in *Bear Lake*, 26-28.

Ashworth, Eliza Dorsey. "History of EDA written by great-granddaughter Sadie Leffler Russon. Information by Mother, Europha Brian and Lola T. Wells," ts, 4 pp., USHS. Family group sheet under name of Benjamin Ashworth, FHL.

Astle, Felicia Raynor. Norma H. Eastley, "Francis Astle and FRA," in *Bear Lake*, 28-31, with photographs.

Baker (Pearce), Jean Rio Griffiths. "Diary of JRBP, obtained from Phyllis Hess, great-granddaughter, May 1952," photocopy of ts, 68 pp, USHS.
   Baker's diary has been widely excerpted. It was serialized

in part in the Logan *Herald Journal* in 1937; published almost in its entirety in Emma Nielsen Mortensen, *Two Mormon Pioneers: History of Alva Benson, Diary of Jean Rio Baker* (Hyrum, UT: Downs Printing, 1986); again in *An Enduring Legacy* (Salt Lake City: DUP, 1987), 10:193-240; and more recently in Kenneth W. Godfrey et al., *Women's Voices: An Untold History of the Latter-day Saints, 1830-1900* (Salt Lake City: Deseret Book Co., 1982), 203-21. Her story is also the subject of a video program shown to visitors to Temple Square.

In spite of this wide exposure, I have included the diary because most versions omit her final pages, which shed a different meaning on her life than that suggested by the early entries.

Ballard, Margaret McNeil. Biography of MMB written by family, 1919, USHS.

Autobiography of MMB cited by M. Russell Ballard in "MMB's Legacy of Faith," *Ensign* 19 (July 1989): 16-19, and by Jessie L. Embry, *Mormon Polygamous Families: Life in the Principle* (Salt Lake City: University of Utah Press, 1987).

Barker, Emily Ann Parsons. Biography of EAPB, manuscript (hereafter ms), USHS.

Family group sheet under name of John Henry Barker, FHL.

Barker, Susan Dermott. "Letters of John H. Barker" in *Our Pioneer Heritage*, 4:77.

This is one of the important exceptions to my rule of using verified DUP histories; no family group sheet could be found on the Barkers (although one was found for a son and his family), nor does the couple appear in the computerized Ancestral File.

Bell, Ann Fish. Eric Andersen, "AFB (1812-1872), A True Pioneer Story," in *Pioneer* 39 (Nov./Dec. 1992): 29 (magazine of the Sons of the Utah Pioneers).

Benbow, Jane Holmes. One of the founders of Mormonism in Great Britain, Jane Benbow is mentioned in B. H. Roberts's *History of the Church* and barely noted in her husband John's

Ancestral File record. She died during the exodus from Nauvoo in 1846. Her husband remarried, and Jane, his first wife, has been forgotten.

Bennett, Margaret Ann McPhail Caldwell. Elvera Manful, "Biography of MAMCB." FWP, 1939, carbon of ts, 11 pp, USHS.
Family group sheet under name of William Calwell (cottonworker), FHL.

Blackburn, Virtue Leah Crompton. Biography in *Our Pioneer Heritage*, 6:41.

Blyth, Margaret Mitchell. "Journal of John L. Blyth, 1878-," photocopy of holograph, 50 pp., USHS.
"History of MMB, 1948," ts, 7 pp, USHS.
Elizabeth Mitchell Boyce Pearl, "History of John Law Blyth for DUP Vilate Kimball Camp," photocopy of holograph, 13 pp, USHS.
Family group sheet under the name of John Law Blythe, FHL.

Brian, Martha Elizabeth Ashworth. "MEAB: History compiled by Euphora Brian Leffler Kinghorn, dtr., et al., Read at DUP meeting, Idaho Falls, spring 1940. Lined portions added from oral information by daughters and granddaughter." Photocopy of ts, 5 pp., USHS. Based partly on a journal started by MEAB in 1897.
Family group sheet under the name of Daniel Gross Brian, FHL.

Brown, Lizzie Weaver. Elvera Manful, "Personal Pioneer History: Mrs. LWB." FWP carbon of ts, 6 pp., 3/9/1937, USHS.
Family group sheet under the name of Moroni Franklin Brown, FHL.

Buckley, Mary Nixon Bate. "Autobiography of MNBB written in 1881, placed in temple cornerstone and returned to daughter in 1931," photocopy of holograph, 16 pp, USHS.
Family group sheet under name of Richard Bate, FHL.

Bullock, Henrietta Rushton. "Travels of the Pioneer Camp of

Israel from Winter Quarters in Search of a Stake of Zion kept by Thomas Bullock, Clerk of the Pioneer Camp," original ts taken from diary, 10 pp., USHS. This journal is another source that has been widely cited, since Thomas was camp clerk to Brigham Young in 1847 and chief clerk in the church offices in Salt Lake City until after Young's death.

Computer Ancestral File, FHL.

Clair Phillips, "Brief History of Thomas Bullock," *Pioneer* 39 (May-June 1992):18-19.

"Thomas Bullock, Pioneer," descendant-written history of the couple found in *Our Pioneer Heritage*, 8:229-356.

Cannon, Ann Quayle. Biography of AQC in Kate B. Carter, comp., *Heartthrobs of the West* (Salt Lake City: DUP, 1947), 3:76 (hereafter *Heartthrobs*).

Computer Ancestral File, FHL.

Cannon, Martha Hughes. Elizabeth C. McCrimmin, "Dr. MHC, First Woman Senator in America," ts, 20 pp., USHS.

Biography of MHC in *Our Pioneer Heritage*, 6:382.

Jean Bickmore White, "Dr. MHC: Doctor, Wife, Legislator, Exile," in Vicky Burgess-Olson, ed., *Sister Saints* (Provo, UT: Brigham Young University Press, 1978), 383-98.

Chisolm, Mary Stuart. Journal of Matthew Rowan, ts, LDS church archives.

Claridge, Charlotte Joy. George S. Ellsworth, *Samuel Claridge: Pioneering the Outposts of Zion* (Logan, UT: the author, 1987).

Computer Ancestral File, FHL.

Clark, Martha Cumming. Frederick James Clark, "The Life Story of MCC," photocopy of ts, 9 pp., USHS.

Coon, Mary Worthington. "A sketch of the lives of Eliza Ann Clark Worthington Horrocks and her Daughter, MWC. As told to her (Mary's) Daughter Mary Eliza (Mamie) Coon Thomas," ts, 2 pp, Thomas family papers in possession of author.

"An Account of MWC by Herself," ts, 2 pp., ibid.

LeNora T. Foster, "Resume of the Early Life of MWC," in

William Kent Goble and Gayle Goble Ord, comps., *Heritage of the Abraham Coon Family* (Salt Lake City, 1989), 90-91.

Family group sheet under the name of James David Coon, FHL.

Copies of vital records in possession of author.

Davies, Rachel Mariah Davies. John Johnson Davies, "Historical Sketch of My Life," ts, 10-plus pp., Special Collections, Marriott Library, University of Utah. John Davies prefaced his autobiography with these words: "I am a very poor speller/ And also very poor writer/ I know but little about grammer/ Then please excuse all my blunders." But he bequeathed a playful, lyrical writing style and a delightful description of the emigration.

Also excerpted in *Our Pioneer Heritage*, 1:29-32.

Family group sheet under the name of John Johnson Davies, FHL.

Dixon, Jane Davis. Sarah Lewis, daughter, "Biography of JDD," USHS.

Dunford, Leah Bailey. Lillie Dunford Mecham, "Isaac Dunford and LBD," *Bear Lake*, 187-97.

Personal papers, Susa Young Gates Collection, USHS. Gates was Brigham Young's 56th child; she became such a prolific Mormon writer and organizer that she was sometimes called "the Thirteenth Apostle." LBD was Gates's mother-in-law, largely raising Gates's two eldest children born during her disastrous teenage marriage.

Dunkley, Margaret Wright. In Leonard J. Arrington and Susan Arrington Madsen, *Mothers of the Prophets* (Salt Lake City: Deseret Book Co., 1987), 198.

Evans, Margaret Powell. Biography from DUP files in *Heartthrobs*, 1:35-36.

Computer Ancestral File, FHL.

Evans, Priscilla Merriman. Autobiography of PME, lithograph of ts, 13 pages, USHS.

Abridged version in *Our Pioneer Heritage*, 9:8.

Family group sheet under the name of Thomas David Evans, FHL.

Ferguson, Ellen Brooke. Blanche E. Rose, "Early Mormon Medical Practice," *Utah Historical Quarterly* 10 (1942): 14-33.

Ann Gardner Stone, "Dr. EBF: Nineteenth-Century Renaissance Women," in Burgess-Olson, *Sister Saints*, 325-40.

"Pioneer Midwives," in *Our Pioneer Heritage*, 6:379.

Fielding, Hannah Greenwood. Diary of Joseph Fielding, photocopy of ts prepared by the Joseph Fielding Smith Family Association, June 1963, ca. 50 pp., LDS church archives. The notation at the top reads "Journal, Preston, 1839-1840," but it begins in September 1937.

Computer Ancestral File, FHL. HGF's computer number is AFN 1MOL-6T. Her sister-wife Mary Ann Peake Fielding's number is AFN 2F53-5Q.

Fox, Ruth May (Polly). Autobiography of RMF, holograph, LDS church archives.

Biography of RMF in *Heartthrobs*, 3:80.

Entry in Andrew Jensen, *LDS Biographical Encyclopedia* (Salt Lake City: the author, 1901), 4 vols.

In Godfrey, *Women's Voices*, 373-86.

Computer Ancestral File, FHL.

Gadd, Eliza Chapman. In *Heartthrobs*, 3:150.

Garner, Janet Sprunt Warner. "Life History of JSWG completed July 16, 1935 by L.P.," ms, USHS.

Gerrard, Elizabeth Tripp. Obituary in *Millennial Star* 30 (1868):320.

Gibson, Janet Aicol. Biography in *Our Pioneer Heritage*, 6:22.

Giles, Veronica Murdoch Caldow. Life sketch in *The James and Mary Murray Murdoch Family History* (Provo, UT: Family Organization, 1982), 761.

Grist, Elicia Allsley. Listed with family in Mini Margetts Card File, British emigration index compiled by an early LDS Genealogical Library (now FHL) employee from ship and emigration office records.

Computer Ancestral File, FHL.

Letter to the *Millennial Star* 21 (1861):2-7.

Information on EAG has been hard to find. Initially I could not find a family group record on the Grist family, but by summer 1992 she and husband John Knapp Grist had been entered in the computerized Ancestral File.

Handley, Elizabeth Clark. Biography in *Our Pioneer Heritage*, 6:477.

Family group sheet under the name of George Handley, FHL.

Hardie, Janet Downing. "Midwives of Pioneer Utah," biography in *Our Pioneer Heritage*, 6:409.

Hart, Emily Ellingham. Mr. and Mrs. Edward Hart, "James H. Hart," in *Bear Lake*, 238-42. Includes excerpts from his short, otherwise unpublished diary.

Heath, Harriet. In Mini Margetts Card File, FHL.

Heggie, Jane Strachan. Biography of Andrew Walter Heggie in *Our Pioneer Heritage*, 4:42.

Heywood, Martha Spence. Maureen Ursenbach, "Three Women and the Life of the Mind," *Utah Historical Quarterly* 43 (1975): 27-40.

Mentioned in Jill Mulvay Derr, "Zion's Schoolmarms," chapter in Claudia Bushman, ed., *Mormon Sisters: Women in Early Utah* (Cambridge, MA: Emmeline Press Ltd., 1976), 66-87.

Computer Ancestral File, FHL.

Hirst, Harriet Tarry. Biography in *Our Pioneer Heritage*, 4:73.

Horne, Mary Isabella. Preston Nibley, *Faith-Promoting Stories* (Salt Lake City: Deseret Book, n.d.), 67-70.

Leon Hartschorn, *Remarkable Stories from the Lives of LDS Women* (Salt Lake City: Deseret Book Co., 1973).

Horrocks, Eliza Ann Clarke Worthington. "A sketch of the lives of EACWH and her Daughters, MWC. As told to her (Mary's) Daughter Mary Eliza (Mamie) Coon Thomas," ts, 2 pp, Thomas family papers in possession of author.

"An Account of MWC by Herself," ts, 2 pp., ibid.

LeNora T. Foster, "Resume of the Early Life of MWC," in William Kent Goble and Gayle Goble Ord, comps., *Heritage of the Abraham Coon Family* (Salt Lake City, 1989), 90-91.

Family group sheet under the name of James David Coon, FHL.

Copies of vital records in possession of author.

Jeremy, Sarah Evans. Florence L. Parry, "SEJ," in *Heartthrobs*, 11:8-9.

Ronald Dennis, *The Call to Zion: The History of the First Welsh Mormon Emigration* (Provo, UT: BYU Religious Studies Center, 1987), 30.

Job (Miles), Hannah. Bliss J. Brimley, *The Book of Thomas Job* (Pleasant Grove, UT, 1988). This is one of the most thorough and professional of the family histories read for this study.

Letter of Hannah Job Miles to her former husband dated 22 June 1876, ibid., 202.

Family group sheet, FHL.

Killian, Rachel Powell. Maria K. Buchanan, "History of RPK." 1932, ts, USHS.

King, Hannah Tapfield. Journals of HTK with foreword by Bertha Eames Loosli, ts, 145 pages, USHS. Mrs. King must have kept several journals at a time, for there are overlapping entries, gaps, and fragmented entries.

HTK writings in the *Woman's Exponent*, including 2 (1 Sept. 1873): 50, 4 (1 Apr. 1876): 161, 4 (1 May 1876): 178, 7 (1 Apr. 1879): 22, and 7 (1 Dec. 1878): 98.

Maureen Ursenbach, "Three Women and the Life of the Mind," *Utah Historical Quarterly* 43 (1975): 27-40.

Computer Ancestral File, FHL.

In Edward W. Tullidge, *History of Salt Lake City* (Salt Lake City, 1886), 797.

In Augusta Joyce Crocheron, *Representative Women of De-seret* (Salt Lake City, 1884), 92-94.

Kingsford, Elizabeth Horrocks Jackson. "Leaves from the Life of EHJK," autobiography, copy of ts, 6 pp., in Thomas family papers in author's possession.
>Jensen, *LDS Biographical Encyclopedia*, 2:528-31.

Knight, Lydia Goldthwait. Hartschorn, *Remarkable Stories*.

Laidlaw, Jane Ferguson Graham. Biography, USHS.
>Family Group Sheet under name of Francis Laidlaw, FHL.

Lapish, Hannah Settle. Autobiography in *Our Pioneer Heritage*, 4:39.

Lewis, Elizabeth. "A Letter of Mrs. Lewis to J. Davis" from Salt Lake Valley, 10 April 1850, in Dennis, *Call to Zion*, Appendix E.
>Also letters labeled, "Manti 1851," ibid., 224.

McCune, Elizabeth Ann Claridge. Susa Young Gates, *Memorial to EACM* (Salt Lake City: the author, 1924).
>Computer Ancestral File, FHL.
>Hartschorn, *Remarkable Stories*.

McKay, Ellen (or Helen) Oman. Computer Ancestral File, FHL.

McKay, Jennette Eveline Evans. Leonard J. Arrington and Susan Arrington Madsen, *Mothers of the Prophets* (Salt Lake City: Deseret Book Co., 1978), 138.

McKenzie, Margaret Campbell. In *Ensign* 8 (Oct. 1978).

McMillan, Mary Murdoch Main Todd. In *The James and Mary Murray Murdoch Family History* (Provo, UT: Family Organization, 1982), 762.

Maughan, Mary Ann (Weston). Autobiography of MAWM, holograph, 3 vols., and ts, USHS, written forty-six years after emigrating but probably from diaries or earlier histories.

Murdoch, Ann Steel. In Journal of John Murdoch, quoted by David Lennox in Murdoch family history, 765.
> Biography of ASM, ibid., 204.
> Family Group Sheet in same volume.

Murdoch, Janet Lennox. Brief biography in Murdoch family history, 766-67. Family group sheet in same.

Murdoch, Mary Murray (Wee Granny) In Murdoch family history, 52-58.
> Family group sheet in same.

Oakey, Mary. Mentioned in James S. Brown Journal in *Our Pioneer Heritage*, 6:24.

Pack, Jessie Belle Stirling. Autobiography/biography in *Our Pioneer Heritage*, 6:31.

Palmer, Mary Jane Ewer. Fannie Palmer Gleave, daughter, "History of MJEP, Pioneer of 1866," photocopy of ts, 16 pp, USHS.
> Family group sheet under the name of James Palmer, FHL.

Parry, Harriet Parry. Granddaughter (written "from Henry's notes,"), History of HPP, USHS.

Piercy, Angelina. Lynn Watkins Jorgensen, "The First London Mormons: 1840-1845: 'What Am I and my Brethren Here For?'" M.A. thesis, Brigham Young University, 1988.

Poulter, Alice Maw. History of AMP, 1857, USHS.

Poulter, Mary Elizabeth Jackson. Family group sheet in Thomas family papers, author's collection.

Powell, Mary. Alfred Cordon Journals, LDS church archives.
> John Powell Autobiography, Special Collections, Lee Library, Brigham Young University. Also cited in John Cotterill, "Midland Saints: The Mormon Mission in the West Midlands, 1937-77," Ph.D. diss., University of Keele, 1985.
> John Powell, "A Summary of the Religious Side of My Life," LDS church archives.

Price, Caroline Blakey. "Martin's 5th Handcart Company of 1856," Journal of Edward Martin, LDS church archives. *Deseret News* 28:448.

Price, Ruth Williams. Diary of John Price cited in "John E. Price of Llandilofan," in *Heartthrobs,* 11:45.

Redman, Ellen Balfour. Mentioned in Wilford Woodruff Journal as cited in London Branch Manuscript History entries beginning 10 Jan. 1840, LDS church archives.

Reese, Emma David. Hannah Reese Phillips, biography of EDR based on autobiography, in *Heartthrobs,* 11:37-38.

Ritchie, Mary Emma. Diary of MER, 18 April-9 June 1868, ts, USHS. The diary recounts her tour of England, visits to Anglican churches, shoppings, museum tours, social calls. Apparently MER was not Mormon, and her diary describing essentially an affluent American lass's coming-of-age tour contrasts vividly with the experiences of most Mormon girls and women. Her experience more closely resembled that of Eliza R. Snow's on her privileged world tour.

Roberts, Ann Everington. Hartschorn, *Remarkable Stories.*
    Also in Edward Tullidge, *Heroines of Mormondom* (Salt Lake City: 2nd vol. in Noble Women's Lives Series, 1884).
    Adah Roberts Naylor, *Relief Society Magazine*, Jan. 1934, 3-8.

Rosser, Ann Sophia Jones. Tribute in *Millenial Star* 78 (1916): 278.

Shipp, Mary Elizabeth Hilstead. Biography in *Our Pioneer Heritage*, 6:378.
    Ellis R. Shipp, M.D., *Her Diary* (Salt Lake City, 1962).
    Family group sheet under the name of Milford Bard Shipp, FHL.
    Ancestral File, FHL.

Smith, Mary Fielding. Don Corbett, *MFS: Daughter of Britain* (Salt Lake City, n.d.).
    Hartschorn, *Remarkable Stories.*

Spencer, Martha Knight. Biography in *Our Pioneer Heritage*, 6:192.

Staines, Priscilla Mogridge. Tullidge, *Heroines of Mormondom*, 285-91.

Stanford, Jane Carol Barker (Jenny). Letters from her brother, John Barker, in *Our Pioneer Heritage*, 4:4.
Family group sheet on John's son, FHL.

Steadman, Elizabeth Wilkins. Letters to her mother dated 22 April, 24 June, and September 1862, February 1863, and spring 1864, in *Our Pioneer Heritage*, 6:34.
Family group sheet under the name of George Steadman (farmer), FHL.

Stenhouse, Fanny Warn. T. B. H. Stenhouse (Mrs.), *Tell It All: The Tyranny of Mormonism or An Englishwoman in Utah* (Reprinted as a Traveller's Classic, London: Praeger Press, 1971).
Family group sheet and Computer Ancestral File under the name of Thomas Brown Holmes Stenhouse, FHL. T. B. H.'s second wife is listed, but only a few details are given on his first wife Fanny.
Ronald W. Walker, "The Stenhouses and the Making of a Mormon Image," *Journal of Mormon History* 1 (1974): 51-72.
Jensen, *LDS Biographical Encyclopedia*, 4:385.
Heartthrobs, 1:44, 184.

Swarts, Jane McKinnon. In *Heartthrobs*, 3.

Taylor, Ann Faulkner. Biography in *Our Pioneer Heritage*, 4:69.

Taylor, Caroline Rogers. Obituary in *Millennial Star* 35:656, cited in London Conference Manuscript History, entry for 7 Sept. 1873, LDS church archives.
Mini Margetts Card File.

Thomas, Elizabeth Phillips. Photograph or cover in Thomas family papers, author's possession.

Thomas, Mary Roberts. Notes on census records in Thomas family papers, author's possession.
Family group sheet, FHL.

Tuckfield, Maria Ann. "History of MAT, my mother," carbon of ts, 2 pp., USHS.

Warner, Mary Ann Chapple. Elvera Manful, "Pioneer Personal History of MACW," carbon of ts, 10 pp., FWP history, USHS.

Weaver, Ann Watkins. Mentioned in Elvera Manful, "Personal Pioneer History: Mrs. Lizzie Weaver Brown," FWP carbon of ts, 6 pp., 3/9/1937.
   Family group sheet under the name of William Weaver, Sr., FHL.

Wells, Sarah Hattersley. Lola T. Wells, "Biography of SHW," ts, 3 pp., USHS.

Wilson, Sarah Elizabeth Isom. "Brief Biography of SEIW and Morris Wilson. Copied by Martin C. Graff at Ogden, UT, Nov. 12, 1936," carbon of ts, 5 pp., FWP Historical Records Survey, USHS.

Windley, Mary Foster. In *Bear Lake*, 883.
   Family group sheet under the name of John Windley (merchant), FHL.

Wood, Alice Horrocks. Mary Comfort Carver Bartlett, granddaughter, "Biography of AHW, with list of children given by Ruth Carver, great-granddaughter," photocopy of ts, 4 pp., USHS.
   "Leaves from the Life of Elizabeth Horrocks Jackson Kingsford," Thomas family papers, author's possession.
   Notes on marriage and baptismal records, ibid.

Woodmansee, Emily Hill. Mentioned as twenty-year-old member of Willie County, in Andrew Jenson notes entitled "Capt. Jas G. Willie's 4th Handcart Co of 1856," ms, LDS church archives.
   Orson F. Whitney, *History of Utah* (Salt Lake City: George Q. Cannon and Sons, 1892-98), 4:593.
   Photograph in Solomon F. Kimball, "Belated Emigrants of 1856," *Improvement Era* 12, nos. 1-4.

Woolley, Ellen Wilding. Leonard J. Arrington, *From Quaker to*

Latter-day Saint: Bishop Edwin D. Woolley (Salt Lake City: Deseret Book Co., 1986).

Catharine E. Woolley Diary, reprinted in J. Cecil Alter, "In the Beginning: Diaries of Mormon Pioneers," *Salt Lake Telegram*, 8 Jan.-2 Mar. 1938.

Preston W. Parkinson, *The Utah Woolley Family* (Salt Lake City, 1967).

"Reminiscences of Mrs. F. D. Richards," ts of handwritten manuscript, Bancroft Library.

Wylie, Elizabeth. In *The James and Mary Murray Murdoch Family History* (Provo, UT: Family Organization, 1982), 204 and 713.

Not among the 100 Finest but of Interest

Barton, Ellen Birchall. In *Our Pioneer History*, 4:33.

Bennett, Elizabeth Wood. In *Our Pioneer History*, 4:67, history of Ann Wood Day.

Burgess, Isabella Lambert Winner. In *Our Pioneer History*, 6:399.

Chapelle, Ursula. In *Heartthrobs*, 3:135.

Corbett, Caroline Lloyd. In *Our Pioneer History*, 6:26.

Cottam, Ellen Bridget Gallagher. In *Our Pioneer History*, 6:481.

Davis, Elizabeth P. In *Heartthrobs*, 11:33-34.

Davis, Margaret R. (Thomas). Biography by Regina G. Erickson in *Heartthrobs*, 11:13-14.

Jenkins, Anna Evans. Esther Jenkins Carpenter, "The Welsh Widow," in *Heartthrobs*, 11:47-48.

Mace, Rebecca Howell. Original holograph, LDS church archives. Godfrey, *Women's Voices*, 252, 387 with photograph.

Mills, Frances Farr. In *Our Pioneer History*, 6:484.

Morgan, Margaret Griffith. In *Our Pioneer History*, 4:61.

Price, Rachel Jones. Biography by Ona Rees Anderson in *Heart-throbs*, 11:18-20.

Rees, Mary William. In *Heartthrobs*, 11:16-18

Ross, Sarah Elizabeth Smyth. In *Our Pioneer History*, 4:32

Rosza, Patience. PR (Archer), "Recollections of Past Days," ts, Lee Library, as cited in Rebecca Cornwall Bartholomew and Leonard J. Arrington, *Rescue of the Handcart Pioneers* (Provo, UT: Redd Center for Western Studies, 1980). See also *Our Pioneer History*, 14:263

Spense, Margery Lisk. In *Our Pioneer History*, 6:489

Stephens, Jane. In *Heartthrobs*, 1:152.

Talton, Mary Johnson. In *Heartthrobs*, 3:83.

Index

A

Abergwilly, 78, 234
Adam-God theory, 226
Aitkenites, 83
Aland, Ellen Sarah Harding, 259
Albion, Rev. James, 47, 48, 49
Albion, Susannah, 47, 85-86, 96
Alexandria, 171, 175
Allred, Clara Alice Robinson, 39, 141, 259
Allred, Isabella Wade, 158, 167, 259
Amelia syndrome, 241
America, 118, 134, 137, 139
—immigrants' first impressions of, 162
American church, x
American Indians, 123, 163, 167, 182-83
American Notes, 170
American press, x
American West, 258
Americans, 162
Ancestral File, xiii
Anderson, Elizabeth Archbold, 138, 259
Anderson, Scott, 113
Anglicanism, 44, 47, 220
Annan, 35
anointing by women, 91
anti-immigrant, 4
anti-Mormon press, xi, 62, 120
anti-Mormon publicity
—cycles of, 1-2
anti-Mormonism, viii, 19, 243
anti-papist, 4, 45
apostasy, 125
Apples of Sodom, 21f
Archibold, Elizabeth, 259
Argyllshire, 29
Arrington, Leonard, 143
Artley, the, 154

Ashley, Sarah Jane Neat, 75, 143, 259
Ashworth, Eliza Dorsey, 43, 52, 58, 144, 154-55, 167, 183, 259
Astle, Felicia Raynor, 58, 75, 165, 168, 243, 259
Atlantic Ocean, 191
Austen, Jane, 13
Australia, 133
Austria, 220
auxiliaries, 106

B

Babylon, 69, 85, 135, 137
Bahamas, 156
Baker, Edward, 193
Baker, Henry, 191
Baker, Jean Rio. *See* Pearce
Baker, Josiah, 141, 157
Ballard, Margaret McNeil, 34, 45, 60, 75, 150, 168, 178, 260
Banbury, 32
baptism, Mormon, 67, 69-71, 79
baptismal sites, 69-70
Baptists, 46, 47, 51, 226, 233
Barker, Christine N. Benson, 218
Barker, Emily Ann Parsons, 141, 260
Barker, Jenny. *See* Stanford
Barker, Johanna, 219
Barker, John H., 138, 149, 151, 243, 257
Barker, Susan Dermott, 75, 138, 149, 174, 216-20, 257, 260
Barker children, 218
Barton, Ellen Birchall, 141, 272
Bate, Richard, 73, 202-203
Bate, Richard, Jr., 171
Bates, Catherine, 91
Bates, Sister, of London, 92
Battery, 165
Beadle, John, 3, 5, 10, 11, 17, 20f

Beard, Auld Mrs., 101-102
Bedfordshire, 84
Bedwelty, 213
Belfast, 94
Belisle, Orvilla, x, 12, 16, 18
Bell, Ann Fish, 260
Benbow, Jane Holmes, 144, 167, 260-61
Bennett, Elizabeth Wood and Charles, 138, 272
Bennett, Margaret Caldwell, 137, 261
Beresford, Harriet, 91
Bible, viii, 43, 44, 52, 69
Bird, Georgine, 111
Birmingham, 27, 29, 36, 100, 147, 212
Bitton, Davis, 143
Black Hills, 180
Blackburn, 84
Blackburn, Bishop Elias, 128
Blackburn, Virtue Leah Crompton, 128, 141, 261
Blackwall, 163
Bland, Mrs. William, 146
blood atonement, 227
blood of Ephraim, 51
Blythe, John, 58, 60, 135-36
Blythe, Margaret Mitchell, 35, 135-36, 243, 261
Bologna, 86
Book of Commandments, 124
Book of Mormon, 57, 81, 120, 124
Booth, Brother and Sister, 48-49, 96
Booth, Elder, 152
Boston, 164, 169, 189,
Bowles, Samuel, vii, ix
Boyd, Jim, 167
Box, Belinda Marden Pratt, 230
Bradford, 87
Bradford Branch, 116
branches, Mormon, 45
—problems in, 99
Brian, Martha Ashworth, 183, 261
Bricktown, 6, 18
Bridgewater, the, 154
Brierleyhill Branch, 100
Bristol, 27, 81
Bristol Branch, 96

British church, x, xi
British Mission, x, xi, 29, 48, 107, 111, 207, 224, 227
British society, religious nature, 47
Bromley Branch, 93
Brown, James S., 149
Brown, Lizzie Weaver, 144, 261
Browne, Charles Farrar, 4f
Brunswick, 161
Buchanan, Pres. James, 14f
Buckebury Bucks, 190
Buckley [Buckly], Mary Nixon Bate, 47, 60, 61, 62, 67, 69, 72, 74, 79, 139, 145, 146, 149, 168-69, 202-203, 261
Budge, Pres. William, 113, 243
Buena Vista, the, 154
buffalo, 177, 182
Bullock, Henrietta Rushton, 35, 37, 123, 137, 171, 261-62
Bullock, Thomas, 37, 47, 100, 123, 137
Bullock, Willard Richards, 171
Bunting, Pres. James L., 113
Burgess, Isabella Lambert Winner, 76, 141, 272
Burgess-Olson, Vicky, 240, 241
Burleigh, 83
Burns, Robert, 45
Burrows Branch, 95
Burslem, 83, 89
Burt, Brother, 115
Burton, R. T., 112
Burton, Sir Richard, vii, 7, 14
Butler, William, 144
Byron, Lord, 176
BYU Harold B. Lee Library, xiii

C

Cable, Mary, 41
Cache Valley, 216, 219
Calcutta, 201
California, 193
Californians, 181
Calvinism, 207
Cambrian, 30
Cambridge, 12, 41
Cambridgeshire, 194

Canada, 133, 137, 172, 224
Candland, Brother, 206
Cannes, 202
Cannon, Ann Quayle, 262
Cannon, George Q., 31, 173
Cannon, Martha Hughes, xii, 170, 245, 262
Capetown, 138
Cardiff, 30, 92
Carmarthen, 143, 232
Carmarthenshire, 39, 40
Carter, Kate B., 25, 26, 31, 33
Carvalho, Solomon, vii, 14
Casterline, Gail, 14, 15
Castle Frome, 41
Castle Garden, 165-66
catechism, 207
Celestial Law, 210
Chalford, 100
Chandler, Sister, 86
Chapelle, Naomi, 139
Chapelle, Ursula, 139, 272
Chapman, Arvis Scott, 196
Chapman, Sarah Ann Briggs Handley, 195
Chapple, Mary Ann. *See* Warner
Charing Cross, 113
charismatic gifts, 93
Cheshire, 149
Cheshire Co., 188
Chester Branch, 70
Chesterton, 194
child labor, 171
Chimney Rock, 180
Chisholm, Mary Stuart, 262
cholera, 5, 172
Christian ideals, 13, 209
church archives, viii, xiii
Church of England, 15, 39, 46, 73, 233
City of God, 251
Civil War, vii, 2, 133, 145, 158, 162, 164
Clackmannan, 29
Claridge, Charlotte Joy, 199-200, 240, 243, 262
Claridge, Rebecca Hughes, 200
Claridge, Samuel, 199-201

Clark, B. Thomas, 194
Clark, Hiram, 89
Clark, Martha Cumming, 172, 244, 262
Clarke, Joseph, 189
Clayton, 116
Clemens, Samuel L., 8
Cockpit, 120
confirmation, 69-72
Congregationalist, 11
Connecticut, 122
Constitutional amendment, 2
contagion theory, 135
contention, causes of, 97, 226
contention in branches, 95
conversion, 57-79
    —contagion theory of, 135
    —Irish, 27
    —motives for, 3, 6, 8, 37, 50-52
    —numbers, 26, 111
    —process, 67-68
    —stereotypes, 15
converts, Mormon
    —acquainted with death, 39
    —ages of, 36
    —European, 27
    —geographic origins, 28
    —Irish, 31
    —landless, 38, 40
    —Scandinavian, 27
    —Scottish, 27
    —Welsh, 30
Cook, John, 107
Coon, Mary Worthington, 145, 188-91, 262-63
Cooper, Brother, 115
Cope, Brother, 89
Copperfield, David, 26
Corbett, Carolyn Lloyd, 76, 136, 145, 170, 178, 272
Cordon, Alfred, 83
cottage industry, 32
Cottam, Ellen Bridget Gallagher, 143, 272
Cottam, Elizabeth Dawson, 83, 95
Council Bluffs, 163, 166, 194
Cowan, Richard O., 26

Crawford, Flora, 115
crossing, plains, 175
—monotony of, 179
Cuerdon, Brother and Sister, 87
Cymric, viii

D

Dakotas, 184
Dan Curlin, the, 154
Danites, 7, 9, 16, 23, 59
Danites in the Sierras, 7
Davies, John J. and Rachel Mariah, 41,
    49, 57, 60, 75, 149, 155, 161, 162, 163,
    170, 177, 182, 183, 175, 263
Davies, Sarah Lewis, 35
Davis, Elizabeth P., 257, 272
Davis, John, 73
Davis, Margaret R., 60, 139, 272
Dawson, Ann, 83, 84, 90, 95, 120, 224
Dawson, Jane, 95
Daynes, Kathryn, 238
Dean Forest Conference, 84
DeBow's Review, 5
Dennis, Ron, xiii
Denver & Rio Grande R.R., 217
depravity, 22
Depression, Great, xii
depression of 1837, 31
Derby Branch, 111
Dernford Dale, 209
desertions, 17, 149, 172, 188, 253
—marital, 38
De Trobriand, Gen. Philip, vii
Devil's Gate (WY), 181
Dew, Sherry, 29
Dickens, Charles, 16, 34, 35, 152, 163,
    170, 172
Dilke, Sir Charles Wentworth, vii
dissenters, Mormon, x, xi
diversity, 254
divorce, 48, 241, 253
Dixon, Jane Davis, 263
Dixon, William Hepworth, vii, 7, 13
doctrinal tension, 98
Doctrine and Covenants, 70, 120
Dow, Lorenzo, 133

Doyle, A. Conan, 11, 17, 18, 21
Dublin, 31, 37
Dumfriesshire, 35
Dunbar, Brother, 73
Dunford, Leah, 164, 170, 263
Dunkley, Margaret Wright, 263
DUP (Daughters of Utah Pioneers), vii,
    xii, 25, 150

E

Eastern press, 254
Eastern States Mission, 173
Eden, British, 6
Edinburgh, 43, 55
Edmunds-Tucker acts, 2
education, Victorian, 45, 233
Elkhorn River, 175
emigrants
—singles, 37-38
emigration, 3, 100, 133
—companies, order of, 152
—cost of, 143
—dangers of, 142, 157-59, 163-65
—family, 36-7
—farewells, 148-49
—handcart, 164
—management of, 146
—motives for, 46, 137
—northern route, 164, 166
—opposition to, 139
—preparations, 145
—railroad, 166
—ship procedures, 150-54
—southern route, 160
—years of, 150
—young, 36
employment opportunities in Utah, 243
Endowment House, 18, 206
England, viii, 68, 133, 134, 138
English Channel, 226
English church, xi
English women, 3
Ephraim (UT), 178
Episcopalians, 194
Epping, 175
Euston Square Station, 147

evangelical groups, 46, 50, 95
Evans, Isaac, 77
Evans, Margaret Powell, 168, 178, 263
Evans, Priscilla Merriman, 40, 44, 47, 48,
    52, 60, 61, 67, 75, 83, 142, 174, 186,
    263-64
Evans, Sister, 91
Evans, Thomas, 168, 178
Evanston (WY), 29
Ewer, Hannah Taylor, 32
Ewer, John, 32
Ewer, Mary Jane. *See* Palmer
excommunications, 49, 100
Express Company, 205

F

family genealogists, ix
family group sheets, xiii
Family History Library, xii, ix
farms, Utah vs. Minnesota, 250
Farrell, George L., 110
Felintawa Mill, 77
Female Relief Society, 88, 89
female support groups, xi
females, preponderance of, 26, 84
feminists, xi, 253
Ferguson, Ellen Brooke, 43, 141, 242,
    245, 264
Ferris, Cornelia Woodcock, 4, 8, 12 (*see
    also* Ward, Maria)
Field, Kate, ix, 20
Fielding, Amos, 88
Fielding, Hannah Greenwood, 87, 89,
    223-25, 264
Fielding, Joseph, 29, 83, 84, 86, 87, 90, 91,
    95, 97, 98, 120, 224-25
Fielding, Mary Ann Greenhalgh, 225
Fife, 29
Fillmore (UT), 223
Finsburg Branch, 67, 72
Florence (NE), 136, 145, 168, 171, 172,
    174, 196
Fort Kearney, 175, 176, 177
Fort Supply, 186
Fox, Ruth May, xii, 264
France, 86

France, Dr., 209
Franklin (ID), 172, 244
Freemason's Hall, 125
Fuller, Metta Victoria, 19

G

Gadd, Eliza Chapman, 142, 185, 245, 264
Gaelic, 30
Garner, Janet Sprunt Warner, 264
Garthwaite, Oliver, 212
Gates, Jacob, 107
Gates, Susa Young, 8, 200, 201, 252
Gathering, The, x, 112, 134-42
Gen. McClelland, the, 154
Geneva, 168
gentiles, 19, 250
George W. Bourne, the, 154
George Washington, the, 154, 157, 189
German, Sister, 121
Germany, 218, 220
Gerrard, Elizabeth Tripp, 143, 264
Gibson, Janet Aicol, 141, 264
Gibson, Pres. William, 141, 153
Gilchrist, Rosetta L., 21
Giles, Veronica Murdoch Caldow, 243,
    264
Glamorganshire Canal, 30
Glasgow, 27, 29, 84, 101
Glasgow-Parkhead Relief Society, 114-15
Gleave, Fanny Palmer, 247-48, 258
Gloucester, 73, 79
Godbe, William S., xi
Godbeites, x, 230
Goddard, Elizabeth H., 110-11
Gogmagog, Earl of, 41
Golconda, the, 154, 156, 210, 234
Gold Rush, 166
Gomer, 62
Goshute Indians, 246
Grand Island (NE), 167
Grant, Jedediah, 207
Grantsville (UT), 247
Great Basin, 167, 171, 251
Great Britain, population of, 133
Great Lakes, 172
Great Plains, vii, 163, 171, 216

Great Platte River Road, 179
Greeley, Horace, ix, 7, 13
Greenland, 84
Griffiths, 191
Grist, Alicia Allsley, 105, 112, 211-12, 264-65
Grist, John Knapp, 36, 211-12
Grist children, 212
Gulf of Mexico, 161
Gunnison, John, 14

H

handcart companies, 184-86
handcarts, 164
Handley, Elizabeth Clark, 145, 188, 194-96, 240, 265
Handley, George, 194
Handley, Sarah Ann Briggs. *See* Chapman
Hanley, 89
Hardie, Janet Downing, 140, 184, 265
hardships, emigration, 243
harem, association of Mormonism with, 13
harem writers, 21
Harmony, the, 154
Harp of Zion, 102
Harris, Dr., 252
Hart, Emily Ellingham, 68, 77, 265
Heath, Hannah, 96
Heath, Harriet, 96, 265
Heber City (UT), 237
Heddingtonshire, 34
Hedlock, Reuben, 85, 89, 92, 96, 98, 124
Heggie, Andrew, 234, 265
Heggie, Jane Strachan, 234, 265
Henry, Dutch, 170
Herefordshire, 30, 41, 46, 57, 63, 171
Hertfordshire, 84
Heywood, Martha Spence, 265
Higbee, John S., 236
Hilstead family, 128
Hirst, Harriet Tarry, 136, 265
Hollywood, 182
Horizon, the, 154
Horne, Joseph, 168

Horne, Mary Isabella, 265
Horrocks, Alice, 47
Horrocks, Edward, 47, 188-91
Horrocks, Eliza Ann Clarke Worthington, 134, 188-91, 196, 245, 266
Horrocks, Mary, 174, 184
Horrocks Bros. Mercantile, 189
Houghton, 199
I Iow, Sister, 92
Howe, Eber D., x
Hulett, James Edward, 42
Hull, York Co., 220
Hunt wagon company, 184
Huntingood, 199
Huntsville (UT), 190
Hyde, Orson, 96-97

I

Illinois, x, 2, 76, 91, 122, 135, 167
immigrants, 133
   —motives, 134, 137
   —numbers, 133
   —Welsh, 16
Independence Rock (WY), 181
Independent Church, 46, 47
Indian Hollow, 167
Indian Relief Society, 106
Iowa, 168, 169-71, 172, 195
   —City, 175, 179, 202
Ireland, 30, 55, 64, 95, 156
Irish revival, 94
Irish Sea, 29, 156
Isle of Man, 92, 107, 156
Isom, Sarah. *See* Wilson
Italian Mission, 227
Italy, 220, 228
Ives, Burl, 24

J

Jackson, Aaron, 174
Jackson, Elizabeth Horrocks. *See* Kingsford
Jenkins, Anna Evans, 244, 272
Jenkins, David, 244

Jenkins, Margaret, 91
Jenkins family, 63
Jeremy, Sarah Evans, 163, 244, 245, 266
Jersey Island, 226
Job, Elizabeth, 233
Job, Elizabeth Davis, 234
Job, Hannah Daniels, 49, 78, 140, 143, 149, 184, 232-36, 266
Job, Thomas, 49, 78, 143, 149, 233-36, 245, 266
John Brent, vii, 4, 16, 223
John Bright, the, 154, 157
John J. Boyd, the, 154
Johnson, Joseph W., 71
Johnson, Mrs., 146
Johnston's Army, 14, 19
Jones, Dan, 30, 45, 59, 62, 63, 157
Jones, Sister, 77

K

Kane, Sarah Wood, 14, 22
Kelsey, Eli, 93
Kennebec, the, 154
Keokuk (IA), 171
Killian, Rachel Powell, 76, 145, 151, 266-67
Kimball, Heber C., 29, 31, 120, 128, 207, 208, 249
King, Bertha, 205
King, Hannah Tapfield, 35, 41, 42, 43, 44, 48, 54, 68, 69, 71, 76, 78, 104, 119, 125-27, 151, 153, 171, 176, 179, 181, 183, 203-11, 266
King, Thomas, 127, 171, 179, 203-11
King, Thomas Owen, 183, 205
Kingsford, Elizabeth Horrocks Jackson, 34, 174-75, 178, 180, 184, 185, 267
Kippen, James, 58
Kirtland (OH), 171
Knight, Lydia Goldthwait, 267

L

Laidlaw, Jane Graham, 35, 53, 149, 267
Lamanites, 123
Lambert, George Cannon, 57

Lamoreaux, Elder, 77
Lanark, 29
Lancashire, 27, 29, 224, 225
—dialect, 4
Lanes End, 89
Lapish, Hannah Settle, 67, 185, 267
Laramie (WY), 172
Lee, John D., x, 179
Leeds Branch, 117
Leeds District, 116
Leicester, 110-11, 117
Lewis, Elizabeth, 59, 62, 75, 137, 212-13, 240, 251, 267
Lewis, Llewellyn and Mary Harry, 213
Lewis, Robert, 213
Liberty Park (SLC), 201
Lincoln Relief Society, 115, 116
Lippincott's, 14
literacy, 44
Littell's Living Age, 14
Little Gentile, 21
Liverpool, 5, 16, 17, 22, 27, 29, 31, 69, 89, 99, 105, 128, 135, 139, 143, 149, 151, 202, 225
—Branch, 84, 111, 117
—emigration office, 144
—Relief Society, 113
—Ward, 37
Llandysfod, 81
Logan (UT), 217
Logan temple, 190
London, x, 47, 48, 49, 57, 67, 72, 85, 92, 96, 107, 139, 146, 149, 202, 216, 250
—Branch, 49, 85
—Conference, 99, 109
—Relief Society, 112-13
—*Times*, 18, 22, 23, 27, 133
London-Lambeth Branch, 113
Loup River, 175
Low, Mrs., 53
Low Church, 48, 54
Lyman, Amasa, 49, 125
Lyon, John (poet), 87, 101-102
Lythgoe, Dennis, 2, 5f, 14f

M

Mabien, John, 72
McAllister, J. D. T., 216
McArthur, Daniel (company), 184
McCammon (ID), 212
Macclesfield, 188
McCune, Albert William, 201-202
McCune, Elizabeth Claridge, 199-202, 240, 256, 267
Mace, Rebecca Howell, 252, 272
McIntyre, Peter, 30
McKay, David O., 168
McKay, Ellen Oman, 267
McKay, Jennette Evans, 267
Mackay, William, 29
McKenzie, Margaret Campbell, 267
McMillan, Mary Murdoch Todd, 68, 267
Magna (UT), 190
Malad (ID), 213, 244
Malmsburg, 139
Manchester, 23, 27, 83, 91, 98, 216, 225, 250
—Branch, 83
Manifesto, 11, 252
Marryat, Francis, 21
Marsden, James, 96, 147
Martin, Lucy, 87
Martin handcart company, 136, 168, 174, 184-86, 189
Martin's Cove (WY), 181
Massachusetts, 237
Maughan, Mary Ann Weston, 59, 63, 67, 69, 73, 79, 124, 171, 243, 267
Maughan, Peter, 171
Meeks, Priddy, 129
Merioneth, Wales, 213
Merthyr Tydfill, 27, 38, 78, 86
—Branch, 75
Methodism, 33, 39, 46, 47, 48, 51, 52, 74, 227, 233
middle-class theory, 31-36, 256
midwives, 221-23
Miles, Albert, 235
Millcreek (UT), 199
Millcreek Canyon, 53
millennial fever, 137
Millennial Star, xi, 37, 48, 62, 81, 82, 88, 91, 94, 101, 105, 107, 119, 124, 135, 173, 211, 228
Miller, Joaquin (Cincinnatus Heiner), 5, 7, 21
Mills, Frances Farr, 141, 156, 272
missionaries, Mormon, xi, 24, 25, 57, 60, 63, 75, 76, 104, 127, 133
—troubles of, 76-8, 79
Mississippi River, 5, 30, 163, 171, 172, 176, 180, 191
Missouri, 2, 170, 179
Missouri River, 163, 164, 166
—settlements, 167, 192
Mittelberger, Gottlieb, 155
monogamy, 129, 187-213
Morgan, Margaret Griffith, 136, 178, 272
Morgan, Owen, 178
Mormon men, 3, 15
Mormon question, ix, 21
Mormon Reformation, 207
Mormon Trail, 177, 181, 185, 195
Mormon Trust Foundation, vii, xiii
Mormon women
—childbearing patterns, 38
—contributions to mission, 82
—cultural roots, 11, 42
—economic origins, 34, 38, 40
—education, 43-45
—family characteristics, 7, 36-37
—geographic origins, 26-27
—history of, viii
—morals, 48
—organizations in British Mission, 88
—physical characteristics, 8, 9
—rally for polygamy, 14
—realistic portraits, 14
—relationships, 41
—religious origins, 10, 46-47
—rights of, 104
—sexuality, 41
—socio-economic roots, 6
—status, 13, 82-3, 85, 97, 103-104, 173, 251
—twentieth-century, 255-56
—voting, 244

Mormonism
 —Britons' awareness of, 63
 —urban success, 30
Mormonism Unveiled, x, 12f
Morris, Annie, 14f
mountain fever, 181, 183
Muddy River Mission, 200
Mulder, William, 2
Murdoch, Ann Steel, 68, 236-38, 240, 268
Murdoch, Isabella Crawford, 237-38, 240, 254
Murdoch, John Murray, 68, 236-38, 240
Murdoch, Wee Granny (Mary Murray), 39, 68, 268
Murdoch family, 256
Musser, Bishop, 174
Mutual Improvement Association, 114, 117
Myres, Sandra, 1

N

Narration of Facts Stranger than Fiction, 19
Nation magazine, 3, 7
National Council of Women, 201
Nauvoo, 121, 130, 135, 167, 169, 224, 225
Nauvoo temple, 127
Nauvoo Temple Fund, 88-89
Nebraska, 136, 180
 —City, 171
Neilson, Sister, 115
Nephi (UT), 200
Nevada, 201
Nevada, the, 154
New England, 24
New Orleans, 5, 16, 69, 144, 156, 161-62, 164, 165
New Orleans Academy of Science, 5
New York
 —Branch, 85
 —City, 144, 155, 158, 161, 164, 165, 166, 168, 197
 —State, 145
Newcastle, 107
Newcastle-on-Tyle Branch, 90, 111, 114
Newport, 61, 81, 196
Newton (UT), 217

Norwich
 —Conference, 125
 —Relief Society, 117
Nottingham, 59, 75, 110, 149
Nottingham Relief Society, 109, 112
Nova Scotia, 35

O

Oakey, Mary, 149, 268
Ogden, 141, 144, 189, 192, 219
Ohio, x, 122, 141, 179
Old Testament, 120, 123, 124, 125
Old World, 4, 8, 50, 109, 249
Olympus, the, 69
Omaha (NE), 158, 171
Oquirrh Mountains, 246
Oregon Trail, 177, 181, 182
Our Pioneer History, 196
Outlook, 11
Oxfordshire, 32

P

Pack, Jessie Belle Stirling, 157, 166, 175, 268
Paint Your Wagon, 7
Palmer, Henry, 247
Palmer, James, 246-48, 256
Palmer, Mary Jane Ewer, 32-34, 53, 59, 69, 143, 146, 157, 174, 187, 240, 243, 245-48, 268
Paris, 22, 51
Parley P. Pratt, 46, 58, 61, 115
Parr, Sister, 96
Parry, Harriet Parry, 268
Parsons, Emily Ann. *See* Barker
patriarchal system, ix
Pawnee Indians, 167
Pearce, Jean Rio Baker, 35, 40, 138, 140, 149, 152-53, 156, 157, 159, 161, 172-73, 175, 176, 178, 187, 188, 191-94, 196, 240, 259-60
Pembrokeshire, 44
Pennsylvania, 76, 121, 136, 138
Penrose, Charles, 59
Penrose, Romania, 117

Penry Field, 88
Perpetual Emigration Fund, 110, 143-44, 166, 197, 199, 205
persecution, 72-6, 79
Philadelphia, 145, 168, 221
Piercy, Angelina, 268
Pikers, 7
Pine Ridge Mountains, 180
Pineview (UT), 190
Pittsburgh, 166
plains, 127
Platte River, 176, 177, 181, 184
Pleasant Green (Magna) (UT), 190
Plum Creek, 167
plural marriage, 50f
polygamist offspring, 5
polygamists, 7
polygamous cults, 258
polygamous families, 1, 42
polygamous vs. monogamous women, 241-42
polygamy, vii, x, 3, 23, 50, 62, 103, 121, 127, 187, 215-48, 251
    —announced, 124
    —denial of, 119
    —in England, 130, 138
    —Principle, the, 252
    —rallies for, 14
    —statistics, 238-45, 252
Polygamy in Utah, 226
Polysophical Society, 207, 255
Pontgwynfe, 38
Pope, the, 4
population of Great Britain, 22
Portsmouth, 110
potato famine, 27
Poulter, Alice Maw, 52, 60, 143, 268
Poulter, Mary Elizabeth Jackson, 268
Powell, Mary, 83, 268
Powell, Mary and John, 52
Pratt, Orson, 124, 128
Pratt, Parley P., 230
Pratt, Romania, 222
Presbyterians 46, 53, 94, 95
Preston, 29, 32, 83, 84, 95, 98, 120, 224, 225

—Branch, 92, 107
Price, Caroline Blakey, 269
Price, John Howell, 69, 76, 170
Price, Rachel Jones, 69, 75, 170, 243, 273
Price, Ruth Williams, 269
priesthood, ix
Primary, 106
Primitive Methodists, 33, 46, 95, 133
prophetesses, 52, 91, 229
proselyting
    —Mormon, 16, 58, 63, 67, 83
    —by women, 83
Protestant revivals, 48
Protestantism, 31, 50, 69
Provo (UT), 203
Putnam's Monthly, 12

Q

Quakers, 51, 121, 155, 248
Quebec, 164
Queen, 25, 57
Quorum of Apostles, 99

R

race, 5
Radley's Hotel, 216
rail travel, 166, 167, 172, 217
records, lack of women's, 81-2
Redman, Ellen Balfour, 43, 85-86, 96, 269
Redmund, Matilda, 96
Rees, Mary Williams, 76, 178, 273
Reese, Emma David, 269
Reform Act of 1832, 32
Reform Act of 1850, 32
reform of polygamy, 2
Reformation of 1856, 99
Reid, Mayne, 6, 15, 16, 17, 21
Relief Society, xi, 88, 106, 109, 111, 112, 117, 202, 221, 229, 255
    —magazine, 200
    —minute book, viii
religious fervor, 48
Remy, Jules, 7, 14, 22
Reorganized Church, 76, 235, 245
Revelle, Ellen Clark, 4f

revivals, 94
Richards, Franklin D., 125, 168
Richards, Levi, 74
Richards, Robert, 6, 7, 12, 15, 16, 17, 67
Richards, Willard, 29, 74, 84, 86, 95, 97, 98, 224
Richfield (UT), 193
Rising, Louisa Chapin, 122
Ritchie, Mary Emma, 269
Roberts, Ann Everington, 134, 269
Roberts, B. H., 241
Roberts, Edward Giles, 213
Robinson, Clara Alice. *See* Allred
Robinson, Phil, 14, 22
Rocky Mountain Saints, 230
Roman Catholicism, 31, 46, 226, 253
Romerell, Pres. Peter, 112
Ross, James Darling, 129
Ross, Sarah Elizabeth Smyth, 129, 141, 273
Rosser, Ann Jones, 81-82, 83, 105, 144, 269
Rosza, Patience, 185, 273
Roughing It, 8, 19
Rushton, Elder, 74

§

St. George temple, 203
St. Heliers, 20, 61, 226
St. Joseph (MO), 166, 171, 175
St. Louis (MO), 164, 166, 167, 169, 170, 175, 202
Saint Mark, the, 154
Salt Lake City, vii, ix, 19, 20, 53, 78, 119, 127, 136, 146, 166, 174, 192, 195, 201, 202, 228, 247
Samaria (ID), 244
Sand Hills (NE), 180
Sanpete County (UT), 243
Saved from the Mormons, 21
Scandinavian women, 3
Scofield, A. J., 109
Scotland, 27, 29, 34, 55, 58, 68, 84, 128, 142, 156, 244
Scott's Bluff (NE), 180
Scripps, Ellen Browning, 4

Scripps College, 4
sermons, Mormon, 16
Sessions, Patty, 24
sex roles, 25
sexism, 15
sexuality, 41-42, 128, 209
Sheffield, 27
Sherman Island (CA), 193
Shipp, Elder Milford, 128, 220-23, 240, 241
Shipp, Dr. Ellis, 220-23, 240, 245, 269
Shipp, Maggie, 221, 241, 254
Shipp, Mary Elizabeth Hilstead, 128, 220-23, 269
Shipp family, 256
ships, Mormon emigration, 154, 164
singles, 37-38
Sioux Indians, 167
Sizzum, Elder, 16
Skinner, Sarah and James Joy, 199
Skull Valley (UT), 243, 246, 256
slavery, American, 162
Sleater, Thomas, 190
Sloan, Elder, 95
Smart, Elder, 16
Smith, Bathsheba, 175
Smith, Hyrum, 121
Smith, Ida, 117
Smith, Joseph, viii, 62, 67, 70, 75, 88, 91, 99, 120, 121, 123, 124, 136, 179, 206
Smith, Mary Fielding, 270
Smith, Mercy Fielding, 88
Snow, Eliza R., 107, 109-10, 112, 114, 123, 221, 229
Snow, Lorenzo, 227
Social Hall, 257
Society of British Dissenters, 47
South Africa, 135, 201
South Cottonwood, 196, 198, 199, 235
Southampton, 216, 226
Spencer, Martha Knight, 270
Spense, Margery Lisk and Captain, 156, 273
Spenser, Antonette Maria, 127
Spenser, Claudius V., 104, 126, 130, 179, 204-205, 206

Spenser, Daniel, 126, 182
Spenser, Georgiana King, 126, 183, 204-205
Spenser, Louie King, 204-205, 207
Spenser, Orson, 256
Spenser, Susannah Neslen, 205
spiritual wifery, 23, 98, 125
spiritualism, 91-94
Springville (UT), 203
Staffordshire Potteries, 29, 89, 99
Staines, Priscilla Mogridge, 270
Stanford, Jane Carol Barker (Jenny), 216-20, 239, 244, 245, 270
Stanford, Stephen, 220
Stars, 62
Steadman, Elizabeth Wilkins, 76, 134, 145, 146, 150, 152, 155, 158, 166, 174, 182, 169-96, 219, 244, 270
Steadman, George, 197, 239
Stebbins (fictional Danite leader), 7
Stenhouse, Belinda Marden Pratt, 230
Stenhouse, Fanny, 2, 10, 18, 20-21, 50, 51, 61, 63, 67, 68, 69, 71, 102, 128, 130, 141, 151, 152, 153, 165, 173, 175, 178, 188, 225-32, 236, 238, 245, 249, 253, 257, 270
Stenhouse, T. B. H., 20, 63, 67, 173, 225-32, 257
Stephens, Jane, 145, 273
stereotypes, 203, 216, 224, 225, 232, 249, 254, 258
—gullible wife, 17
—myrmidon, 7
—shopgirl, 18
stereotyping process, 22
Stevenson, Fanny/Robert Louis, 15, 17
Stopford, Archdeacon, 94-95
Stowe, Harriet Beecher, 20
Study in Scarlet, 11, 17, 18f
Sunday school, 117
Surke, Mr., 212
Sussex, 196
Swarts, Jane McKinnon, 185, 270
Swiss Mission, 141
Switzerland, 228
Sydney, Sir Philip, vii

Sydney Mining Co., 35

T

Tabernacle, 106, 251
—Choir, 246
Talton, Mary Johnson, 144, 273
Tapfield, Mary, 208
Tarry, Harriet. *See* Hirst
tarrying in the East, 167-70, 174
Taylor, Ann Faulkner, 128, 270
Taylor, Caroline Rogers, 87, 144, 270
Taylor, John Possels, 128
Taylor, P. A. M., 28, 33, 34, 37, 46, 134, 173
Taylorsville (UT), 199
Teasdale, Emily, 105
Tell It All, 220
Temperance Hall, 60
Temple Fund, 88
Tenby, 44
Texas, 216
Thames River, 163
Thatcher (AZ), 201
Theosophy, 245
Thomas, Brother and Sister, 152, 153
Thomas, Elizabeth Phillips, 38, 40, 270
Thomas, Frederick, 139
Thomas, Mary Coslet, 44
Thomas, Mary Roberts, 270
Thomas, Thomas, 39
Thomas families, 34, 47
Thompson, Mercy R., 88
Thorp, Malcolm R., 20, 32, 33, 46, 52
time, marriage for, 190
Times, 62
tithing, 47
Tollcross, 115
Tooele (UT), 246
Tract Society, 114
Tranent, 34
Truth about the Mormons, x
Tuckfield, Maria Ann, 155, 271
Twain, Mark, vii, 8, 9

U

Ugdorn Seion, 61, 63
Uncommercial Traveler, 17
Union Army, 196
United Brethren, 30, 83
United States, 133, 139
University of Utah Marriott Library, xiii
Utah, x, 53, 58, 79, 81, 106, 110, 112, 124,
    134, 138, 139
—farming in, 244
—employment opportunities, 243
Utah Agricultural College, 201
Utah church, x
Utah Northern Railroad, 216
Utah State Historical Society, xii
Utah State University library, xiii
Utah War, 106, 192

V

Victorian ideals, 210-11, 223, 225, 252,
    256, 258
Victorian magazines, 1
Victorian women, 101, 103
—family size, 39
Victorians, 20, 42
—Mormon, 188
Vinehill Branch, 84
Voice of Warning, 46, 61
voting reform, 32, 244
voyage, Atlantic, 154
—length of, 155

W

Wade, Isabella. *See* Allred
wagon trains, Mormon, 174
Waite, Mrs. C. V., 9
Waldensians, 228
Wales, viii, 12, 27, 30, 34, 44, 45, 47, 61,
    64, 75, 78, 83, 86, 137, 156, 170, 212,
    232
Wallace, Thomas, 107
Walmsley, Sister, 97
Ward, Artemus, 5
Ward, Austin, 5, 7, 18, 19

Ward, Maria, ix, 4, 7, 8, 12, 13, 19, 23, 67,
    78, 203
wards, Salt Lake 13th, 15th, 16th, 257
Warner, Mary Ann Chapple, 59, 146,
    156, 157, 172, 178, 271
Water, 91
Weaver, Ann Watkins, 271
Weaver, Lizzie Brown, 168
Wells, Samuel, 41, 137-38
Wells, Sarah Hattersley, 41, 59, 137-38,
    146, 149, 178, 243, 271
Wellsville (OH), 122
Welsh
—emigration, 157, 166, 175, 186
—history, xiii
—Mission, 61, 63
—settlements, 244, 257
—women, viii, 3, 44, 59, 62, 86, 91
Wesleyans, 52
West Midlands, 27, 55
West Riding, 27
Western Isles, 30
Weston, Mary Ann. *See* Maughan
Westport, 171
White Huntress, 6
Whitechapel
—Branch, x, 43, 49, 82, 109, 111, 191,
    194
—Relief Society, 109, 112-13
Whitehead, Elder James, 95
Whittier, John Greenleaf, 10
Wilding, David, 83
wildlife, plains, 181
Wilkins, Charles, 196, 197
Wilkins, Christopher, 196
Wilkins, Elizabeth. *See* Steadman
Willie handcart company, 136, 142, 174,
    184-86
William Tapscott, 154
Williamsburg (VA), 158, 164
Wilshire, 139
Wilson, Sarah Isom, 158, 172, 178, 182,
    266, 271
Windley, Mary Foster, 144, 271
Winner, Isabella. *See* Burgess
Winner, James, 141

Winter Quarters, 127, 167, 171

Winthrop, Theodore, vii, viii, 4, 5, 16, 17, 186, 224

Woman Suffrage, 105, 107

Woman's Exponent, xi, 37, 82, 106, 109, 110, 111, 114, 118, 209, 255

women, Scandinavian, 3

Wood, Alice Horrocks, 59, 186, 271

Wood, Elizabeth and Charles. *See* Bennett

Woodmansee, Emily Hill, 271

Woodruff, Wilford, 30, 31, 43, 46, 58, 59, 63, 74, 85-86, 88-89, 91, 93

Woolley, Bishop E. D., 106, 121-22

Woolley, Ellen Wilding, 120, 121-22, 130, 240, 271

Woolley, Mary Wickersham, 121-23

Woolley, Rachel (md. name Simmons), 121

Woolley, Samuel, 121

Wordsworth, William, 176

working women, 87

Worthington, James, 188, 191

WPA histories, xi

Wylie, Elizabeth, 68, 272

Wyoming, 180-81

Y

Yale University, vii

Yorkshire, 27, 86

Yorkshire, the, 154

Young, Ann Eliza, 2

Young, Brigham, vii, 4, 9, 11, 19, 29, 62, 110, 120, 123, 127, 128, 136, 164, 182, 185, 200, 201, 205, 207, 208, 221, 232, 236, 243, 249, 250, 253

Young, Clara Federata Stenhouse, 230

Young, Kimball, 253

Young, Zina Huntington, 8

Young Ladies Improvement Association, 106, 202

Young Women's Journal, 200

Z

Zion, 3, 6, 13, 17, 24, 33, 38, 53, 76, 104, 107, 113, 124, 131, 134, 135, 136, 138, 141, 194, 195, 199, 209
—arrival in, 187
—expectations of, 187-88, 242
—honeymoon period, 249
—treatment of women by, 187-89

Zionism, 46